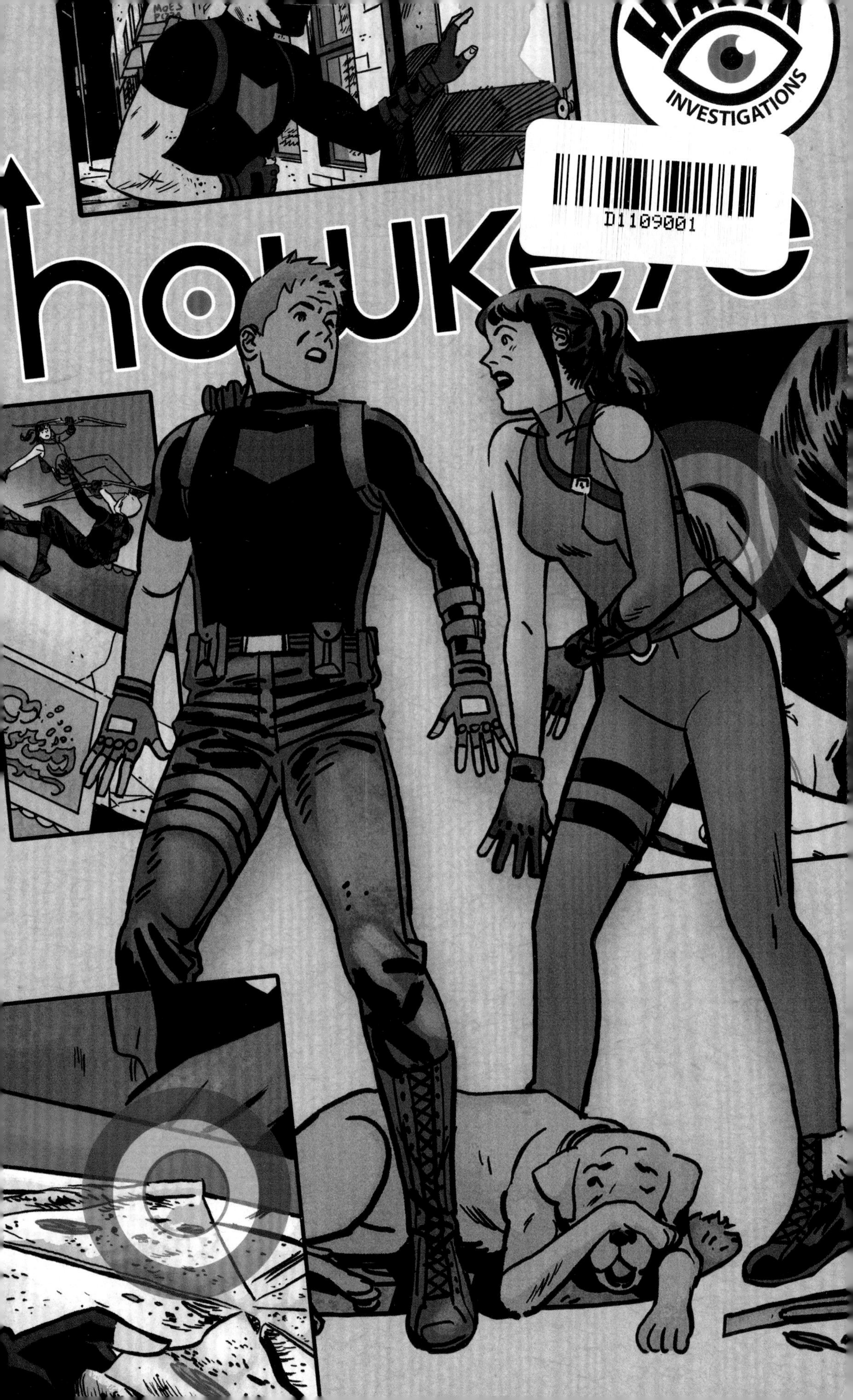
INVESTIGATIONS

HAWKEYE: KATE BISHOP VOL. 3 — FAMILY REUNION. Contains material originally published in magazine form as HAWKEYE #13-16 and GENERATIONS: HAWKEYE & HAWKEYE #1. First printing 2018. ISBN 978-1-302-91097-6. Published by MARVEL WORLDWIDE, INC., a subsidiary of MARVEL ENTERTAINMENT, LLC. OFFICE OF PUBLICATION: 135 West 50th Street, New York, NY 10020. Copyright © 2018 MARVEL. No similarity between any of the names, characters, persons, and/or institutions in this magazine with those of any living or dead person or institution is intended, and any such similarity which may exist is purely coincidental. **Printed in Canada.** DAN BUCKLEY, President, Marvel Entertainment; JOHN NEE, Publisher; JOE QUESADA, Chief Creative Officer; TOM BREVOORT, SVP of Publishing; DAVID BOGART, SVP of Business Affairs & Operations, Publishing & Partnership; DAVID GABRIEL, SVP of Sales & Marketing, Publishing; JEFF YOUNGQUIST, VP of Production & Special Projects; DAN CARR, Executive Director of Publishing Technology; ALEX MORALES, Director of Publishing Operations; SUSAN CRESPI, Production Manager; STAN LEE, Chairman Emeritus. For information regarding advertising in Marvel Comics or on Marvel.com, please contact Vit DeBellis, Custom Solutions & Integrated Advertising Manager, at vdebellis@marvel.com. For Marvel subscription inquiries, please call 888-511-5480. **Manufactured between 3/16/2018 and 4/17/2018 by SOLISCO PRINTERS, SCOTT, QC, CANADA.**

10 9 8 7 6 5 4 3 2 1

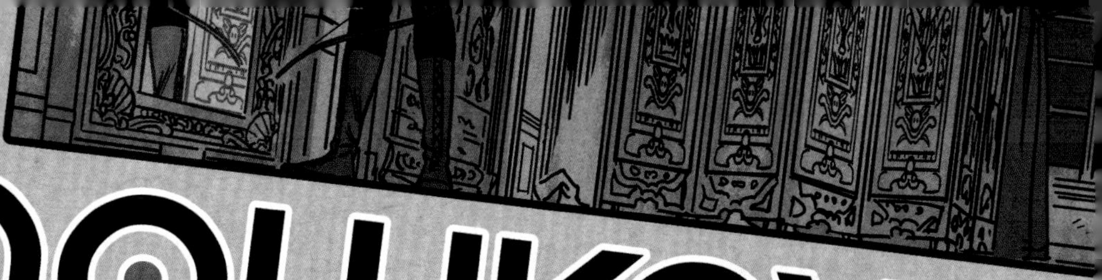

hawkeye

family reunion

Kelly Thompson
writer

Generations: Hawkeye & Hawkeye #1

Stefano Raffaele
artist

Digikore
color artist

Greg Smallwood
cover art

Hawkeye #13-16

Leonardo Romero
artist

Jordie Bellaire
color artist

Julian Totino Tedesco
cover art

VC's Joe Sabino
letterer

Alanna Smith & **Charles Beacham**
editors

Sana Amanat
supervising editor

HAWK INVESTIGATIONS

collection editor **Jennifer Grünwald** • assistant editor **Caitlin O'Connell**
associate managing editor **Kateri Woody** • editor, special projects **Mark D. Beazley**
vp production & special projects **Jeff Youngquist** • svp print, sales & marketing **David Gabriel**
book designer **Jay Bowen**

editor in chief **C.B. Cebulski** • chief creative officer **Joe Quesada**
president **Dan Buckley** • executive producer **Alan Fine**

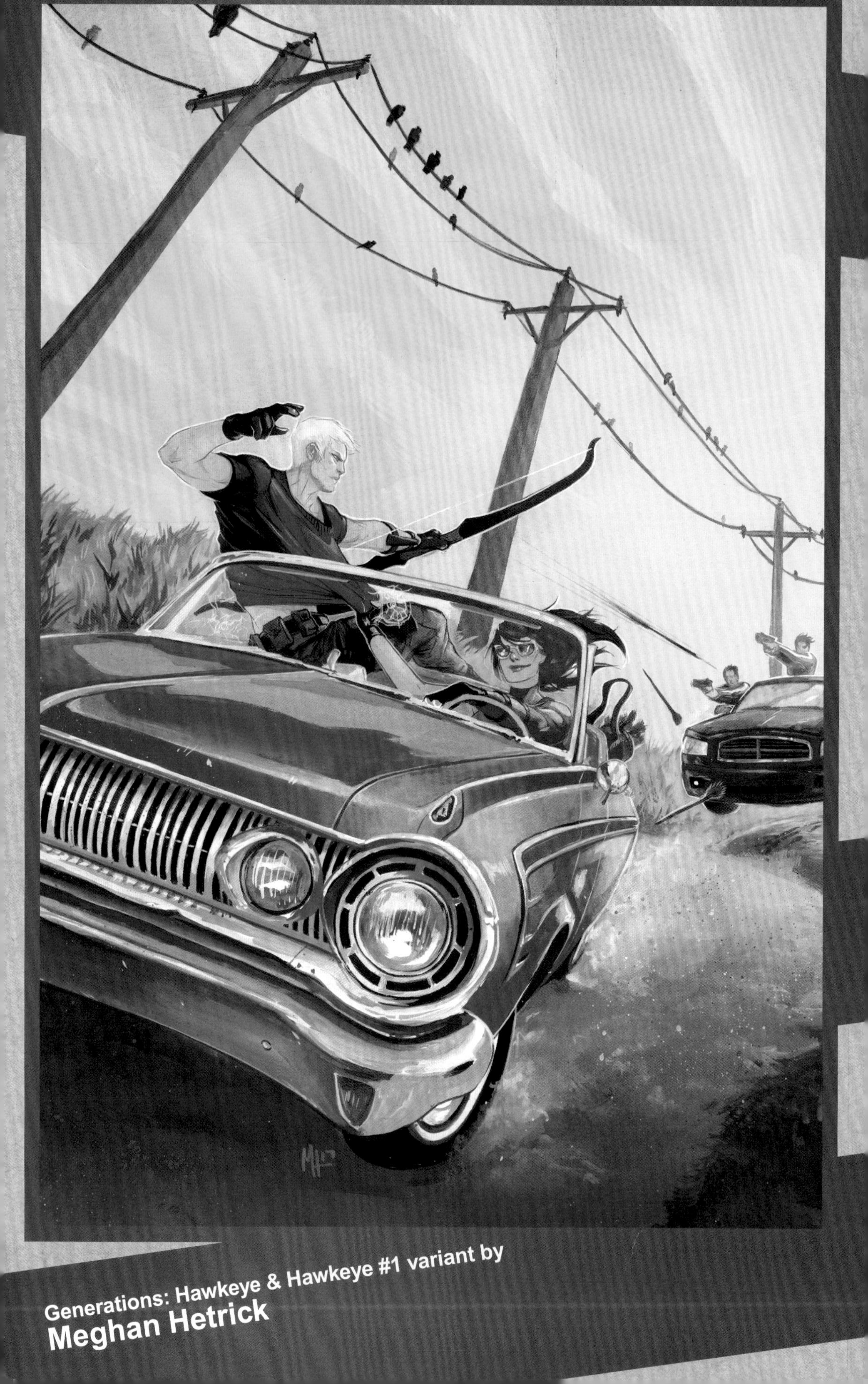

Generations: Hawkeye & Hawkeye #1 variant by
Meghan Hetrick

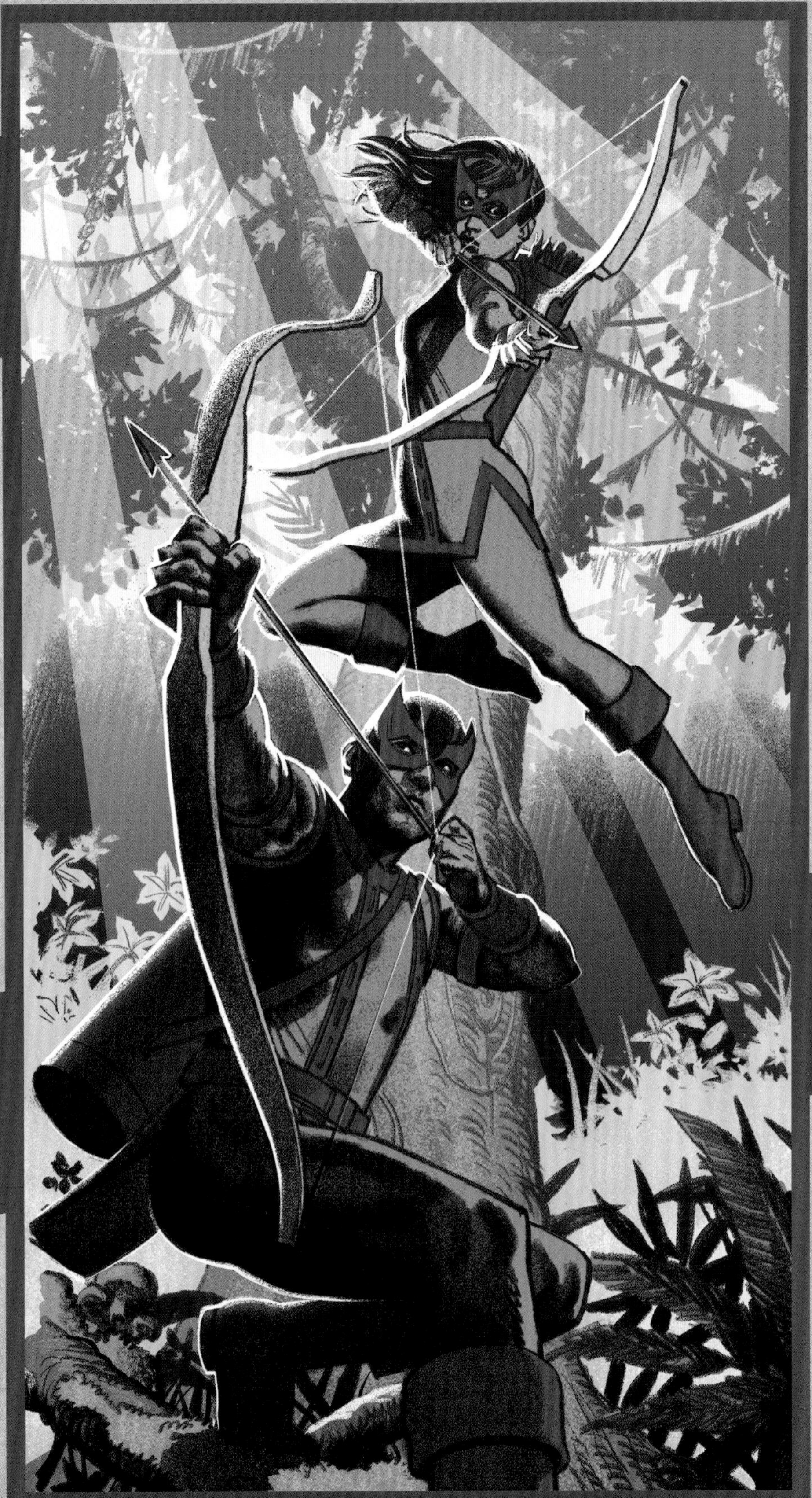

Generations: Hawkeye & Hawkeye #1

THE VANISHING POINT

AN INSTANT APART!

A MOMENT BEYOND!

LOOSED FROM THE SHACKLES OF PAST, PRESENT, FUTURE— A PLACE WHERE TIME HAS NO MEANING!

BUT WHERE TRUE INSIGHT CAN BE GAINED!

MAKE YOUR CHOICE! SELECT YOUR DESTINATION!

THIS JOURNEY IS A GIFT...

AS A BOY, CLINT BARTON RAN AWAY FROM HIS ABUSIVE FOSTER FATHER TO JOIN THE CIRCUS. HIS APTITUDE FOR ARCHERY LANDED HIM AN APPRENTICESHIP UNDER THE SWORDSMAN WHO—THOUGH HE HELPED CLINT HONE HIS SKILLS—TURNED OUT TO BE A CRIMINAL. NOW CLINT'S AN AVENGER AND ONE OF THE TWO GREATEST SHARPSHOOTERS KNOWN TO MAN. HE IS...

HAWKEYE

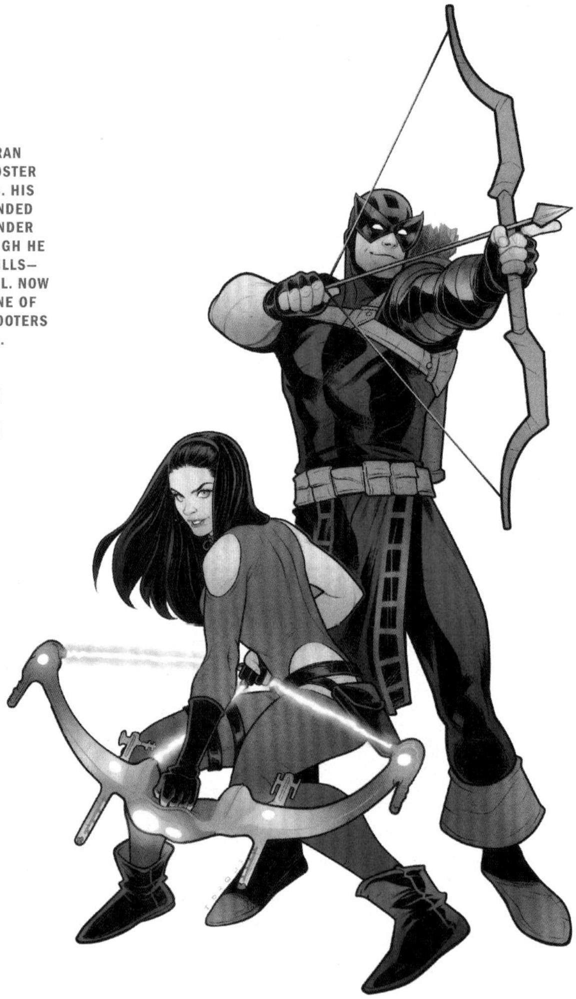

KATE BISHOP WAS BORN THE DAUGHTER OF A WEALTHY BUSINESSMAN, BUT WHEN SHE LEARNED THAT HER FATHER'S FORTUNE WAS BUILT ON A LIFE OF CRIME, SHE VOWED TO RISE ABOVE THOSE WHO'D LET HER DOWN. SHE SET OUT TO BETTER THE WORLD AND HAS BECOME A DAMN GOOD SUPER HERO. NOW KATE'S ONE OF THE GREATEST PRIVATE DETECTIVES IN LOS ANGELES AND THE WORLD'S GREATEST SHARPSHOOTER. SHE IS...

HAWKEYE

GENERATIONS

THE ARCHERS

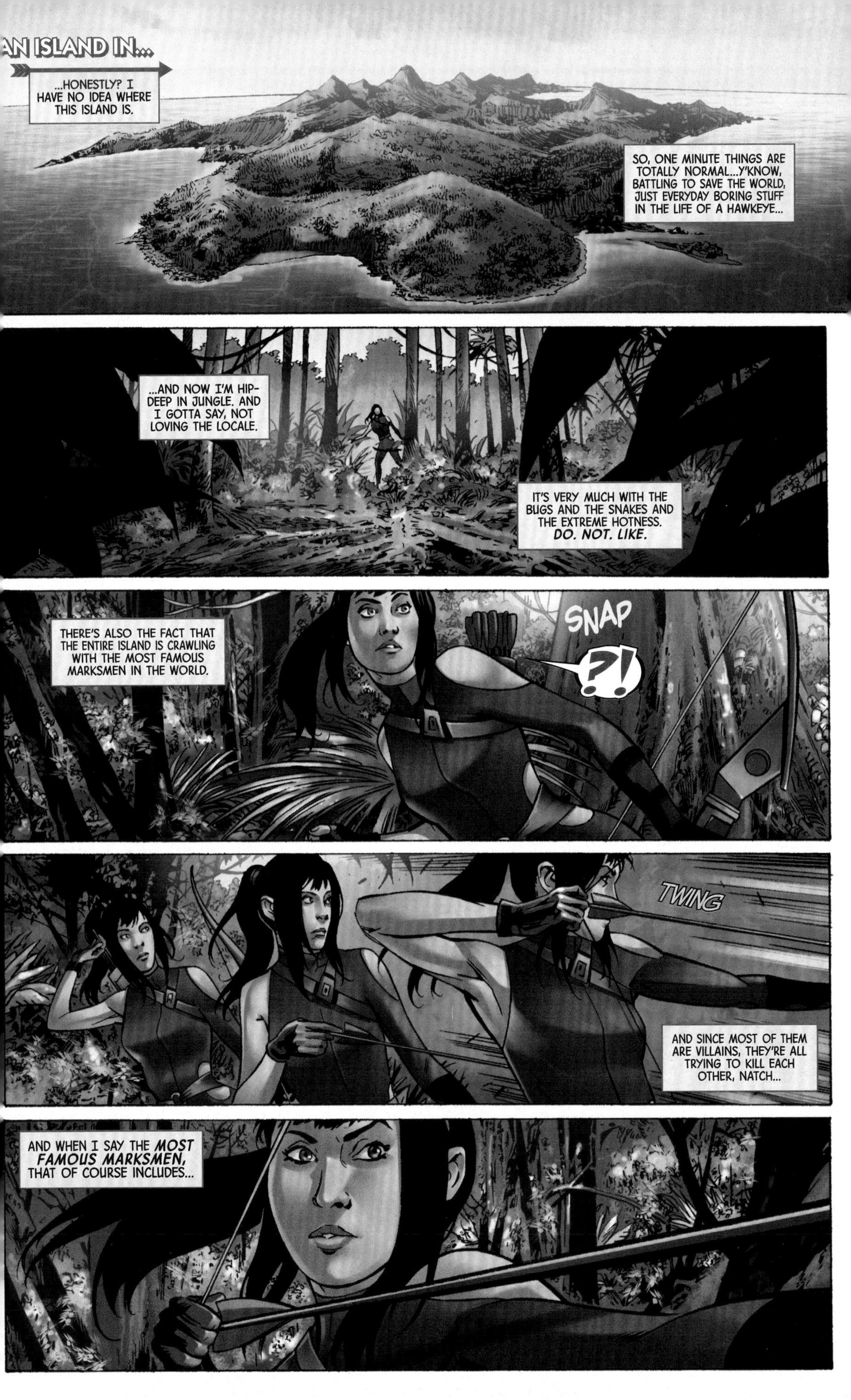
AN ISLAND IN...
...HONESTLY? I HAVE NO IDEA WHERE THIS ISLAND IS.
SO, ONE MINUTE THINGS ARE TOTALLY NORMAL...Y'KNOW, BATTLING TO SAVE THE WORLD, JUST EVERYDAY BORING STUFF IN THE LIFE OF A HAWKEYE...
...AND NOW I'M HIP-DEEP IN JUNGLE. AND I GOTTA SAY, NOT LOVING THE LOCALE.
IT'S VERY MUCH WITH THE BUGS AND THE SNAKES AND THE EXTREME HOTNESS. DO. NOT. LIKE.
THERE'S ALSO THE FACT THAT THE ENTIRE ISLAND IS CRAWLING WITH THE MOST FAMOUS MARKSMEN IN THE WORLD.
SNAP
?!
TWING
AND SINCE MOST OF THEM ARE VILLAINS, THEY'RE ALL TRYING TO KILL EACH OTHER, NATCH...
AND WHEN I SAY THE MOST FAMOUS MARKSMEN, THAT OF COURSE INCLUDES...

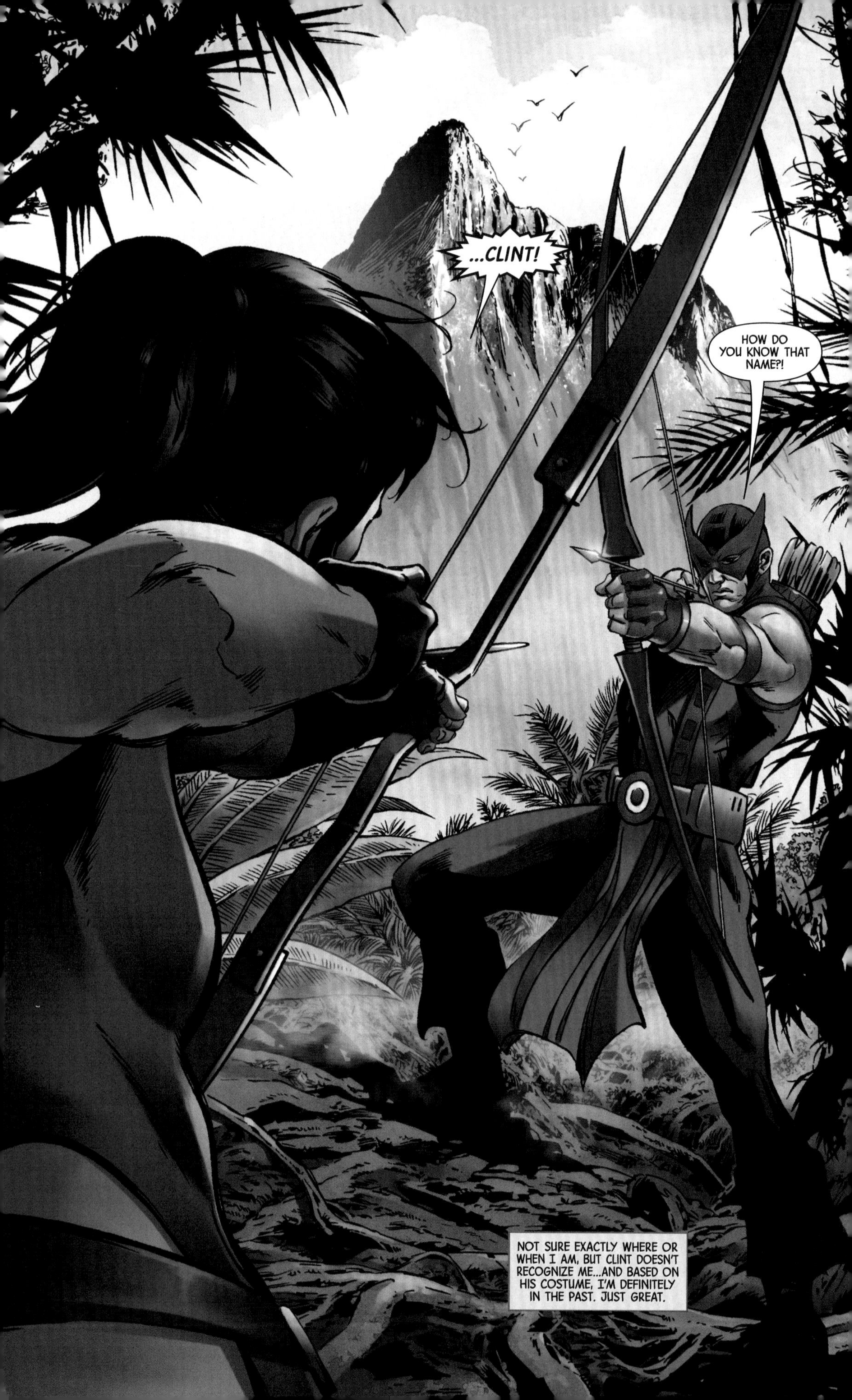
...CLINT!
HOW DO YOU KNOW THAT NAME?!
NOT SURE EXACTLY WHERE OR WHEN I AM, BUT CLINT DOESN'T RECOGNIZE ME...AND BASED ON HIS COSTUME, I'M DEFINITELY IN THE PAST. JUST GREAT.

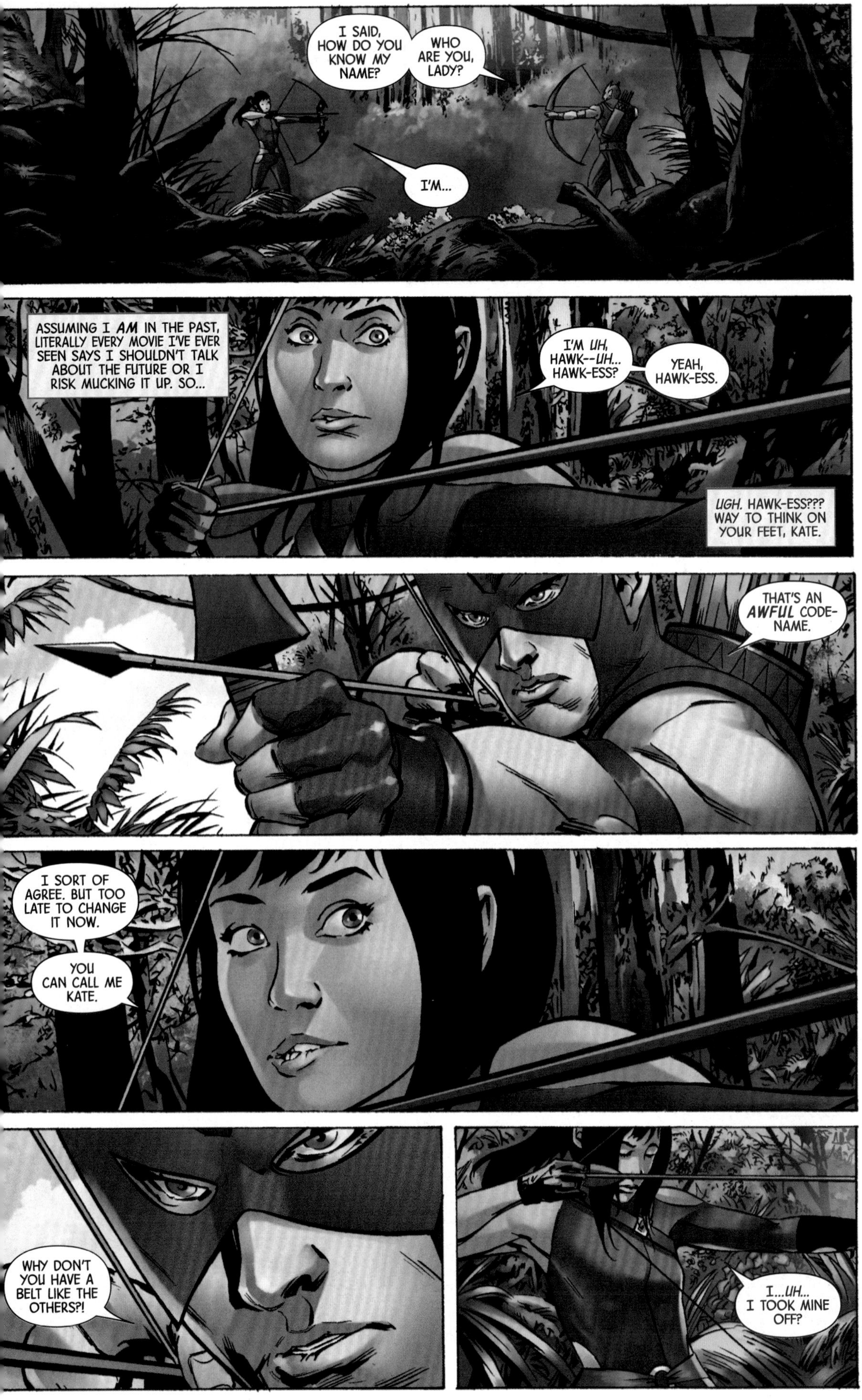
I SAID, HOW DO YOU KNOW MY NAME?
WHO ARE YOU, LADY?
I'M...
ASSUMING I AM IN THE PAST, LITERALLY EVERY MOVIE I'VE EVER SEEN SAYS I SHOULDN'T TALK ABOUT THE FUTURE OR I RISK MUCKING IT UP. SO...
I'M UH, HAWK--UH... HAWK-ESS?
YEAH, HAWK-ESS.
UGH. HAWK-ESS??? WAY TO THINK ON YOUR FEET, KATE.
THAT'S AN AWFUL CODE-NAME.
I SORT OF AGREE. BUT TOO LATE TO CHANGE IT NOW.
YOU CAN CALL ME KATE.
WHY DON'T YOU HAVE A BELT LIKE THE OTHERS?!
I...UH... I TOOK MINE OFF?

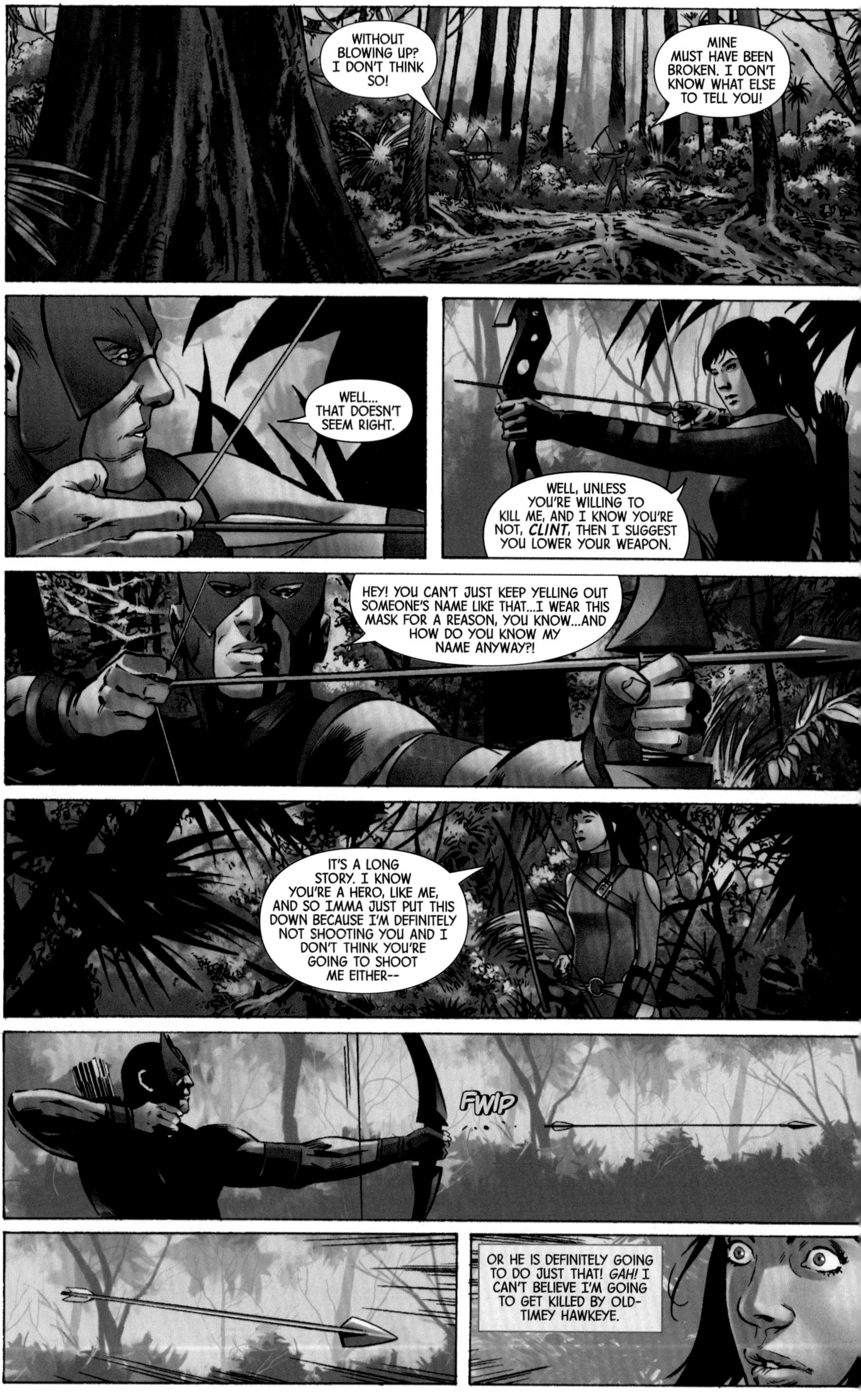
WITHOUT BLOWING UP? I DON'T THINK SO!
MINE MUST HAVE BEEN BROKEN. I DON'T KNOW WHAT ELSE TO TELL YOU!
WELL... THAT DOESN'T SEEM RIGHT.
WELL, UNLESS YOU'RE WILLING TO KILL ME, AND I KNOW YOU'RE NOT, *CLINT*, THEN I SUGGEST YOU LOWER YOUR WEAPON.
HEY! YOU CAN'T JUST KEEP YELLING OUT SOMEONE'S NAME LIKE THAT...I WEAR THIS MASK FOR A REASON, YOU KNOW...AND HOW DO YOU KNOW MY NAME ANYWAY?!
IT'S A LONG STORY. I KNOW YOU'RE A HERO, LIKE ME, AND SO IMMA JUST PUT THIS DOWN BECAUSE I'M DEFINITELY NOT SHOOTING YOU AND I DON'T THINK YOU'RE GOING TO SHOOT ME EITHER--
FWIP
OR HE IS DEFINITELY GOING TO DO JUST THAT! *GAH!* I CAN'T BELIEVE I'M GOING TO GET KILLED BY OLD-TIMEY HAWKEYE.

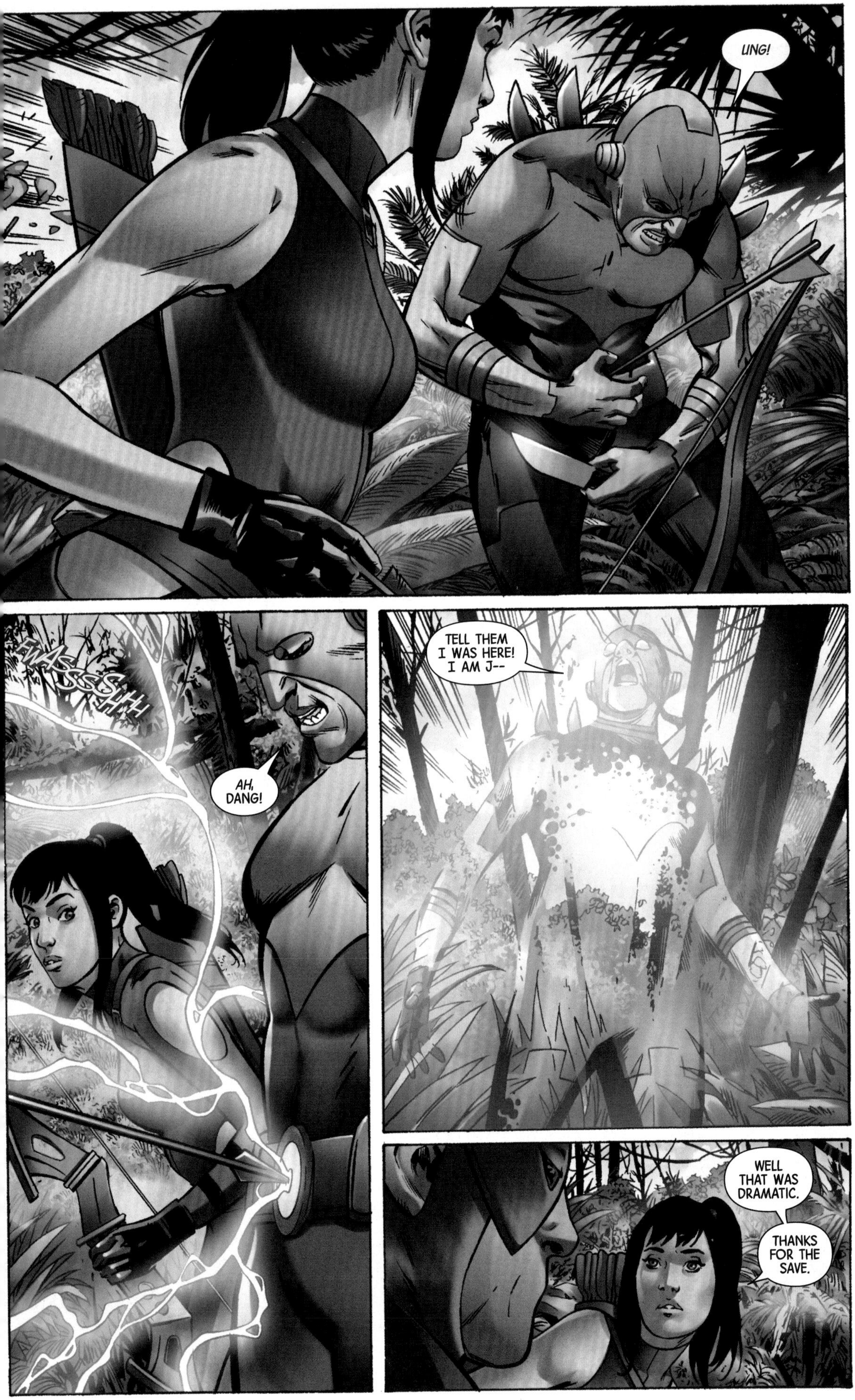
UNG!
FWASSSSHHH
AH, DANG!
TELL THEM I WAS HERE! I AM J--
WELL THAT WAS DRAMATIC.
THANKS FOR THE SAVE.

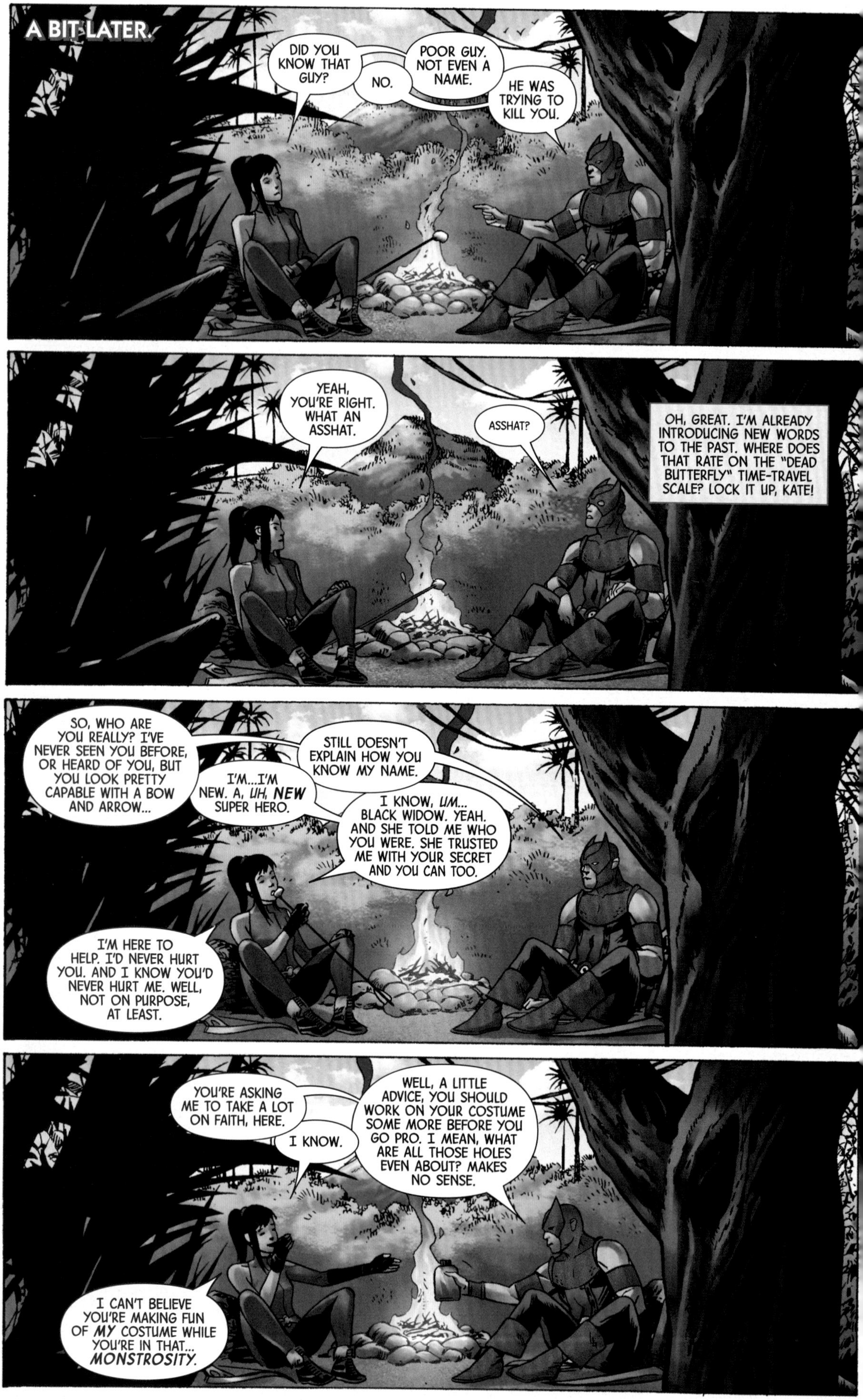
A BIT LATER.
DID YOU KNOW THAT GUY?
NO.
POOR GUY. NOT EVEN A NAME.
HE WAS TRYING TO KILL YOU.
YEAH, YOU'RE RIGHT. WHAT AN ASSHAT.
ASSHAT?
OH, GREAT. I'M ALREADY INTRODUCING NEW WORDS TO THE PAST. WHERE DOES THAT RATE ON THE "DEAD BUTTERFLY" TIME-TRAVEL SCALE? LOCK IT UP, KATE!
SO, WHO ARE YOU REALLY? I'VE NEVER SEEN YOU BEFORE, OR HEARD OF YOU, BUT YOU LOOK PRETTY CAPABLE WITH A BOW AND ARROW...
I'M...I'M NEW. A, *UH*, ***NEW*** SUPER HERO.
STILL DOESN'T EXPLAIN HOW YOU KNOW MY NAME.
I KNOW, *UM*... BLACK WIDOW. YEAH. AND SHE TOLD ME WHO YOU WERE. SHE TRUSTED ME WITH YOUR SECRET AND YOU CAN TOO.
I'M HERE TO HELP. I'D NEVER HURT YOU. AND I KNOW YOU'D NEVER HURT ME. WELL, NOT ON PURPOSE, AT LEAST.
YOU'RE ASKING ME TO TAKE A LOT ON FAITH, HERE.
I KNOW.
WELL, A LITTLE ADVICE, YOU SHOULD WORK ON YOUR COSTUME SOME MORE BEFORE YOU GO PRO. I MEAN, WHAT ARE ALL THOSE HOLES EVEN ABOUT? MAKES NO SENSE.
I CAN'T BELIEVE YOU'RE MAKING FUN OF *MY* COSTUME WHILE YOU'RE IN THAT... ***MONSTROSITY.***

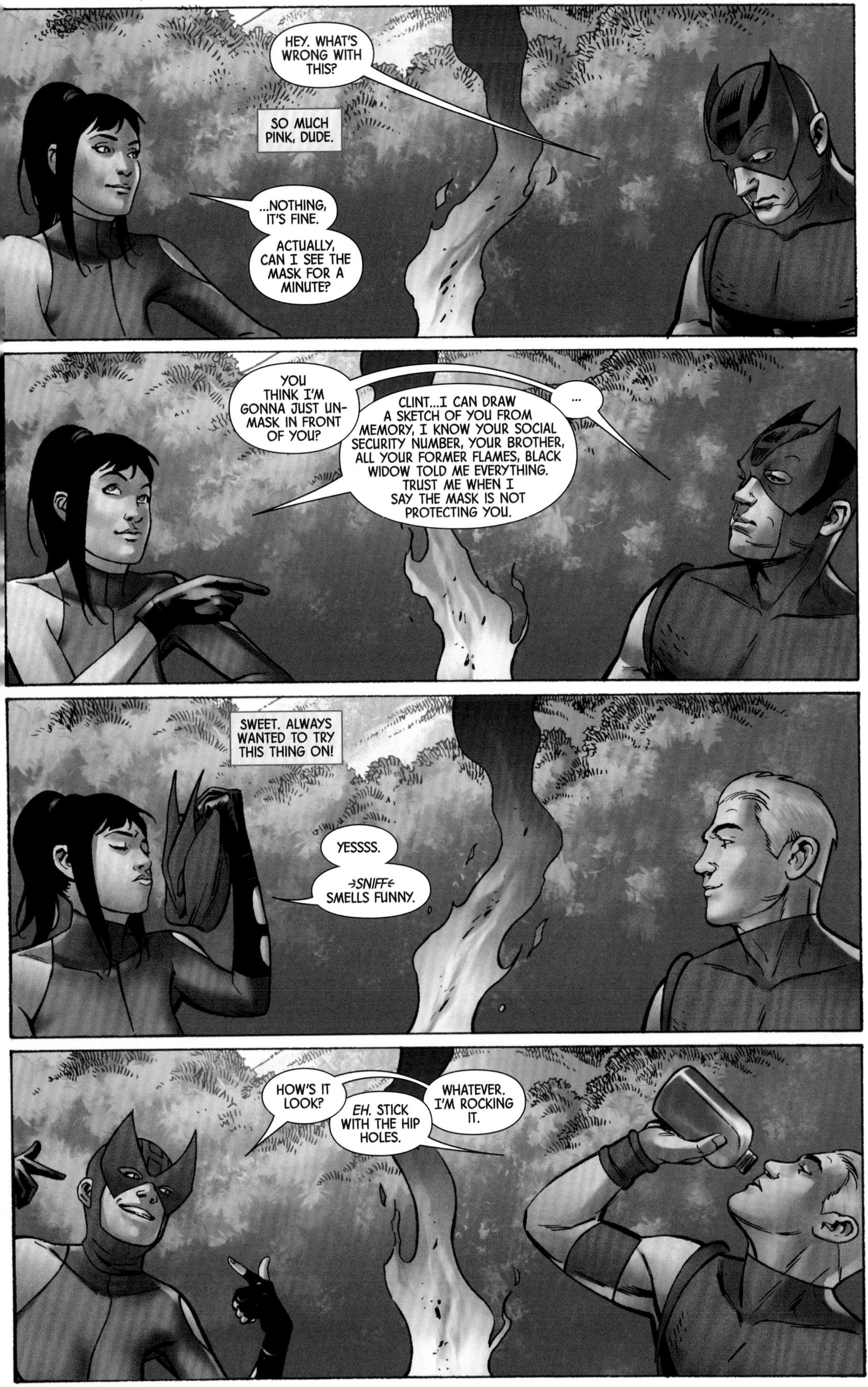
HEY. WHAT'S WRONG WITH THIS?
SO MUCH PINK, DUDE.
...NOTHING, IT'S FINE.
ACTUALLY, CAN I SEE THE MASK FOR A MINUTE?
YOU THINK I'M GONNA JUST UN-MASK IN FRONT OF YOU?
...
CLINT...I CAN DRAW A SKETCH OF YOU FROM MEMORY, I KNOW YOUR SOCIAL SECURITY NUMBER, YOUR BROTHER, ALL YOUR FORMER FLAMES, BLACK WIDOW TOLD ME EVERYTHING. TRUST ME WHEN I SAY THE MASK IS NOT PROTECTING YOU.
SWEET. ALWAYS WANTED TO TRY THIS THING ON!
YESSSS.
→SNIFF← SMELLS FUNNY.
HOW'S IT LOOK?
EH. STICK WITH THE HIP HOLES.
WHATEVER. I'M ROCKING IT.

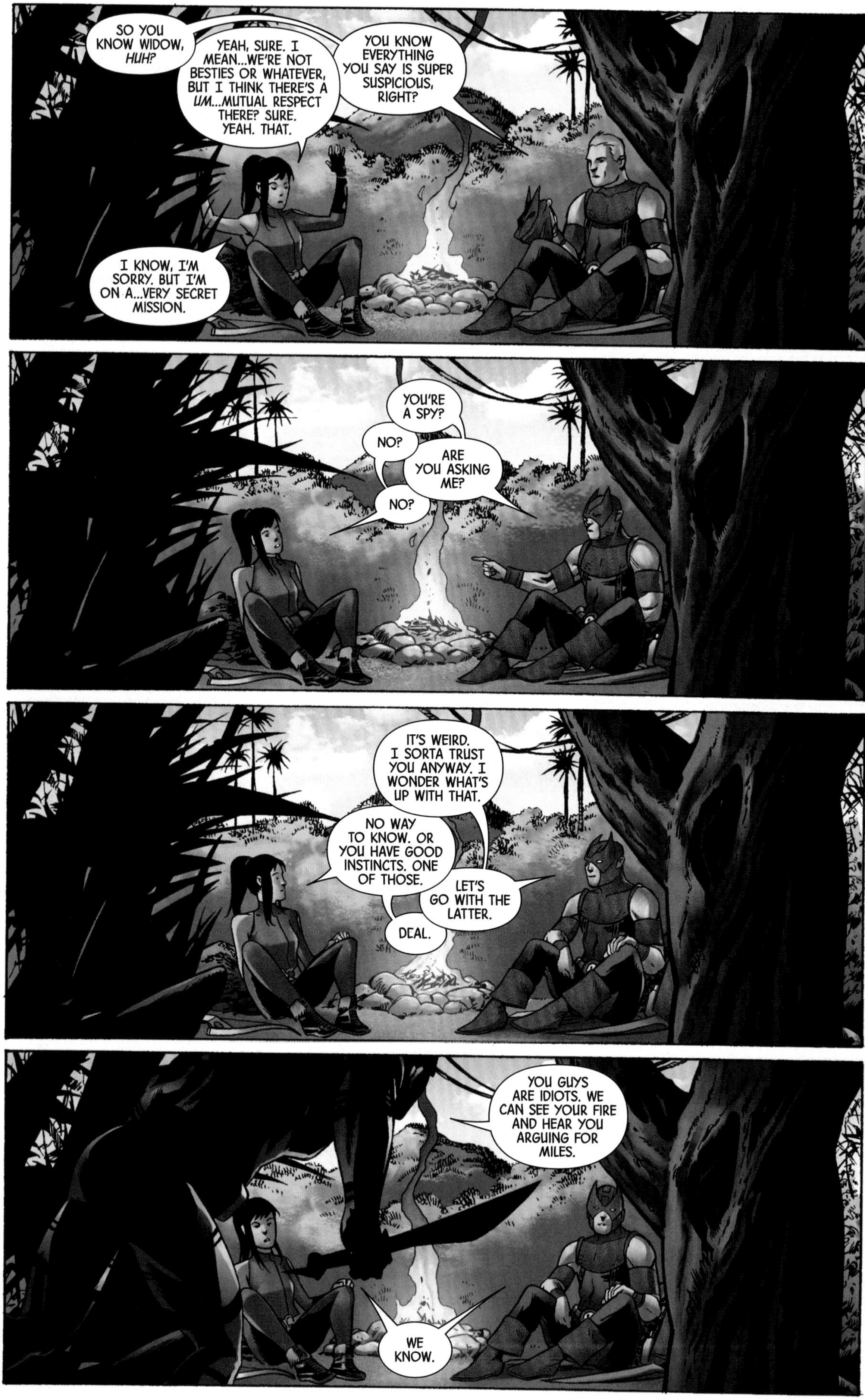
SO YOU KNOW WIDOW, *HUH?*
YEAH, SURE. I MEAN...WE'RE NOT BESTIES OR WHATEVER, BUT I THINK THERE'S A *UM*...MUTUAL RESPECT THERE? SURE. YEAH. THAT.
YOU KNOW EVERYTHING YOU SAY IS SUPER SUSPICIOUS, RIGHT?
I KNOW, I'M SORRY. BUT I'M ON A...VERY SECRET MISSION.
YOU'RE A SPY?
NO?
ARE YOU ASKING ME?
NO?
IT'S WEIRD. I SORTA TRUST YOU ANYWAY. I WONDER WHAT'S UP WITH THAT.
NO WAY TO KNOW. OR YOU HAVE GOOD INSTINCTS. ONE OF THOSE.
LET'S GO WITH THE LATTER.
DEAL.
YOU GUYS ARE IDIOTS. WE CAN SEE YOUR FIRE AND HEAR YOU ARGUING FOR MILES.
WE KNOW.

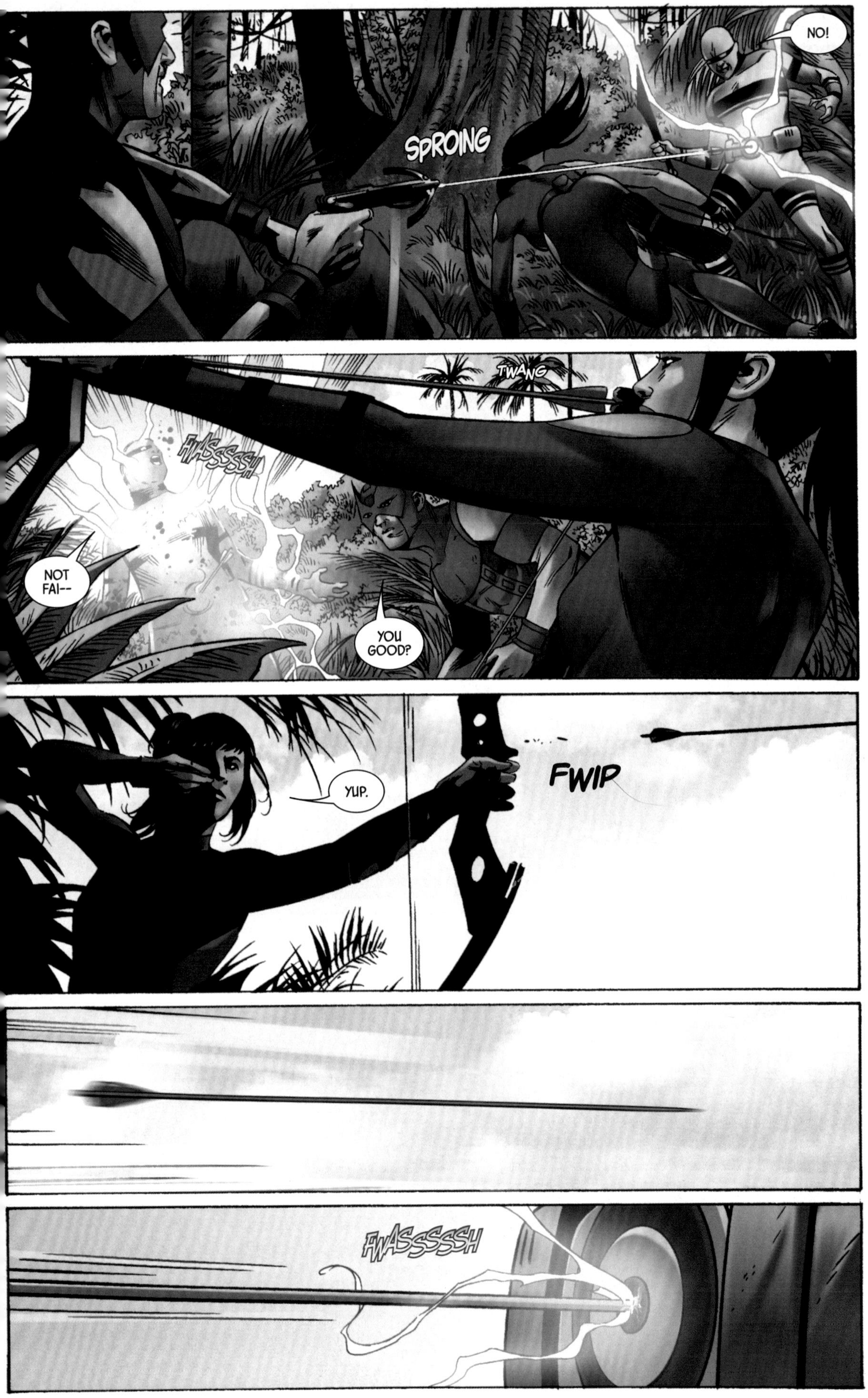
SPROING
NO!
TWANG
FWASSSSH
NOT FAI--
YOU GOOD?
YUP.
FWIP
FWASSSSSH

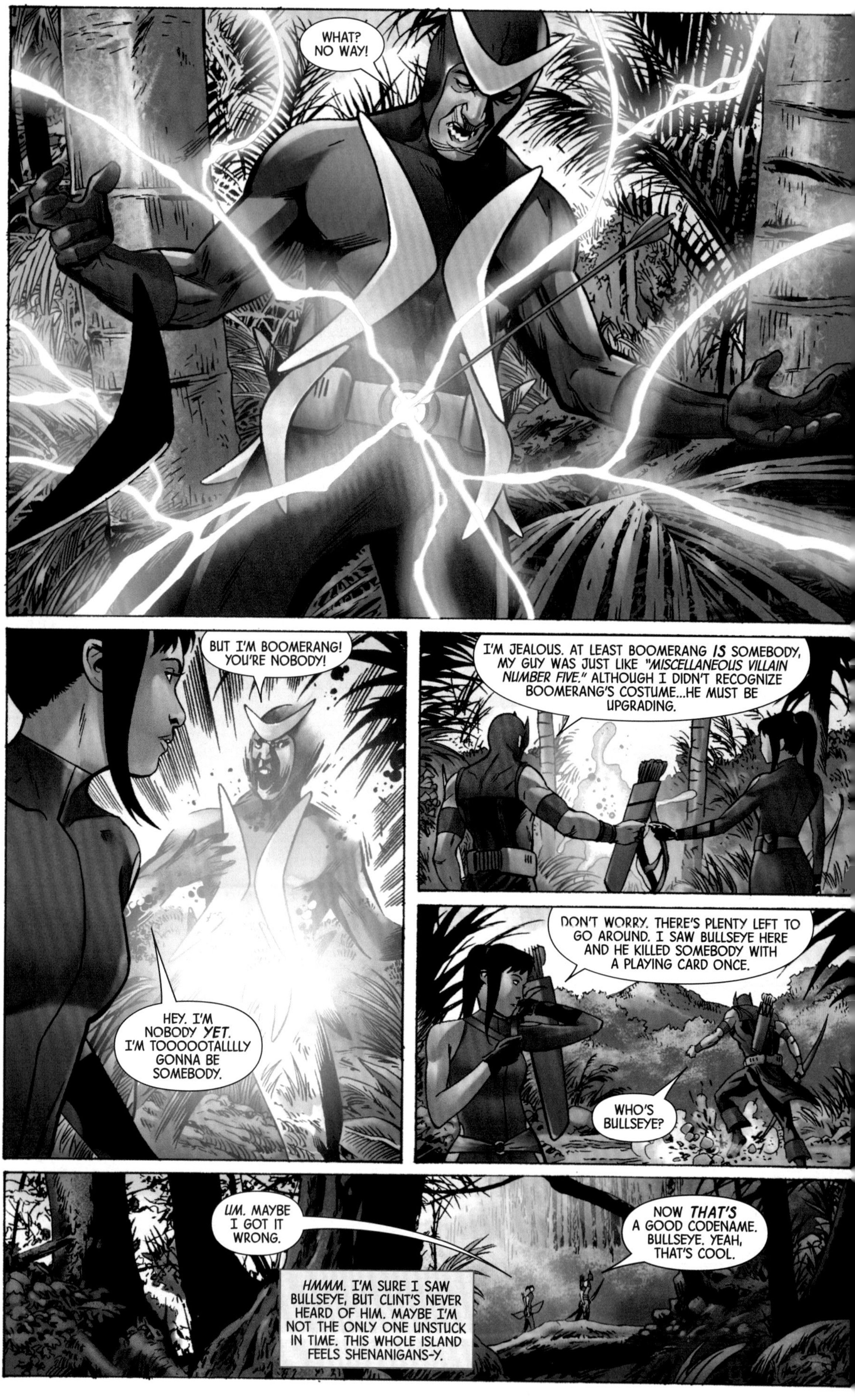
WHAT? NO WAY!
BUT I'M BOOMERANG! YOU'RE NOBODY!
HEY. I'M NOBODY *YET*. I'M TOOOOOTALLLLY GONNA BE SOMEBODY.
I'M JEALOUS. AT LEAST BOOMERANG *IS* SOMEBODY. MY GUY WAS JUST LIKE *"MISCELLANEOUS VILLAIN NUMBER FIVE."* ALTHOUGH I DIDN'T RECOGNIZE BOOMERANG'S COSTUME...HE MUST BE UPGRADING.
DON'T WORRY. THERE'S PLENTY LEFT TO GO AROUND. I SAW BULLSEYE HERE AND HE KILLED SOMEBODY WITH A PLAYING CARD ONCE.
WHO'S BULLSEYE?
NOW *THAT'S* A GOOD CODENAME. BULLSEYE. YEAH, THAT'S COOL.
UM. MAYBE I GOT IT WRONG.
HMMM. I'M SURE I SAW BULLSEYE, BUT CLINT'S NEVER HEARD OF HIM. MAYBE I'M NOT THE ONLY ONE UNSTUCK IN TIME. THIS WHOLE ISLAND FEELS SHENANIGANS-Y.

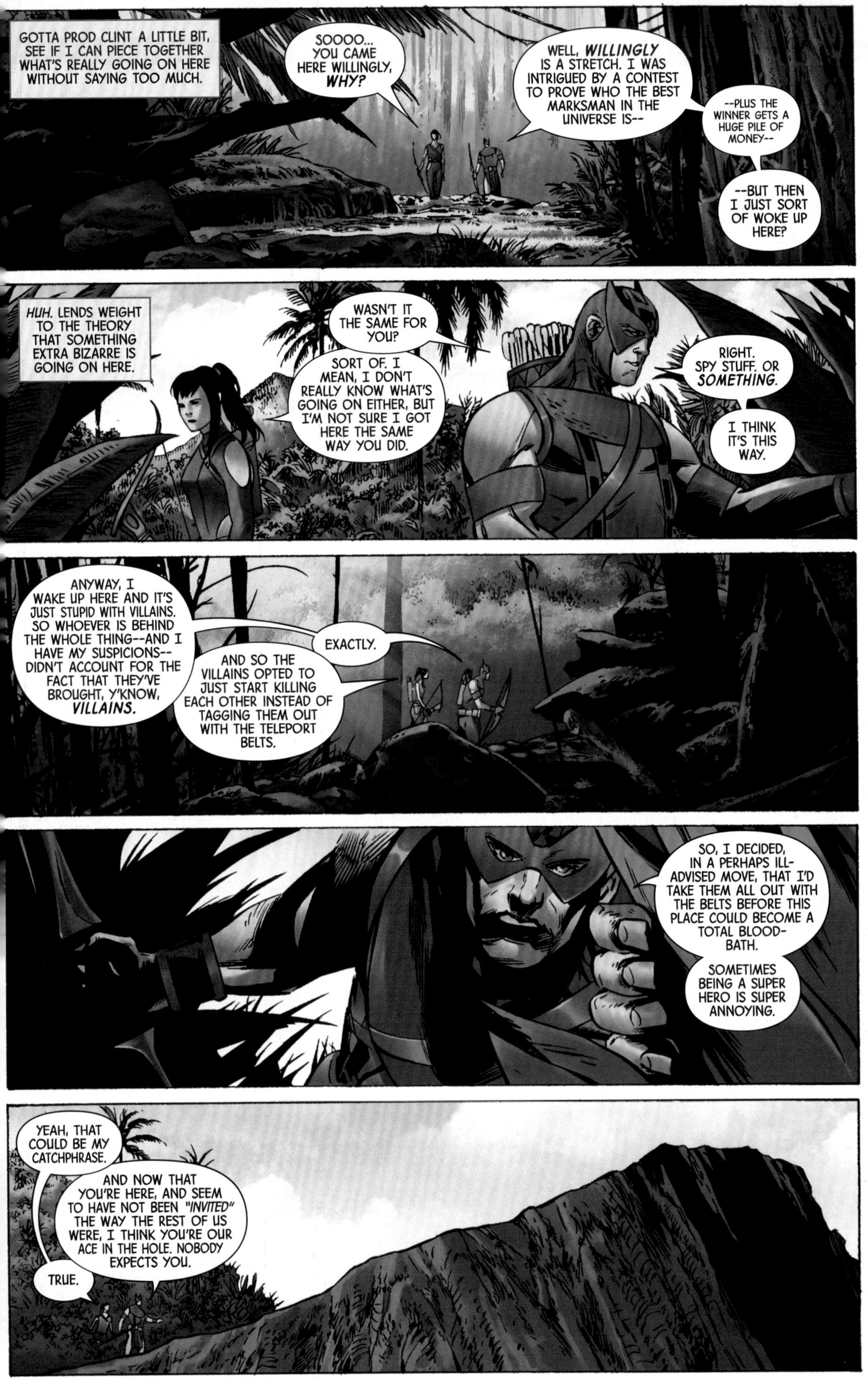

GOTTA PROD CLINT A LITTLE BIT, SEE IF I CAN PIECE TOGETHER WHAT'S REALLY GOING ON HERE WITHOUT SAYING TOO MUCH.
SOOOO... YOU CAME HERE WILLINGLY, WHY?
WELL, WILLINGLY IS A STRETCH. I WAS INTRIGUED BY A CONTEST TO PROVE WHO THE BEST MARKSMAN IN THE UNIVERSE IS--
--PLUS THE WINNER GETS A HUGE PILE OF MONEY--
--BUT THEN I JUST SORT OF WOKE UP HERE?
HUH. LENDS WEIGHT TO THE THEORY THAT SOMETHING EXTRA BIZARRE IS GOING ON HERE.
WASN'T IT THE SAME FOR YOU?
SORT OF. I MEAN, I DON'T REALLY KNOW WHAT'S GOING ON EITHER, BUT I'M NOT SURE I GOT HERE THE SAME WAY YOU DID.
RIGHT. SPY STUFF. OR SOMETHING.
I THINK IT'S THIS WAY.
ANYWAY, I WAKE UP HERE AND IT'S JUST STUPID WITH VILLAINS. SO WHOEVER IS BEHIND THE WHOLE THING--AND I HAVE MY SUSPICIONS--DIDN'T ACCOUNT FOR THE FACT THAT THEY'VE BROUGHT, Y'KNOW, VILLAINS.
EXACTLY.
AND SO THE VILLAINS OPTED TO JUST START KILLING EACH OTHER INSTEAD OF TAGGING THEM OUT WITH THE TELEPORT BELTS.
SO, I DECIDED, IN A PERHAPS ILL-ADVISED MOVE, THAT I'D TAKE THEM ALL OUT WITH THE BELTS BEFORE THIS PLACE COULD BECOME A TOTAL BLOOD-BATH.
SOMETIMES BEING A SUPER HERO IS SUPER ANNOYING.
YEAH, THAT COULD BE MY CATCHPHRASE.
AND NOW THAT YOU'RE HERE, AND SEEM TO HAVE NOT BEEN "INVITED" THE WAY THE REST OF US WERE, I THINK YOU'RE OUR ACE IN THE HOLE. NOBODY EXPECTS YOU.
TRUE.

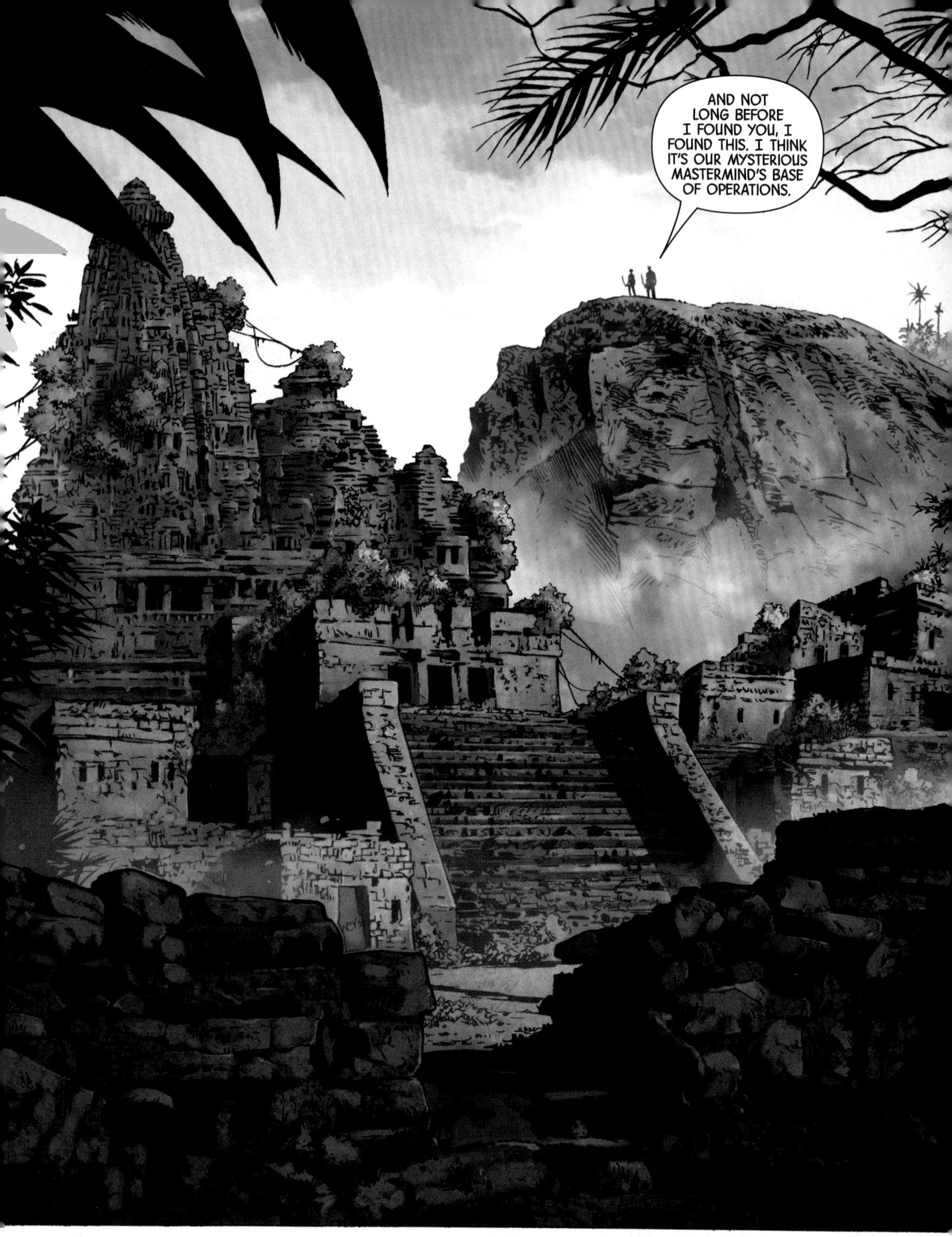
AND NOT LONG BEFORE I FOUND YOU, I FOUND THIS. I THINK IT'S OUR MYSTERIOUS MASTERMIND'S BASE OF OPERATIONS.

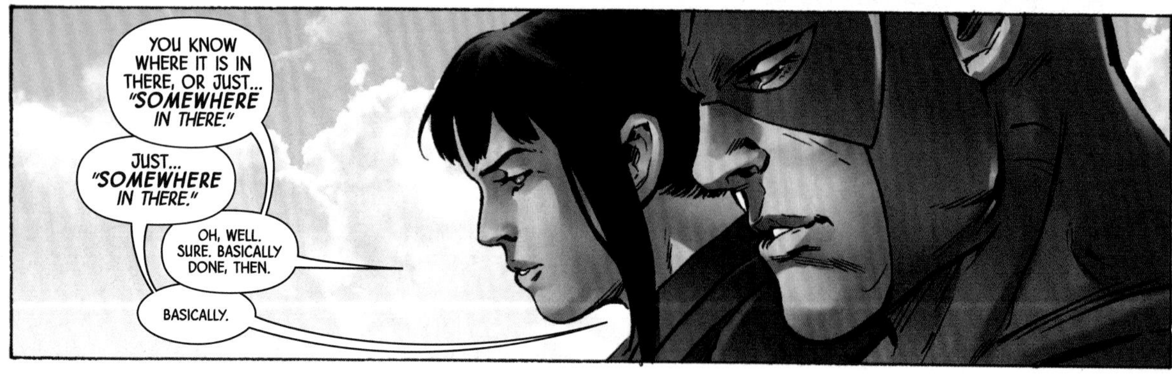
YOU KNOW WHERE IT IS IN THERE, OR JUST... *"SOMEWHERE IN THERE."*
JUST... *"SOMEWHERE IN THERE."*
OH, WELL. SURE. BASICALLY DONE, THEN.
BASICALLY.

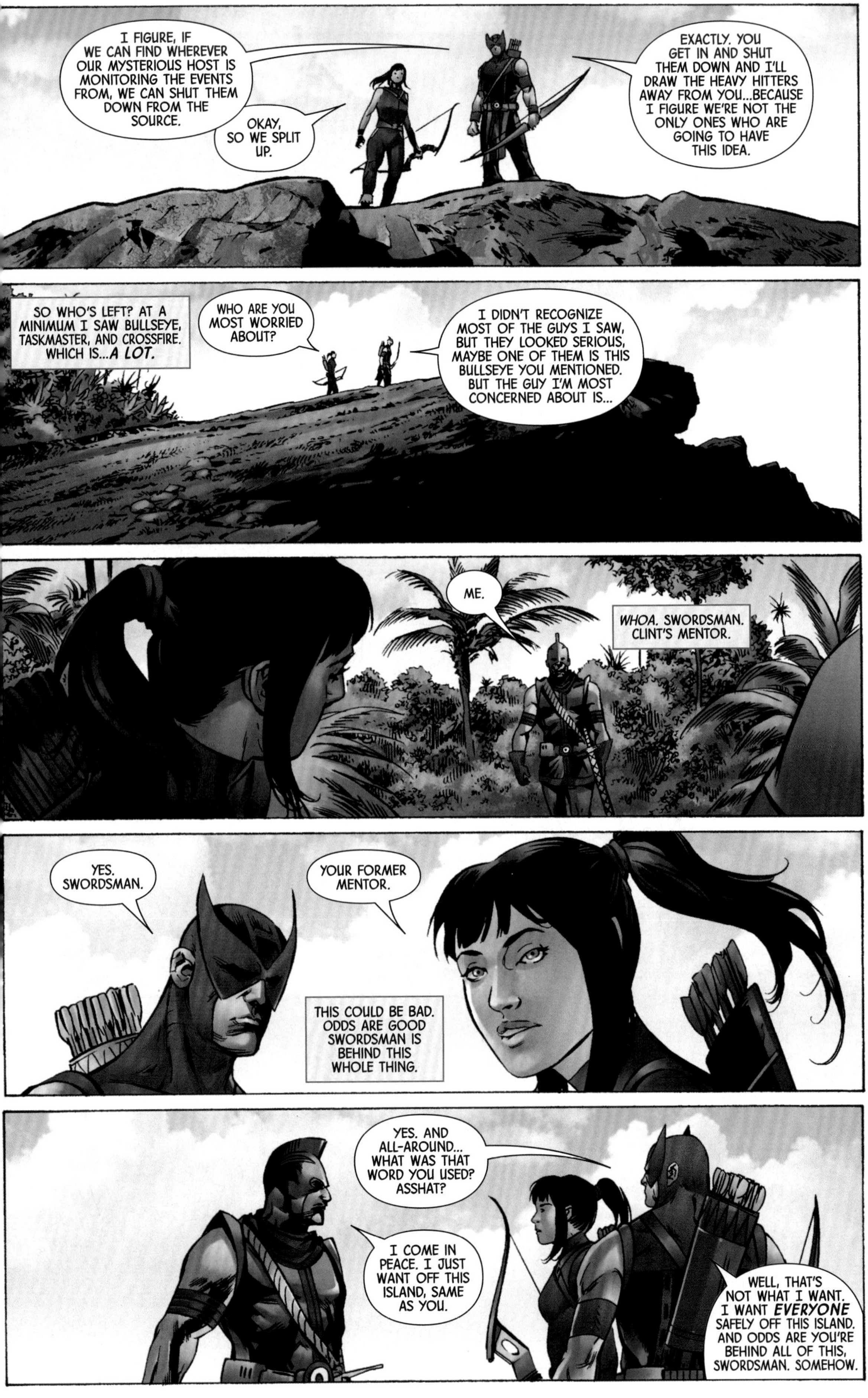
I FIGURE, IF WE CAN FIND WHEREVER OUR MYSTERIOUS HOST IS MONITORING THE EVENTS FROM, WE CAN SHUT THEM DOWN FROM THE SOURCE.
OKAY, SO WE SPLIT UP.
EXACTLY. YOU GET IN AND SHUT THEM DOWN AND I'LL DRAW THE HEAVY HITTERS AWAY FROM YOU...BECAUSE I FIGURE WE'RE NOT THE ONLY ONES WHO ARE GOING TO HAVE THIS IDEA.
SO WHO'S LEFT? AT A MINIMUM I SAW BULLSEYE, TASKMASTER, AND CROSSFIRE. WHICH IS...*A LOT.*
WHO ARE YOU MOST WORRIED ABOUT?
I DIDN'T RECOGNIZE MOST OF THE GUYS I SAW, BUT THEY LOOKED SERIOUS, MAYBE ONE OF THEM IS THIS BULLSEYE YOU MENTIONED. BUT THE GUY I'M MOST CONCERNED ABOUT IS...
ME.
WHOA. SWORDSMAN. CLINT'S MENTOR.
YES. SWORDSMAN.
YOUR FORMER MENTOR.
THIS COULD BE BAD. ODDS ARE GOOD SWORDSMAN IS BEHIND THIS WHOLE THING.
YES. AND ALL-AROUND... WHAT WAS THAT WORD YOU USED? ASSHAT?
I COME IN PEACE. I JUST WANT OFF THIS ISLAND, SAME AS YOU.
WELL, THAT'S NOT WHAT I WANT. I WANT *EVERYONE* SAFELY OFF THIS ISLAND. AND ODDS ARE YOU'RE BEHIND ALL OF THIS, SWORDSMAN. SOMEHOW.

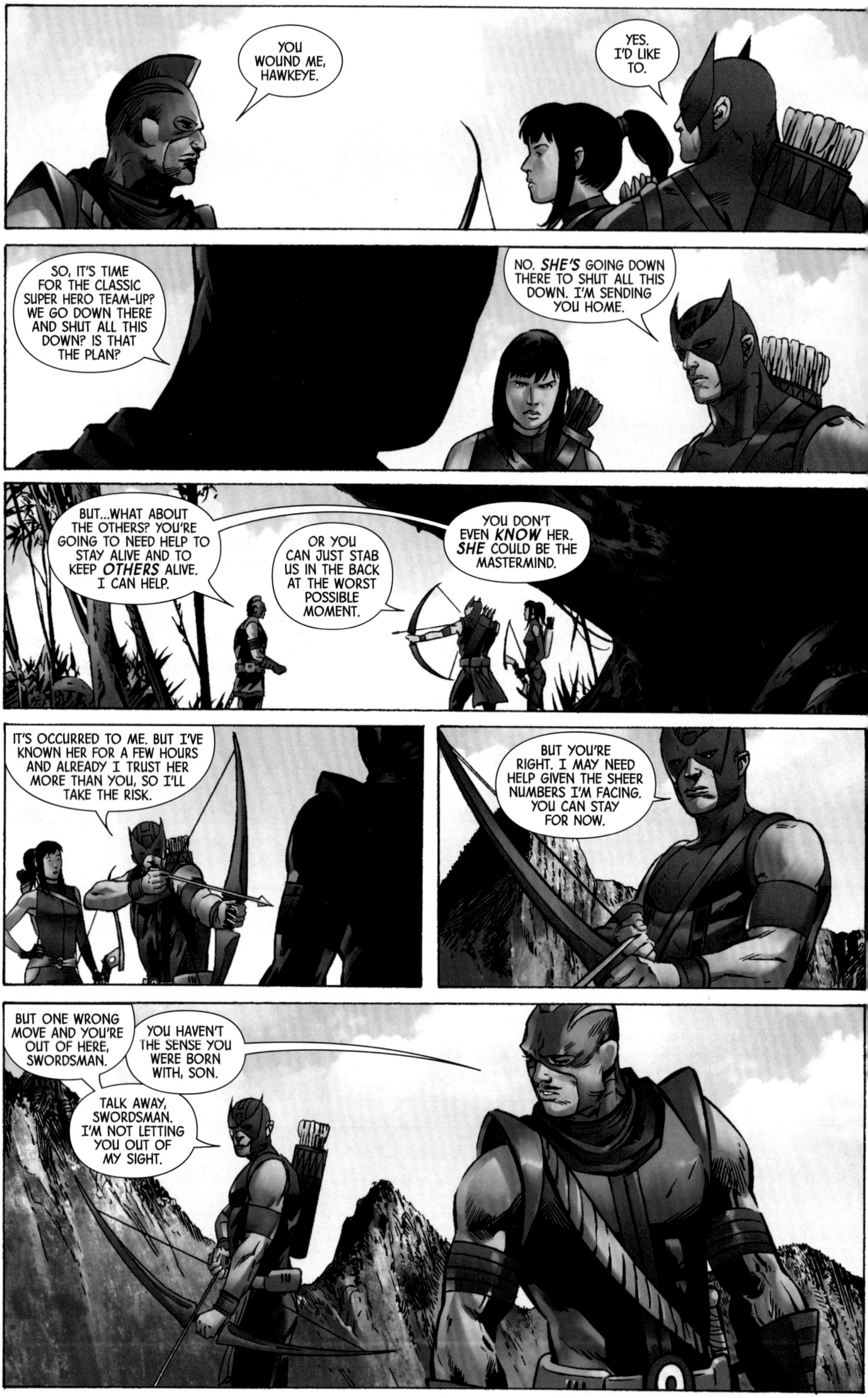
YOU WOUND ME, HAWKEYE.
YES. I'D LIKE TO.
SO, IT'S TIME FOR THE CLASSIC SUPER HERO TEAM-UP? WE GO DOWN THERE AND SHUT ALL THIS DOWN? IS THAT THE PLAN?
NO. SHE'S GOING DOWN THERE TO SHUT ALL THIS DOWN. I'M SENDING YOU HOME.
BUT...WHAT ABOUT THE OTHERS? YOU'RE GOING TO NEED HELP TO STAY ALIVE AND TO KEEP OTHERS ALIVE. I CAN HELP.
YOU DON'T EVEN KNOW HER. SHE COULD BE THE MASTERMIND.
OR YOU CAN JUST STAB US IN THE BACK AT THE WORST POSSIBLE MOMENT.
IT'S OCCURRED TO ME. BUT I'VE KNOWN HER FOR A FEW HOURS AND ALREADY I TRUST HER MORE THAN YOU, SO I'LL TAKE THE RISK.
BUT YOU'RE RIGHT. I MAY NEED HELP GIVEN THE SHEER NUMBERS I'M FACING. YOU CAN STAY FOR NOW.
BUT ONE WRONG MOVE AND YOU'RE OUT OF HERE, SWORDSMAN.
YOU HAVEN'T THE SENSE YOU WERE BORN WITH, SON.
TALK AWAY, SWORDSMAN. I'M NOT LETTING YOU OUT OF MY SIGHT.

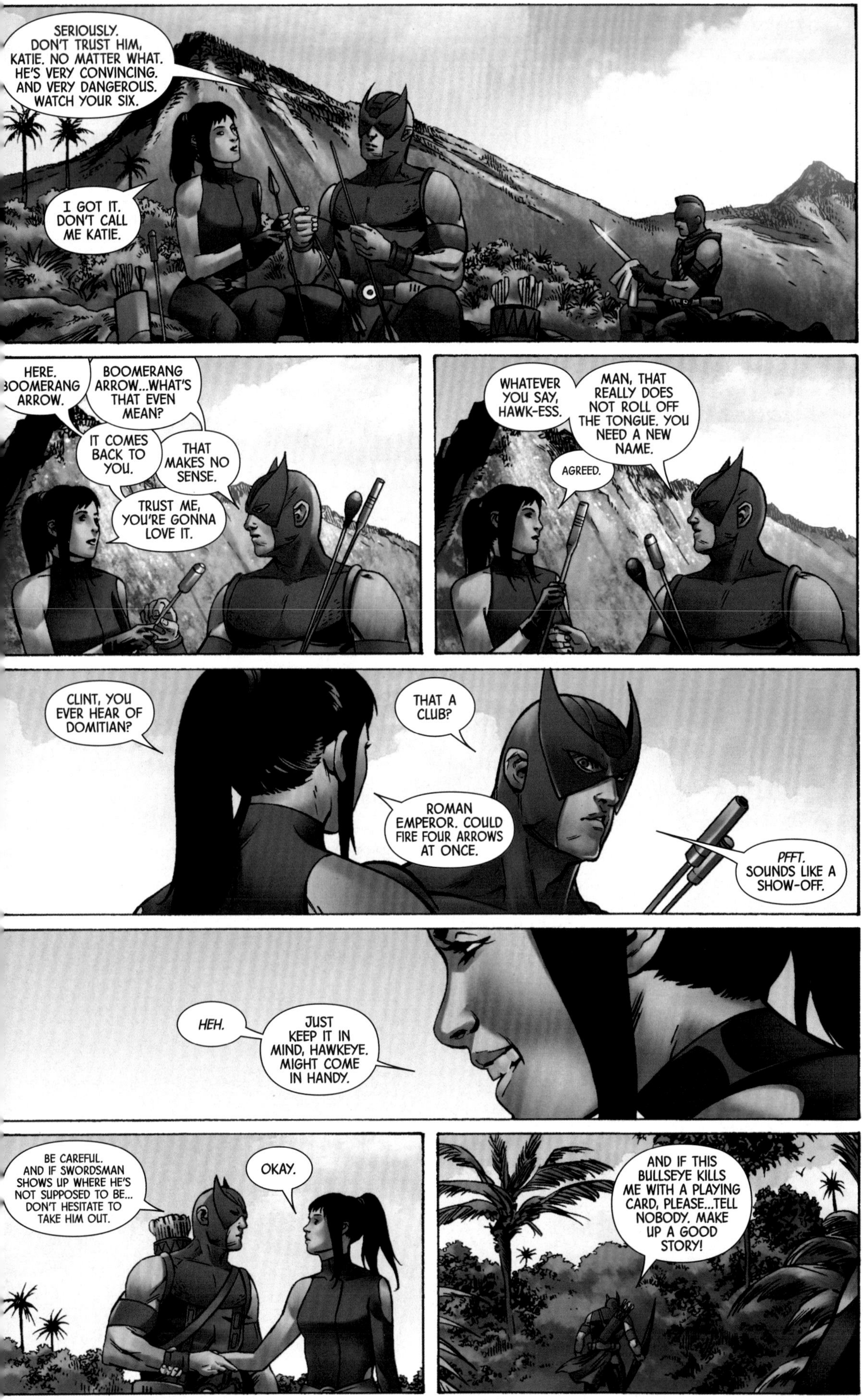
SERIOUSLY. DON'T TRUST HIM, KATIE. NO MATTER WHAT. HE'S VERY CONVINCING. AND VERY DANGEROUS. WATCH YOUR SIX.
I GOT IT. DON'T CALL ME KATIE.
HERE. BOOMERANG ARROW.
BOOMERANG ARROW...WHAT'S THAT EVEN MEAN?
IT COMES BACK TO YOU.
THAT MAKES NO SENSE.
TRUST ME, YOU'RE GONNA LOVE IT.
WHATEVER YOU SAY, HAWK-ESS.
MAN, THAT REALLY DOES NOT ROLL OFF THE TONGUE. YOU NEED A NEW NAME.
AGREED.
CLINT, YOU EVER HEAR OF DOMITIAN?
THAT A CLUB?
ROMAN EMPEROR. COULD FIRE FOUR ARROWS AT ONCE.
PFFT. SOUNDS LIKE A SHOW-OFF.
HEH.
JUST KEEP IT IN MIND, HAWKEYE. MIGHT COME IN HANDY.
BE CAREFUL. AND IF SWORDSMAN SHOWS UP WHERE HE'S NOT SUPPOSED TO BE... DON'T HESITATE TO TAKE HIM OUT.
OKAY.
AND IF THIS BULLSEYE KILLS ME WITH A PLAYING CARD, PLEASE...TELL NOBODY. MAKE UP A GOOD STORY!

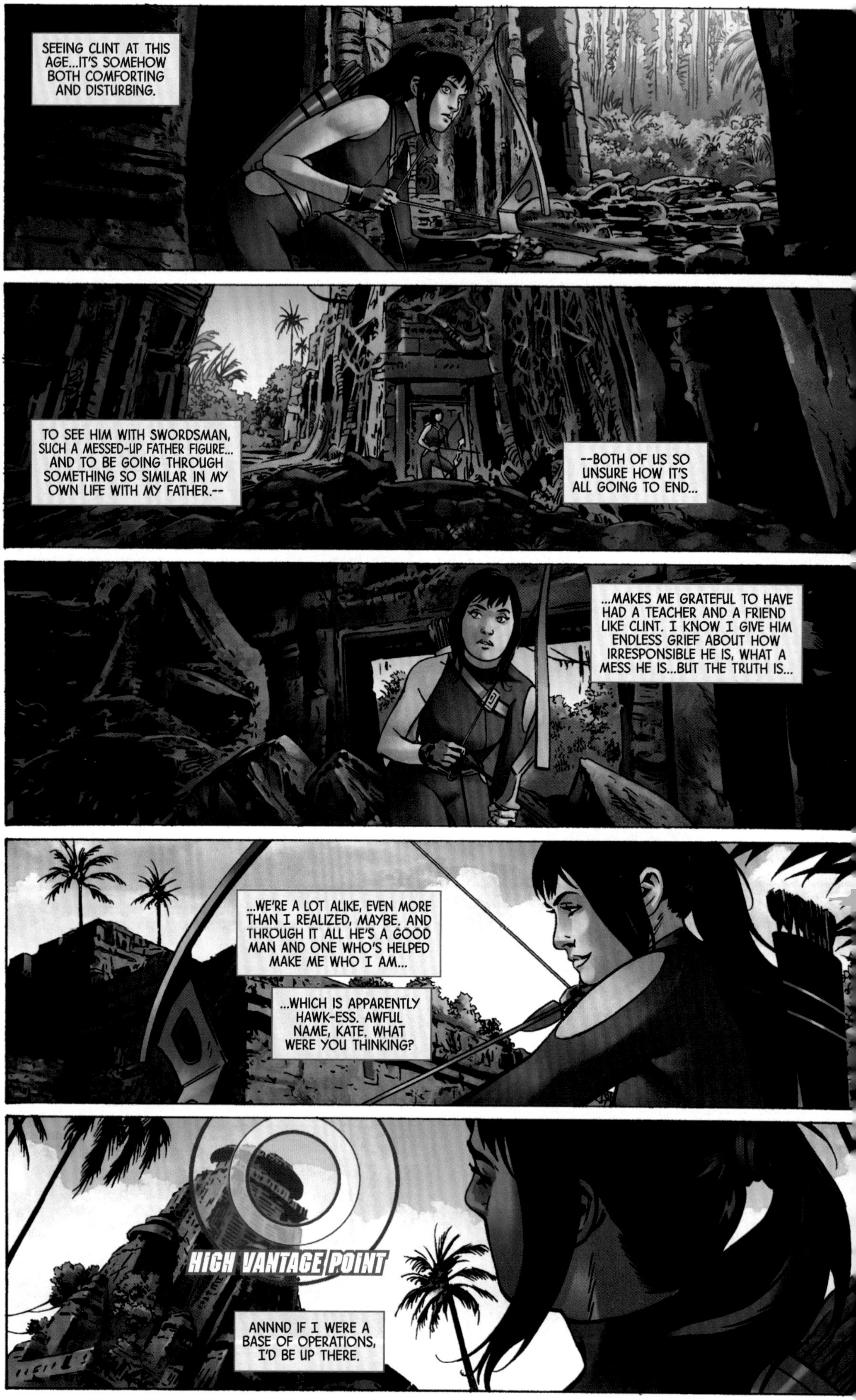
SEEING CLINT AT THIS AGE...IT'S SOMEHOW BOTH COMFORTING AND DISTURBING.
TO SEE HIM WITH SWORDSMAN, SUCH A MESSED-UP FATHER FIGURE... AND TO BE GOING THROUGH SOMETHING SO SIMILAR IN MY OWN LIFE WITH MY FATHER.--
--BOTH OF US SO UNSURE HOW IT'S ALL GOING TO END...
...MAKES ME GRATEFUL TO HAVE HAD A TEACHER AND A FRIEND LIKE CLINT. I KNOW I GIVE HIM ENDLESS GRIEF ABOUT HOW IRRESPONSIBLE HE IS, WHAT A MESS HE IS...BUT THE TRUTH IS...
...WE'RE A LOT ALIKE, EVEN MORE THAN I REALIZED, MAYBE, AND THROUGH IT ALL HE'S A GOOD MAN AND ONE WHO'S HELPED MAKE ME WHO I AM...
...WHICH IS APPARENTLY HAWK-ESS. AWFUL NAME, KATE. WHAT WERE YOU THINKING?
HIGH VANTAGE POINT
ANNND IF I WERE A BASE OF OPERATIONS, I'D BE UP THERE.

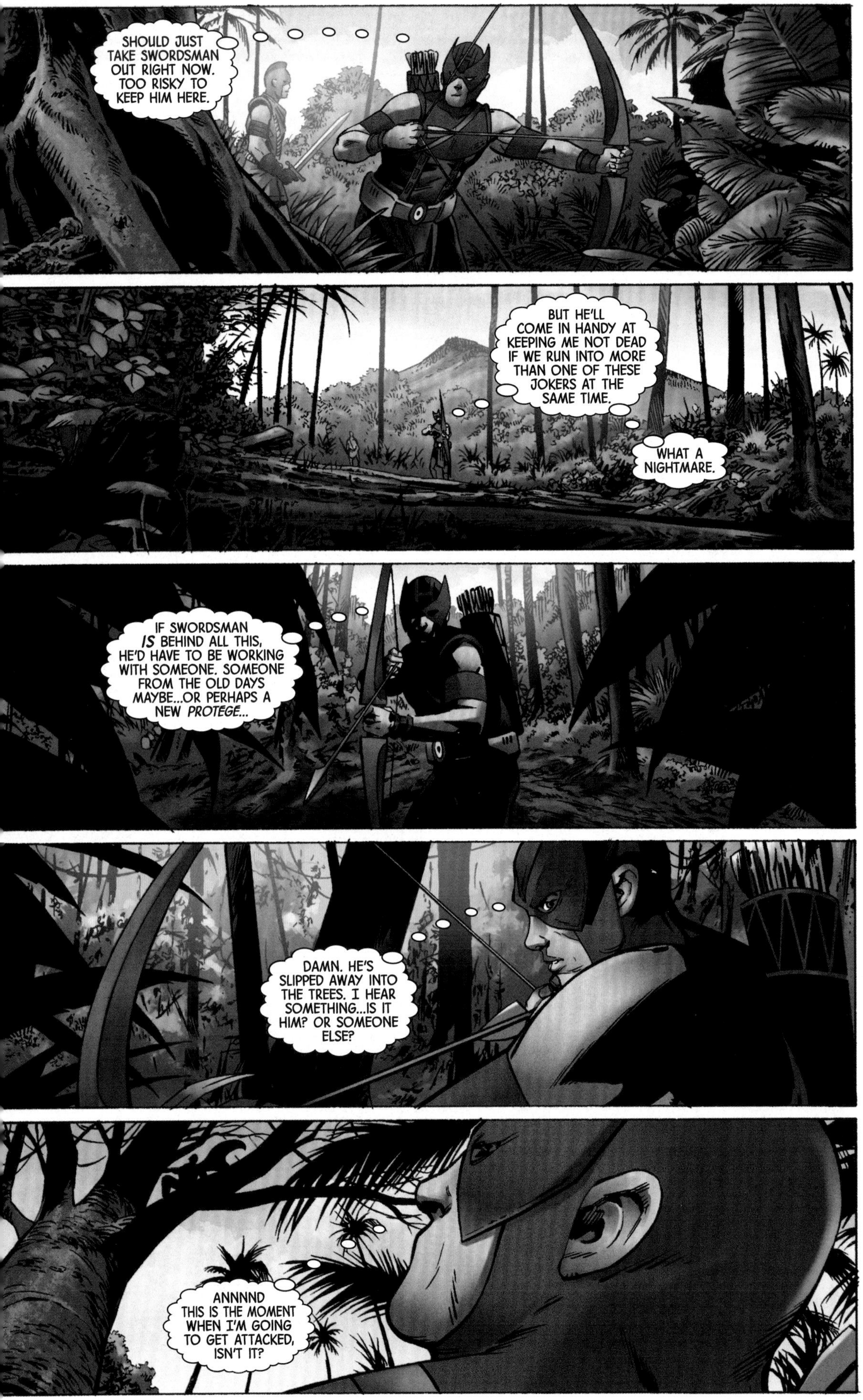
SHOULD JUST TAKE SWORDSMAN OUT RIGHT NOW. TOO RISKY TO KEEP HIM HERE.
BUT HE'LL COME IN HANDY AT KEEPING ME NOT DEAD IF WE RUN INTO MORE THAN ONE OF THESE JOKERS AT THE SAME TIME.
WHAT A NIGHTMARE.
IF SWORDSMAN *IS* BEHIND ALL THIS, HE'D HAVE TO BE WORKING WITH SOMEONE. SOMEONE FROM THE OLD DAYS MAYBE...OR PERHAPS A NEW *PROTÉGÉ*...
DAMN. HE'S SLIPPED AWAY INTO THE TREES. I HEAR SOMETHING...IS IT HIM? OR SOMEONE ELSE?
ANNNND THIS IS THE MOMENT WHEN I'M GOING TO GET ATTACKED, ISN'T IT?

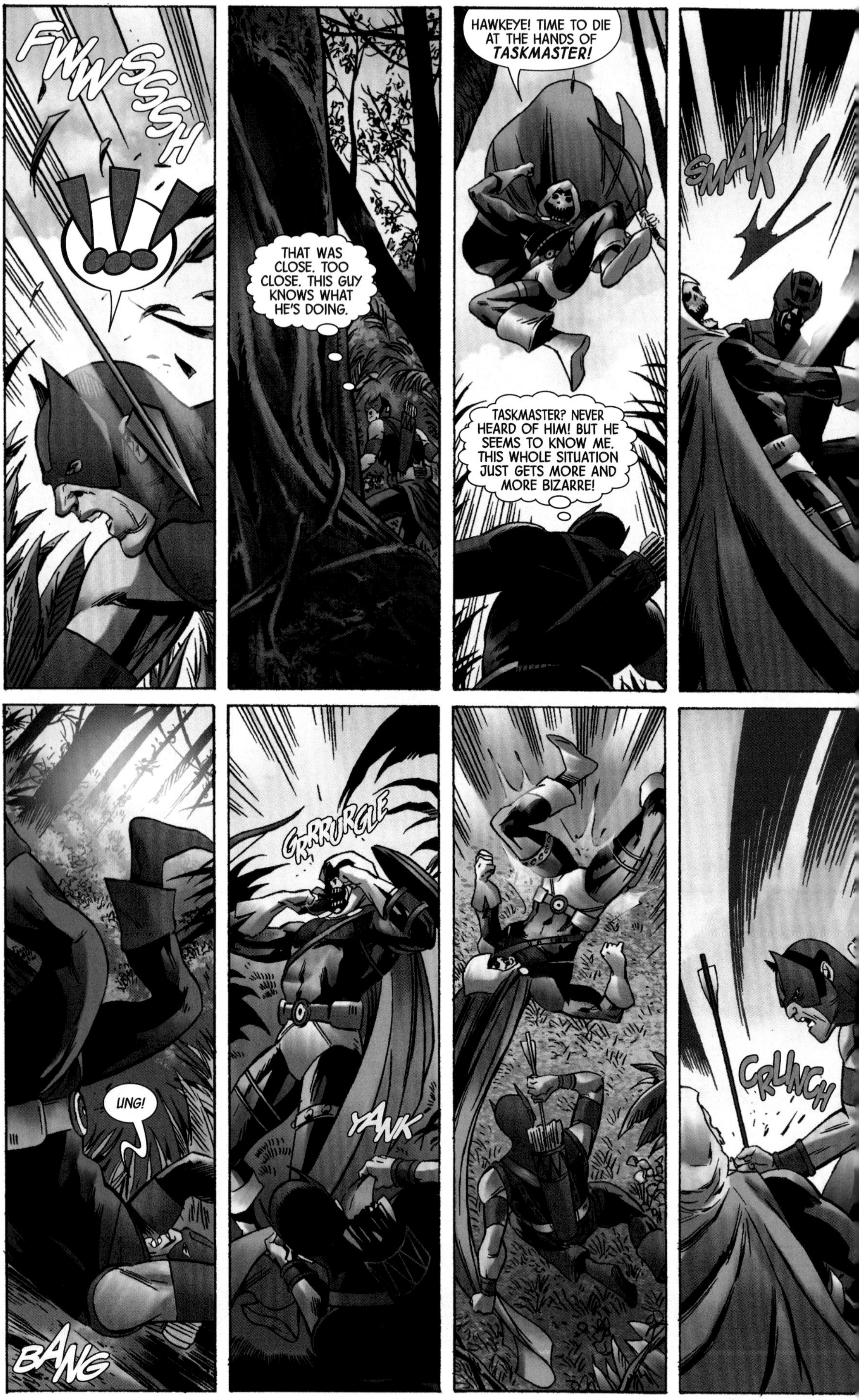
FWWSSSH
!!!...
THAT WAS CLOSE. TOO CLOSE. THIS GUY KNOWS WHAT HE'S DOING.
HAWKEYE! TIME TO DIE AT THE HANDS OF TASKMASTER!
TASKMASTER? NEVER HEARD OF HIM! BUT HE SEEMS TO KNOW ME. THIS WHOLE SITUATION JUST GETS MORE AND MORE BIZARRE!
SMAK
UNG!
BANG
GRRRURGLE
YANK
CRUNCH

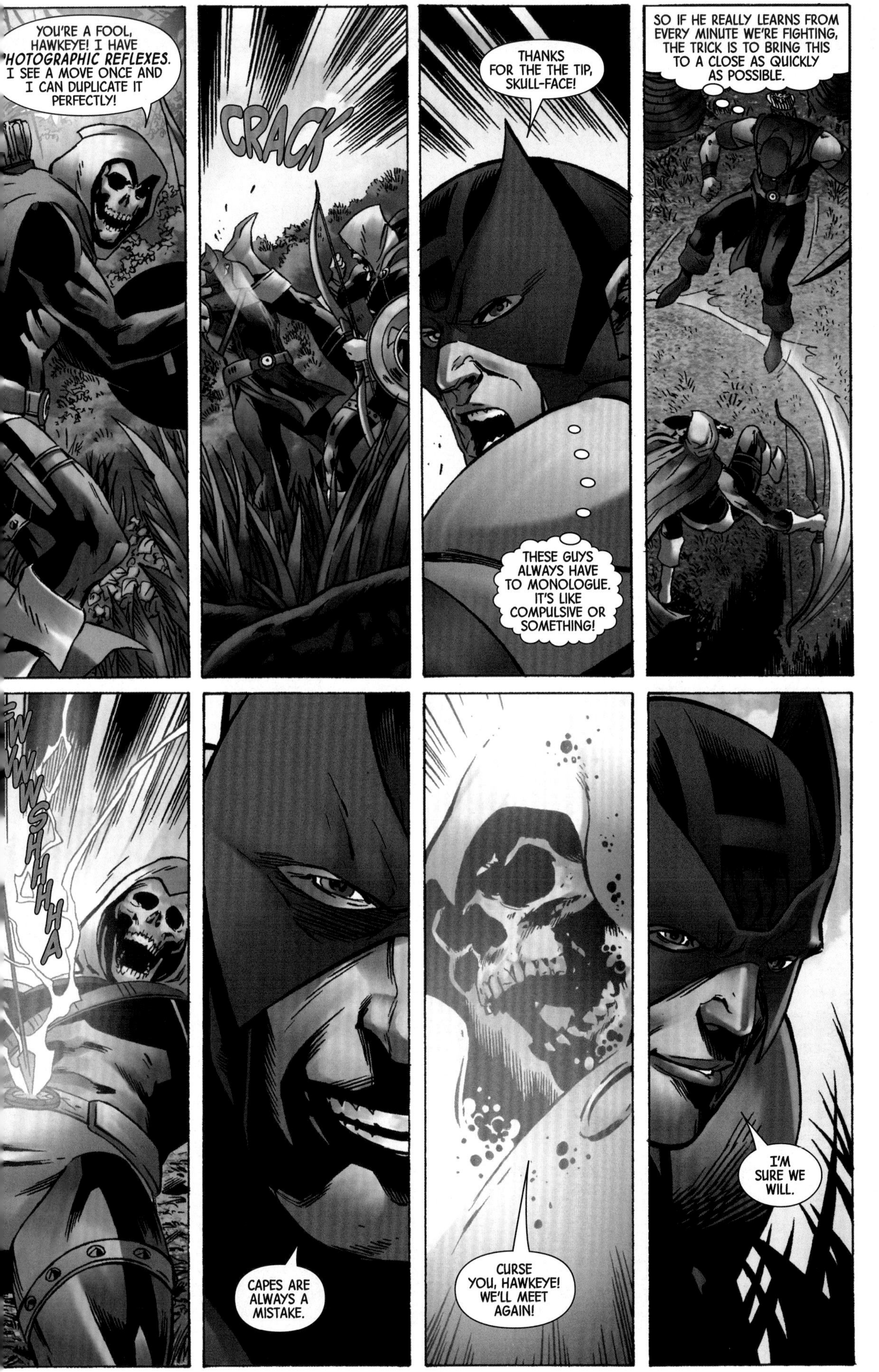
YOU'RE A FOOL, HAWKEYE! I HAVE PHOTOGRAPHIC REFLEXES. I SEE A MOVE ONCE AND I CAN DUPLICATE IT PERFECTLY!
CRACK
THANKS FOR THE THE TIP, SKULL-FACE!
THESE GUYS ALWAYS HAVE TO MONOLOGUE. IT'S LIKE COMPULSIVE OR SOMETHING!
SO IF HE REALLY LEARNS FROM EVERY MINUTE WE'RE FIGHTING, THE TRICK IS TO BRING THIS TO A CLOSE AS QUICKLY AS POSSIBLE.
FWWWSHHHHA
CAPES ARE ALWAYS A MISTAKE.
CURSE YOU, HAWKEYE! WE'LL MEET AGAIN!
I'M SURE WE WILL.

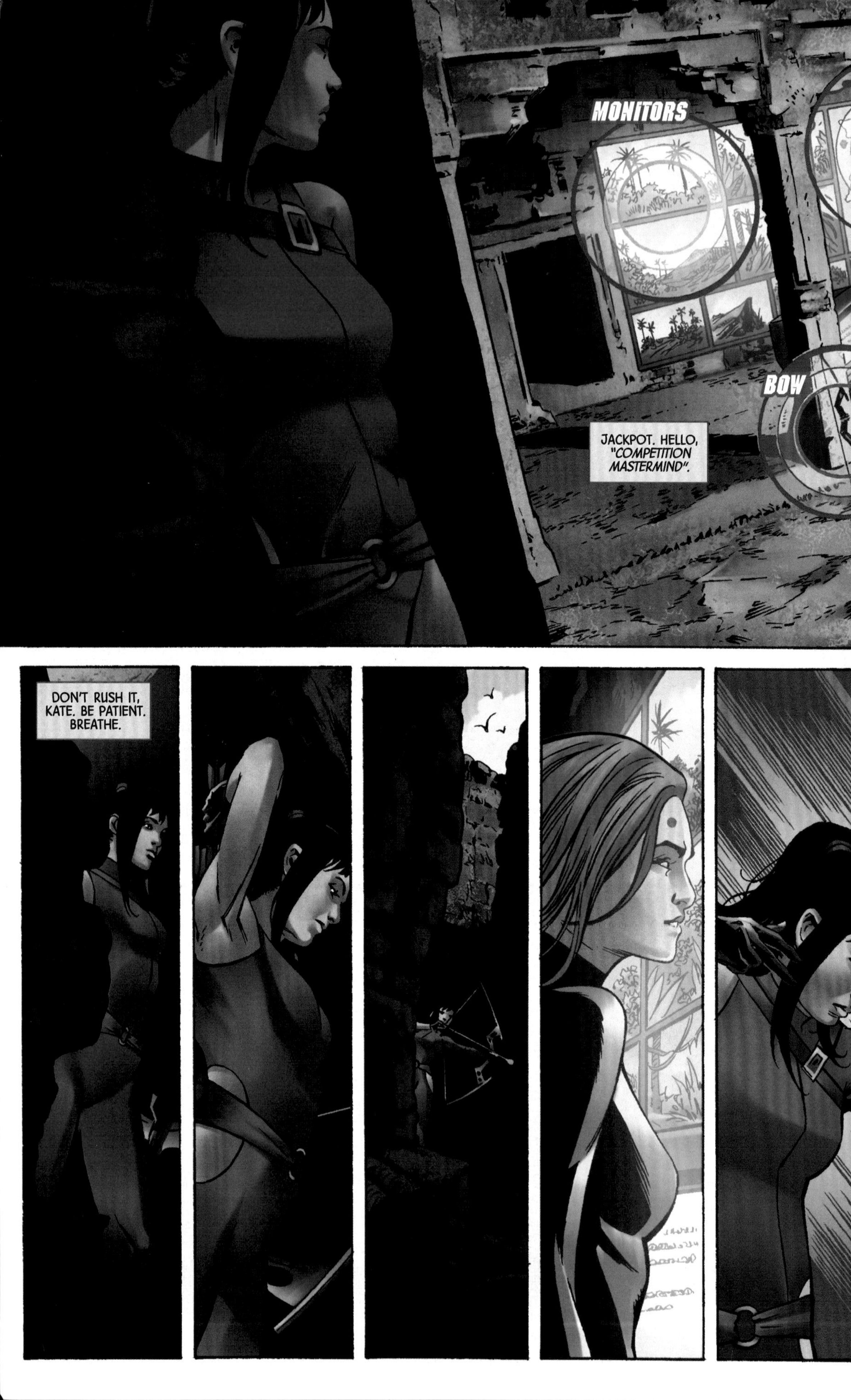
MONITORS
BOW
JACKPOT. HELLO, "COMPETITION MASTERMIND".
DON'T RUSH IT, KATE. BE PATIENT. BREATHE.

COMPETITOR TRACKING

COMPETITION MASTERMIND?

ARROWS

RADIO

GLINT OF METAL?

WE'VE GOT EVERYTHING HERE... INCLUDING SOMETHING...ER *SOMEONE* THAT DEFINITELY DOESN'T BELONG.

AND I KNOW EXACTLY WHO YOU ARE.

FWWWSH

THUNK

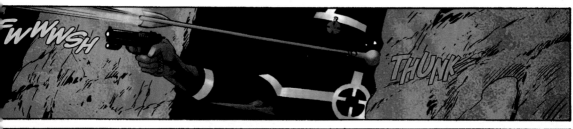

FOOOOM

?!

AHHHH!

UNNNGGG!

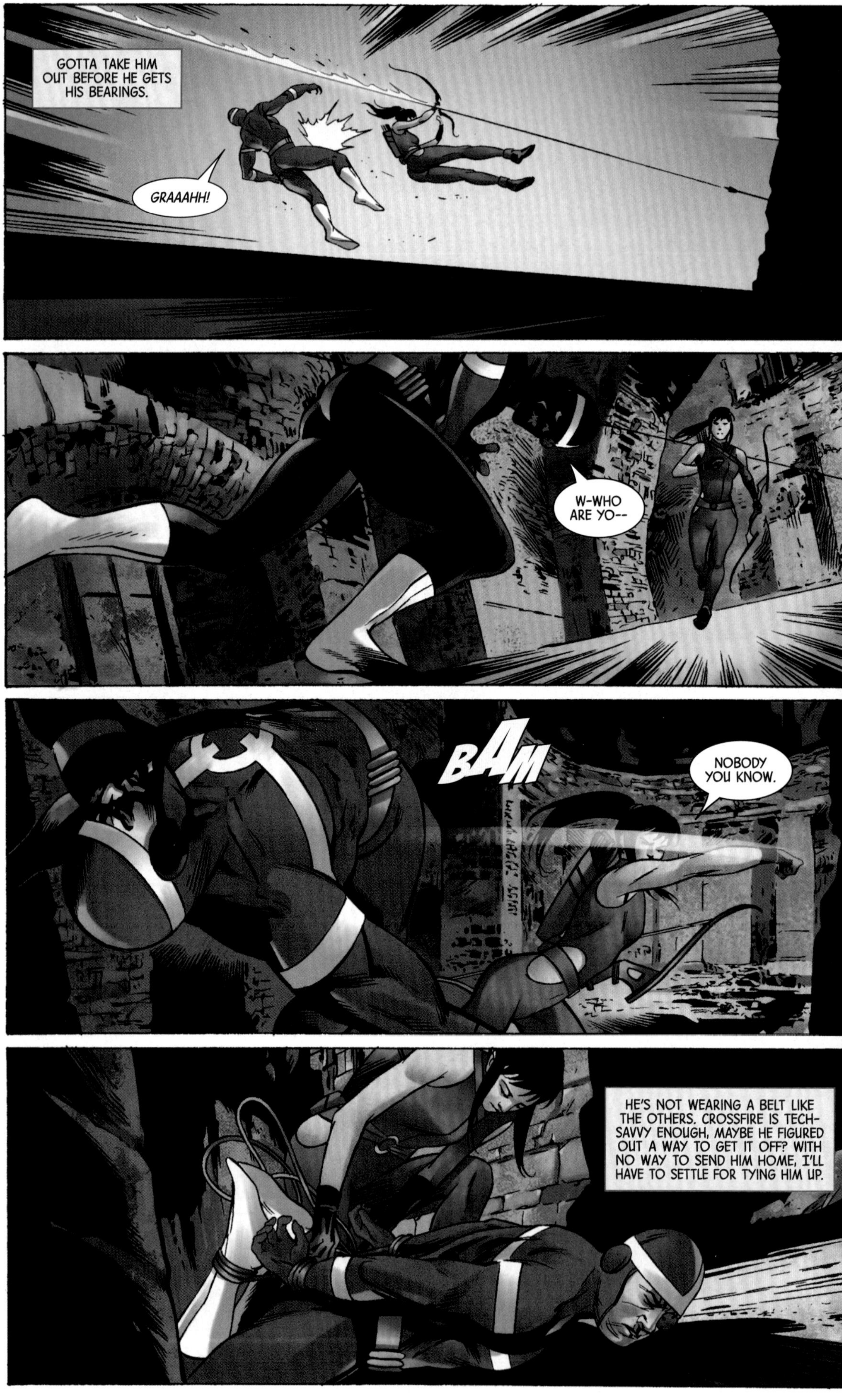
GOTTA TAKE HIM OUT BEFORE HE GETS HIS BEARINGS.
GRAAAHH!
W-WHO ARE YO--
BAM
NOBODY YOU KNOW.
HE'S NOT WEARING A BELT LIKE THE OTHERS. CROSSFIRE IS TECH-SAVVY ENOUGH, MAYBE HE FIGURED OUT A WAY TO GET IT OFF? WITH NO WAY TO SEND HIM HOME, I'LL HAVE TO SETTLE FOR TYING HIM UP.

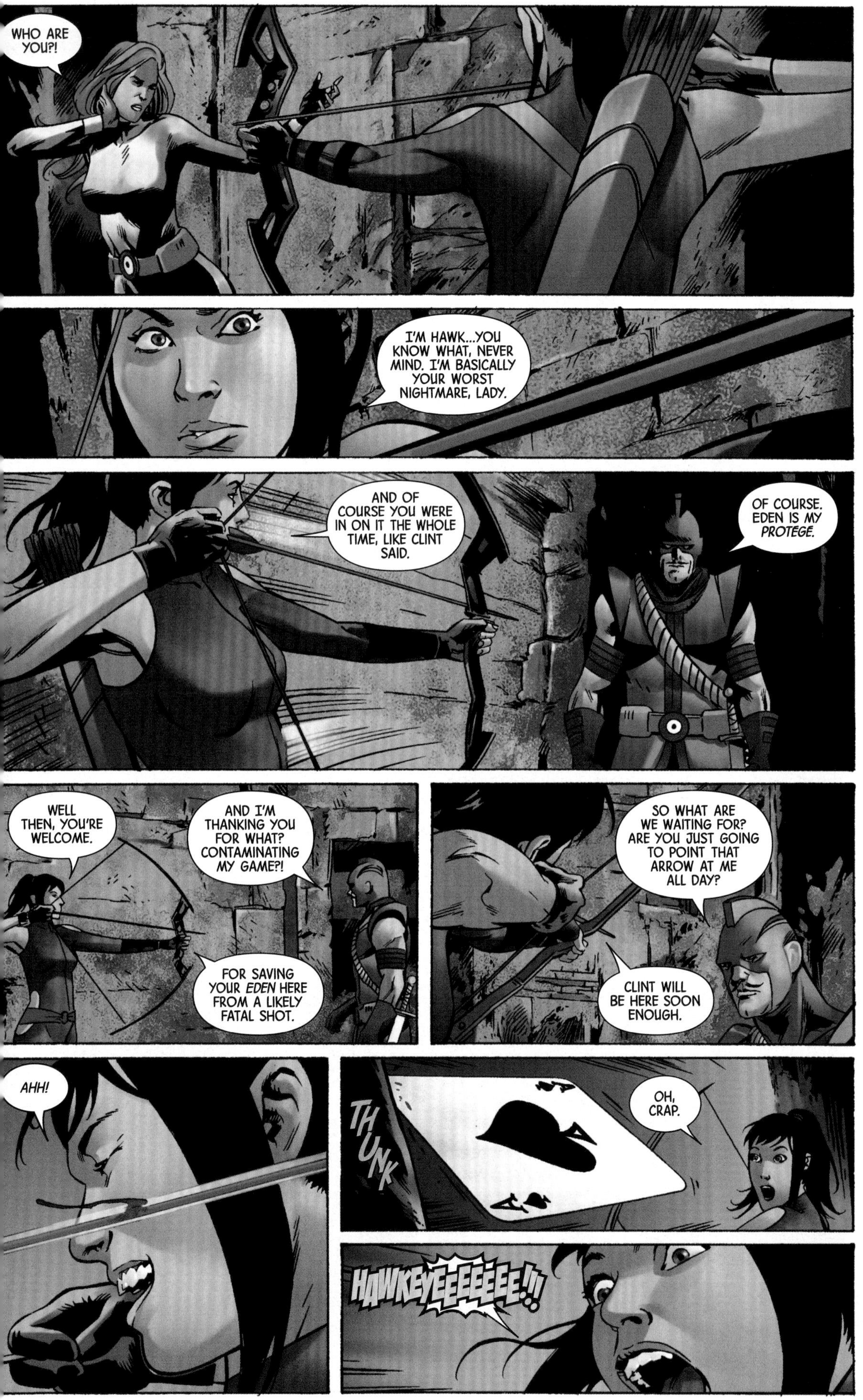
WHO ARE YOU?!
I'M HAWK...YOU KNOW WHAT, NEVER MIND. I'M BASICALLY YOUR WORST NIGHTMARE, LADY.
AND OF COURSE YOU WERE IN ON IT THE WHOLE TIME, LIKE CLINT SAID.
OF COURSE. EDEN IS MY *PROTEGE.*
WELL THEN, YOU'RE WELCOME.
AND I'M THANKING YOU FOR WHAT? CONTAMINATING MY GAME?!
FOR SAVING YOUR *EDEN* HERE FROM A LIKELY FATAL SHOT.
SO WHAT ARE WE WAITING FOR? ARE YOU JUST GOING TO POINT THAT ARROW AT ME ALL DAY?
CLINT WILL BE HERE SOON ENOUGH.
AHH!
THUNK
OH, CRAP.
HAWKEYEEEEEEE!!!

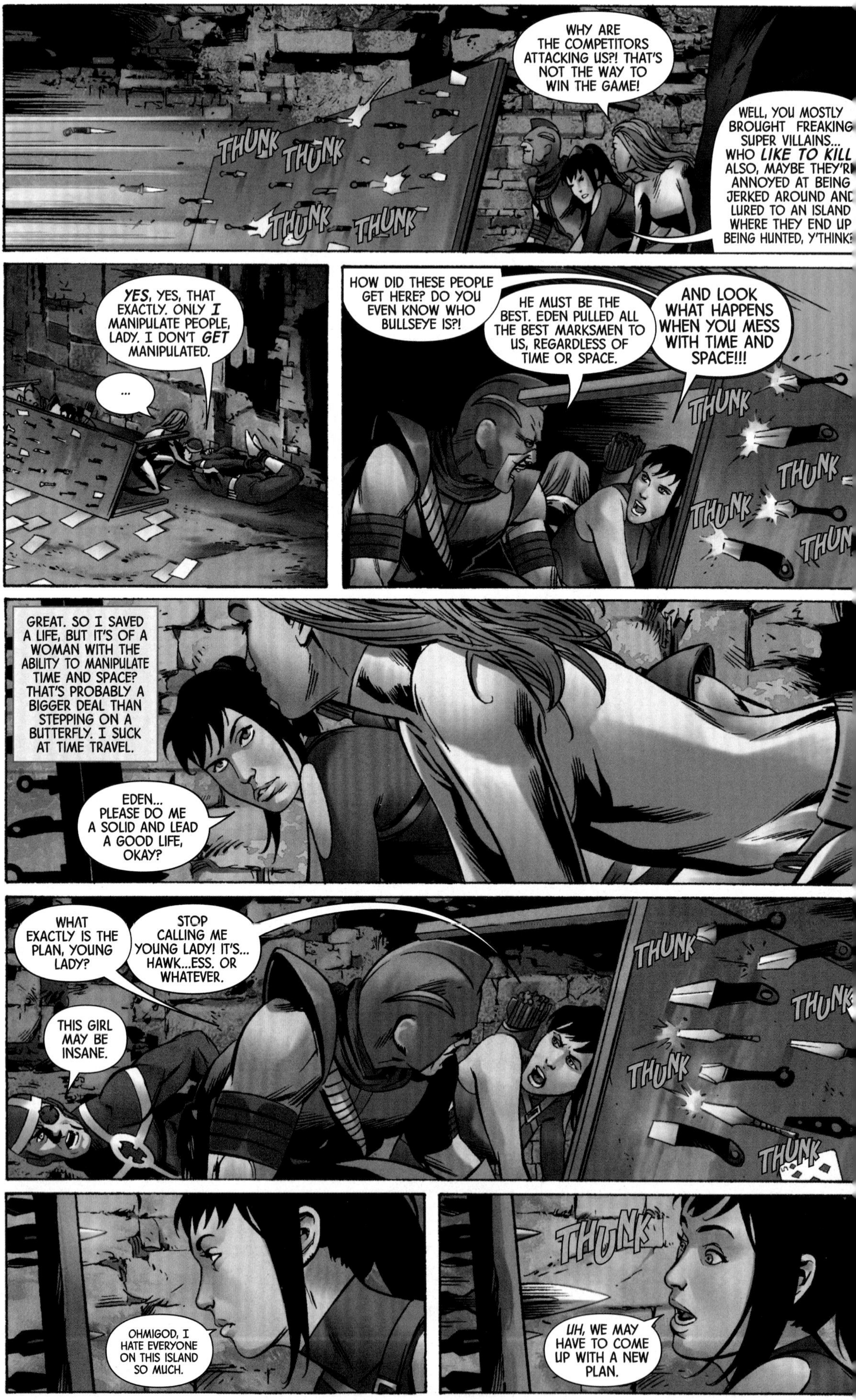
WHY ARE THE COMPETITORS ATTACKING US?! THAT'S NOT THE WAY TO WIN THE GAME!
THUNK THUNK THUNK THUNK
WELL, YOU MOSTLY BROUGHT FREAKING SUPER VILLAINS... WHO LIKE TO KILL. ALSO, MAYBE THEY'RE ANNOYED AT BEING JERKED AROUND AND LURED TO AN ISLAND WHERE THEY END UP BEING HUNTED, Y'THINK?
YES, YES, THAT EXACTLY. ONLY I MANIPULATE PEOPLE, LADY. I DON'T GET MANIPULATED.
...
HOW DID THESE PEOPLE GET HERE? DO YOU EVEN KNOW WHO BULLSEYE IS?!
HE MUST BE THE BEST. EDEN PULLED ALL THE BEST MARKSMEN TO US, REGARDLESS OF TIME OR SPACE.
AND LOOK WHAT HAPPENS WHEN YOU MESS WITH TIME AND SPACE!!!
THUNK THUNK THUNK THUNK
GREAT. SO I SAVED A LIFE, BUT IT'S OF A WOMAN WITH THE ABILITY TO MANIPULATE TIME AND SPACE? THAT'S PROBABLY A BIGGER DEAL THAN STEPPING ON A BUTTERFLY. I SUCK AT TIME TRAVEL.
EDEN... PLEASE DO ME A SOLID AND LEAD A GOOD LIFE, OKAY?
WHAT EXACTLY IS THE PLAN, YOUNG LADY?
STOP CALLING ME YOUNG LADY! IT'S... HAWK...ESS. OR WHATEVER.
THIS GIRL MAY BE INSANE.
THUNK THUNK THUNK THUNK
OHMIGOD, I HATE EVERYONE ON THIS ISLAND SO MUCH.
THUNK
UH, WE MAY HAVE TO COME UP WITH A NEW PLAN.

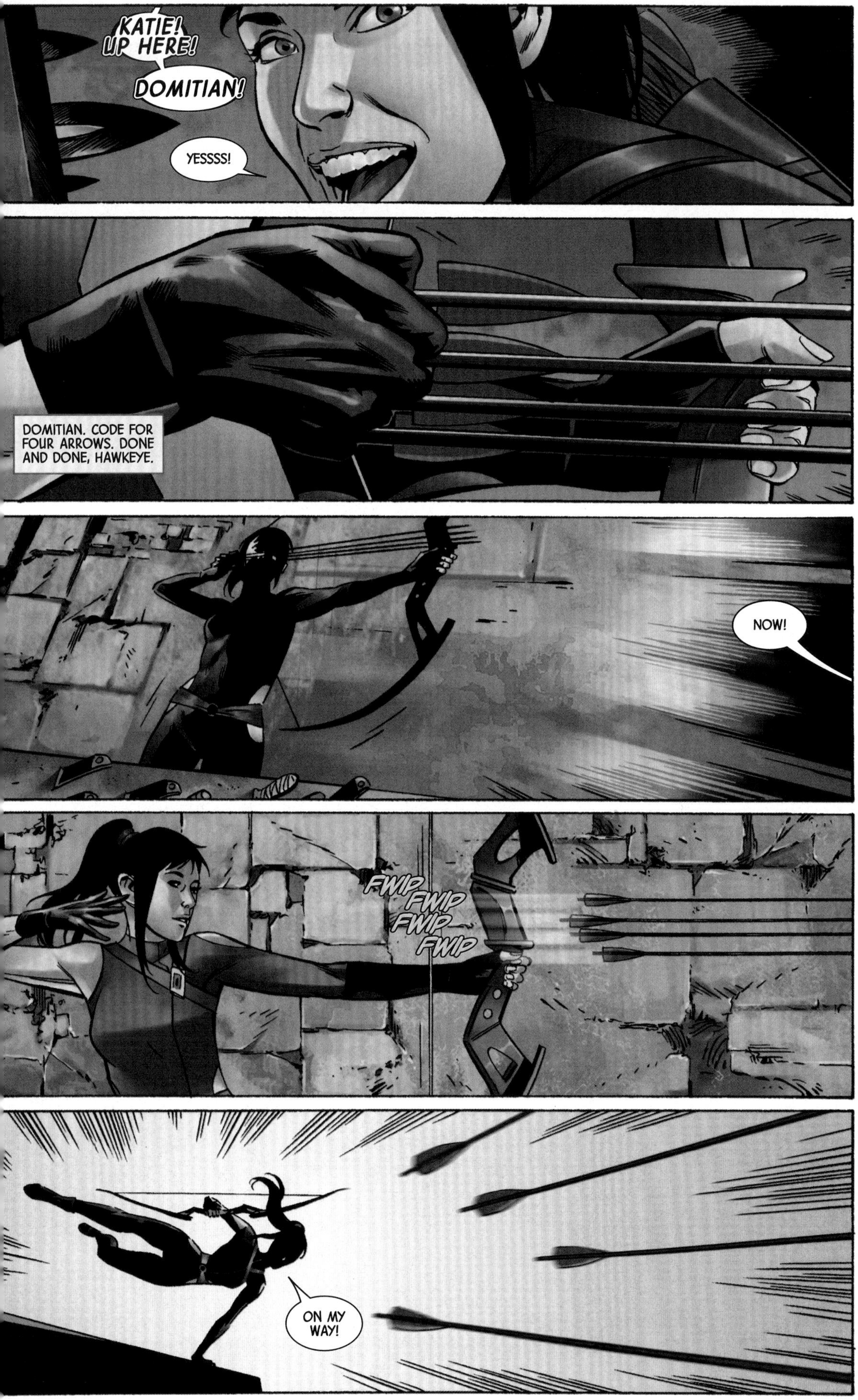

KATIE! UP HERE!
DOMITIAN!
YESSSS!
DOMITIAN. CODE FOR FOUR ARROWS. DONE AND DONE, HAWKEYE.
NOW!
FWIP FWIP FWIP FWIP
ON MY WAY!

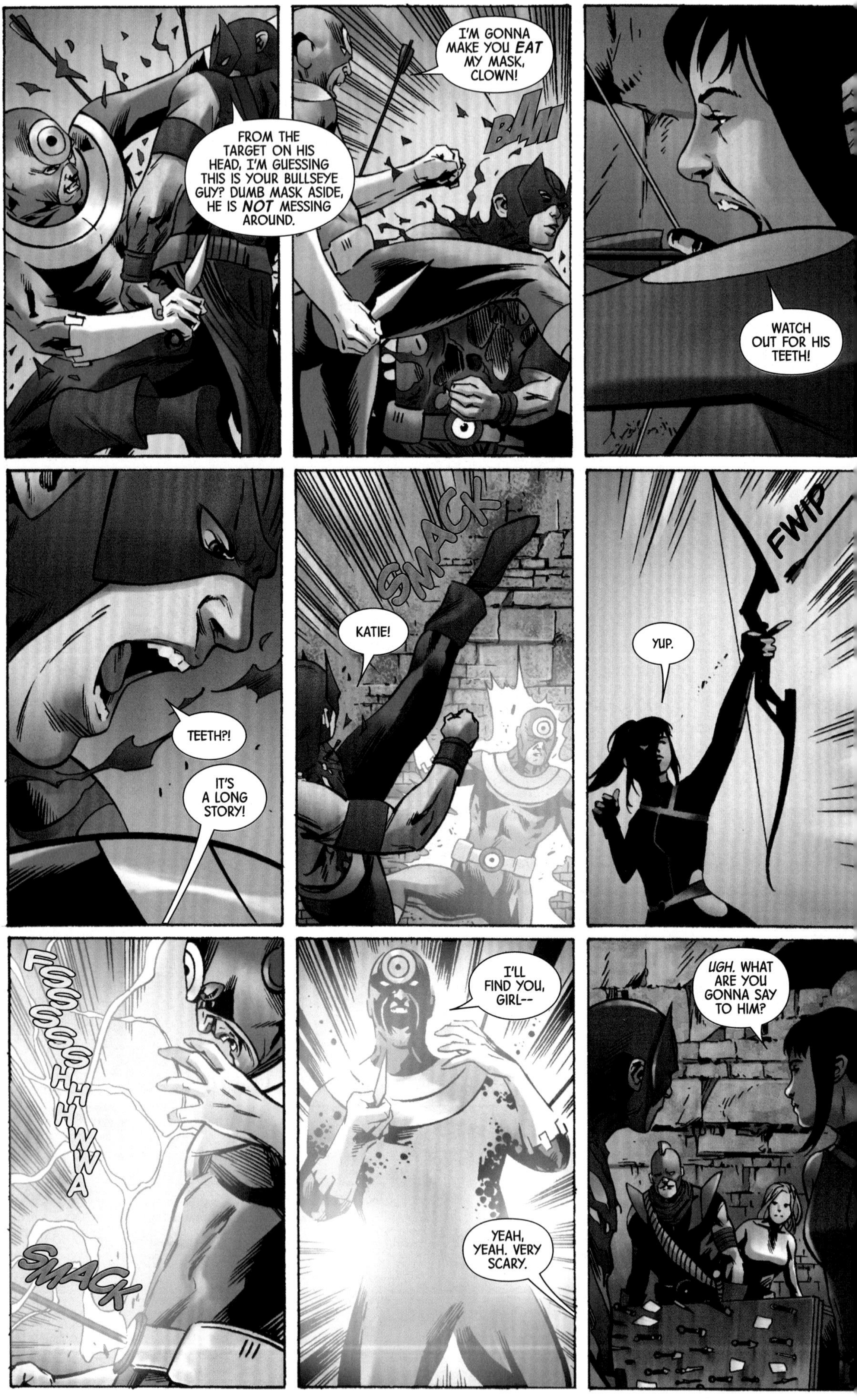
FROM THE TARGET ON HIS HEAD, I'M GUESSING THIS IS YOUR BULLSEYE GUY? DUMB MASK ASIDE, HE IS *NOT* MESSING AROUND.
I'M GONNA MAKE YOU *EAT* MY MASK, CLOWN!
BAM
WATCH OUT FOR HIS TEETH!
TEETH?!
IT'S A LONG STORY!
SMACK
KATIE!
FWIP
YUP.
FSSSSHHWWA
SMACK
I'LL FIND YOU, GIRL--
YEAH, YEAH. VERY SCARY.
UGH. WHAT ARE YOU GONNA SAY TO HIM?

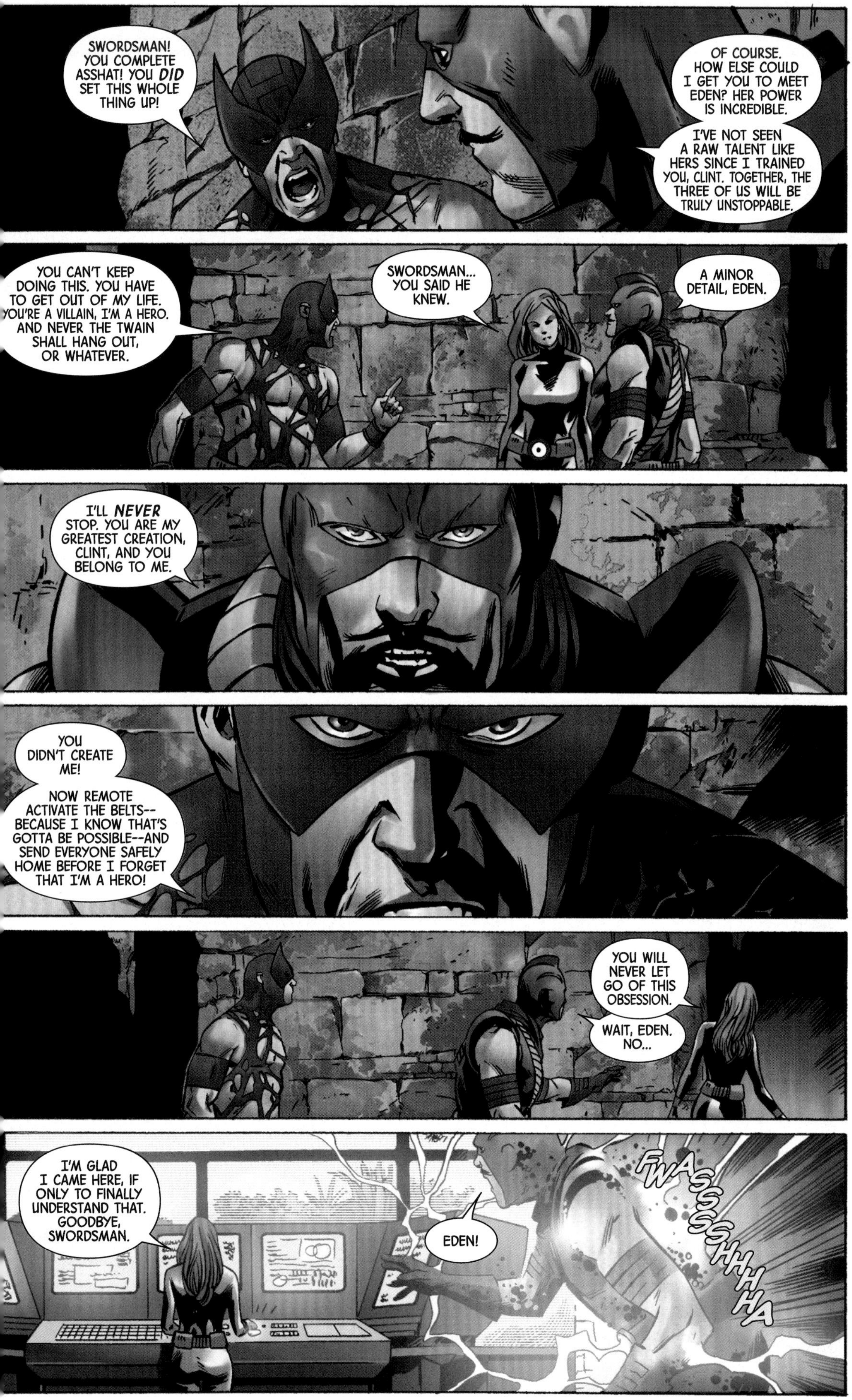

SWORDSMAN! YOU COMPLETE ASSHAT! YOU *DID* SET THIS WHOLE THING UP!
OF COURSE. HOW ELSE COULD I GET YOU TO MEET EDEN? HER POWER IS INCREDIBLE.
I'VE NOT SEEN A RAW TALENT LIKE HERS SINCE I TRAINED YOU, CLINT. TOGETHER, THE THREE OF US WILL BE TRULY UNSTOPPABLE.
YOU CAN'T KEEP DOING THIS. YOU HAVE TO GET OUT OF MY LIFE. YOU'RE A VILLAIN, I'M A HERO. AND NEVER THE TWAIN SHALL HANG OUT, OR WHATEVER.
SWORDSMAN... YOU SAID HE KNEW.
A MINOR DETAIL, EDEN.
I'LL *NEVER* STOP. YOU ARE MY GREATEST CREATION, CLINT, AND YOU BELONG TO ME.
YOU DIDN'T CREATE ME!
NOW REMOTE ACTIVATE THE BELTS--BECAUSE I KNOW THAT'S GOTTA BE POSSIBLE--AND SEND EVERYONE SAFELY HOME BEFORE I FORGET THAT I'M A HERO!
YOU WILL NEVER LET GO OF THIS OBSESSION.
WAIT, EDEN. NO...
I'M GLAD I CAME HERE, IF ONLY TO FINALLY UNDERSTAND THAT. GOODBYE, SWORDSMAN.
EDEN!
FWASSSHHHHA

FWASSSSHHHHA

AND GOODBYE TO YOU, CROSSFIRE.

GIRL, YOU COULDN'T EVEN UNDO THE CABLES FIRST? C'MON--

I HAVE SENT EVERYONE BACK TO WHERE THEY BELONG, SAVE YOU AND YOUR COMPANION, OF COURSE.

USE THIS REMOTE TO ACTIVATE YOUR BELT WHENEVER YOU'RE READY TO LEAVE.

...THANKS.

FWASSSSHHHHA

I APOLOGIZE FOR ALL OF THIS AND WISH YOU WELL, CLINT BARTON.

...YOU TOO.

SHE WAS PRETTY CUTE, RIGHT?

OHMIGOD. I CAN'T BELIEVE YOU.

WHAT? I WAS DIGGING THE LOOK. PLUS YOU KNOW WE'D HAVE A LOT IN COMMON...MANIPULATED BY THE SAME ASSHAT.

UGH. STOP.

ANNNND SURPRISING NOBODY, YOUR SHIRT INEXPLICABLY GOT TORN TO SHREDS. C'MON.

IT HAPPENS.

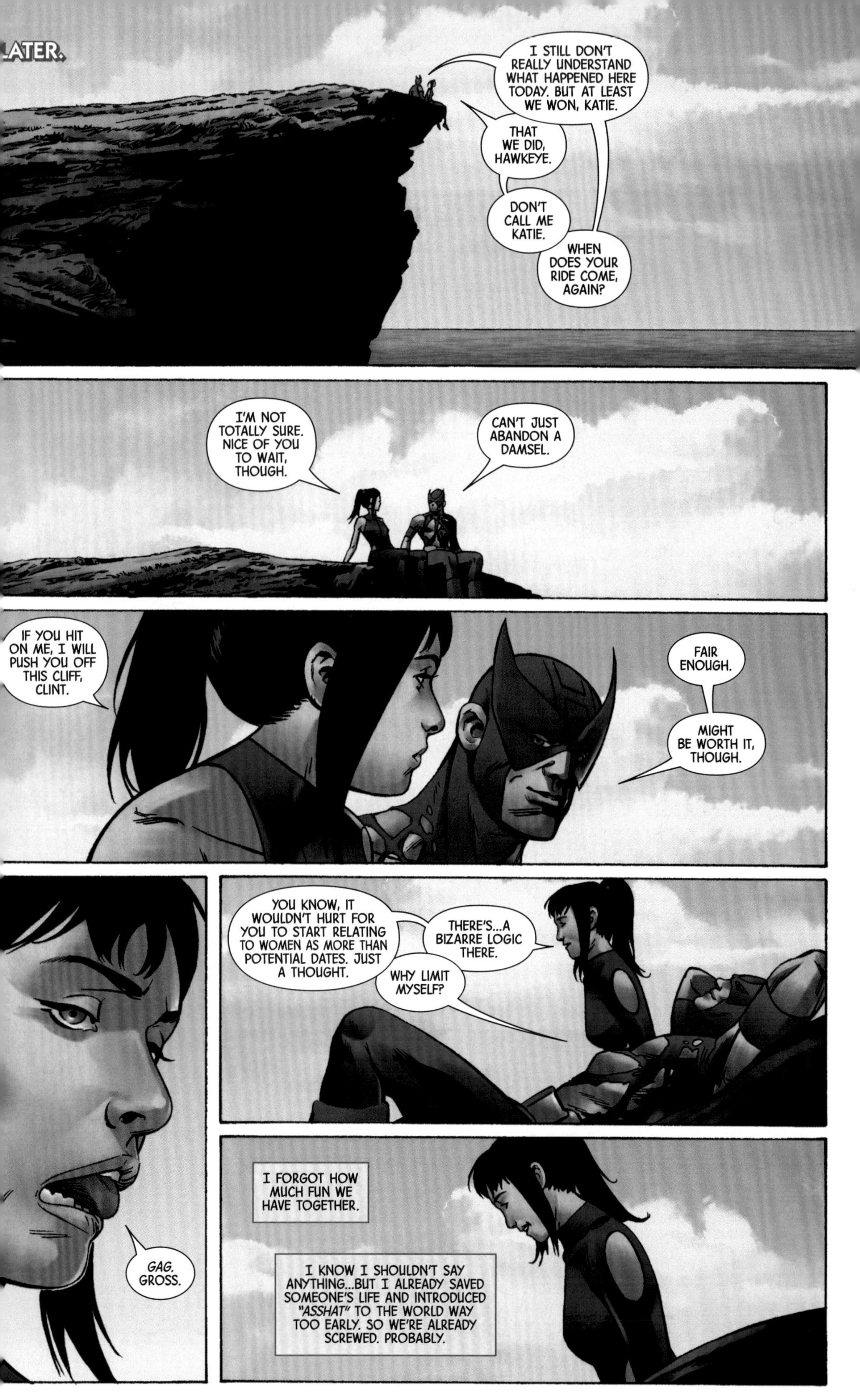
LATER.
I STILL DON'T REALLY UNDERSTAND WHAT HAPPENED HERE TODAY. BUT AT LEAST WE WON, KATIE.
THAT WE DID, HAWKEYE.
DON'T CALL ME KATIE.
WHEN DOES YOUR RIDE COME, AGAIN?
I'M NOT TOTALLY SURE. NICE OF YOU TO WAIT, THOUGH.
CAN'T JUST ABANDON A DAMSEL.
IF YOU HIT ON ME, I WILL PUSH YOU OFF THIS CLIFF, CLINT.
FAIR ENOUGH.
MIGHT BE WORTH IT, THOUGH.
GAG. GROSS.
THERE'S...A BIZARRE LOGIC THERE.
WHY LIMIT MYSELF?
YOU KNOW, IT WOULDN'T HURT FOR YOU TO START RELATING TO WOMEN AS MORE THAN POTENTIAL DATES. JUST A THOUGHT.
I FORGOT HOW MUCH FUN WE HAVE TOGETHER.
I KNOW I SHOULDN'T SAY ANYTHING...BUT I ALREADY SAVED SOMEONE'S LIFE AND INTRODUCED "ASSHAT" TO THE WORLD WAY TOO EARLY. SO WE'RE ALREADY SCREWED. PROBABLY.

I'VE BEEN GOING THROUGH SOME STUFF BACK HOME, CLINT. A LOT OF PEOPLE IN MY LIFE ARE TURNING OUT TO BE NOT WHO I THOUGHT THEY WERE...PEOPLE LETTING ME DOWN.

AND I HAVEN'T EXACTLY BEEN COMPLETELY HONEST WITH YOU...MY NAME ISN'T HAWK-ESS...I MEAN, OF COURSE IT ISN'T, THAT'S AN AWFUL NAME. MY NAME IS HAWKEYE.

DON'T... DON'T SAY ANYTHING, JUST LEMME TALK FOR A MINUTE, OKAY?

SO YOU'RE NOT DEAD OR ANYTHING WEIRD, YOU'RE JUST MY MENTOR AND SOMETIMES MY COLLEAGUE, AND YOU SHARED YOUR NAME WITH ME...

...AND WELL, I DON'T ALWAYS AGREE WITH WHAT YOU DO, BUT YOU'RE ALWAYS *TRYING* TO DO RIGHT. AND THAT MEANS A LOT.

SEEING *YOUR* MENTOR, SWORDSMAN, BEING...WELL, A REAL PIECE OF WORK...IT MAKES ME REALIZE HOW LUCKY I AM TO HAVE YOU.

EVEN WHEN YOU MAKE ME WANT TO TEAR MY HAIR OUT, I STILL ALWAYS KNOW YOU'RE GOOD.

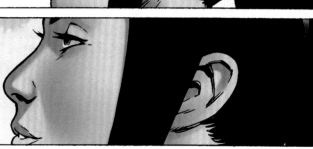

THE THINGS I ADMIRE THE MOST ABOUT YOU NOW-- YOUR HEART, HOW YOU NEVER GIVE UP EVEN AS YOU FAIL OVER AND OVER AGAIN--YOU CAME TO THOSE THINGS WITHOUT A *YOU* TO HELP YOU.

AND I GUESS, WELL, I JUST WANTED TO SAY...

...THANK YOU. YOU'RE A GOOD MENTOR, CLINT, A GOOD FRIEND.

→SNORE←

CLINT?!

OH, YOU HAVE *GOT* TO BE KIDDING ME.

HONESTLY? IT'S SORT OF COMFORTING THAT SOME THINGS NEVER CHA--

PLINK

→SNORE←

With friends like these...

81A8437
BARTON, C
VENICE BEACH, C

81A2574
BISHOP, K
NICE BEA

81A84
BARTON
CE BE

81A84

13

JONATHAN
<3 LUCKY???

WOLVERINE
TEAM-UP!!!

HAWK INVESTIGATIONS

22 1/2 N. Venice Blvd.
Venice, CA 90291

CASE NO.: 016007
INVESTIGATOR: KATE BISHOP, A.K.A. HAWKEYE
CLIENT: ME AND SOME WOLVERINES

CASE OVERVIEW:

While following up on some leads I got from Madame Masque's place, I ran into Laura Kinney, Gabby and Jonathan--A.K.A. Wolverine, Tiny Wolverine (?) and Literal Wolverine (??? I don't even know)--tearing things up at the same "sidekick hangout" I was investigating. Turns out we were looking for the same guy (poor sap).

DETAIL OF EVENTS:

We teamed up to make mincemeat of the minions, which was a super-nice distraction from the whole my-dad-may-have-murdered-my-mom-unless-she's-still-alive thing and the Madame-Masque-became-me-and-made-poor-life-decisions thing.

Hawkey
Remember
by and lot's

All my lov,

N

Santa monica boulevard
penthouse, Los Angeles
California.

ACTION TAKEN:

We made mincemeat again (this time of the bad guy and his clones) and fortunately kept all our feet (long story). We trussed them up in roughly 500 rolls of duct tape for the LAPD to find, with a confession. Also, I'm realizing just now that nobody paid me. Dammit.

EXHIBI
A

ADDITIONAL NOTES:

I think Lucky and Jonathan the Wolverine are in love. Is that legal?

(Oh, and I may have, uh, realized I needed help with the investigation into my mom's murder and uh...called Clint "this won't be awkward at all" Barton. GAH.)

STATUS:

CLOSED

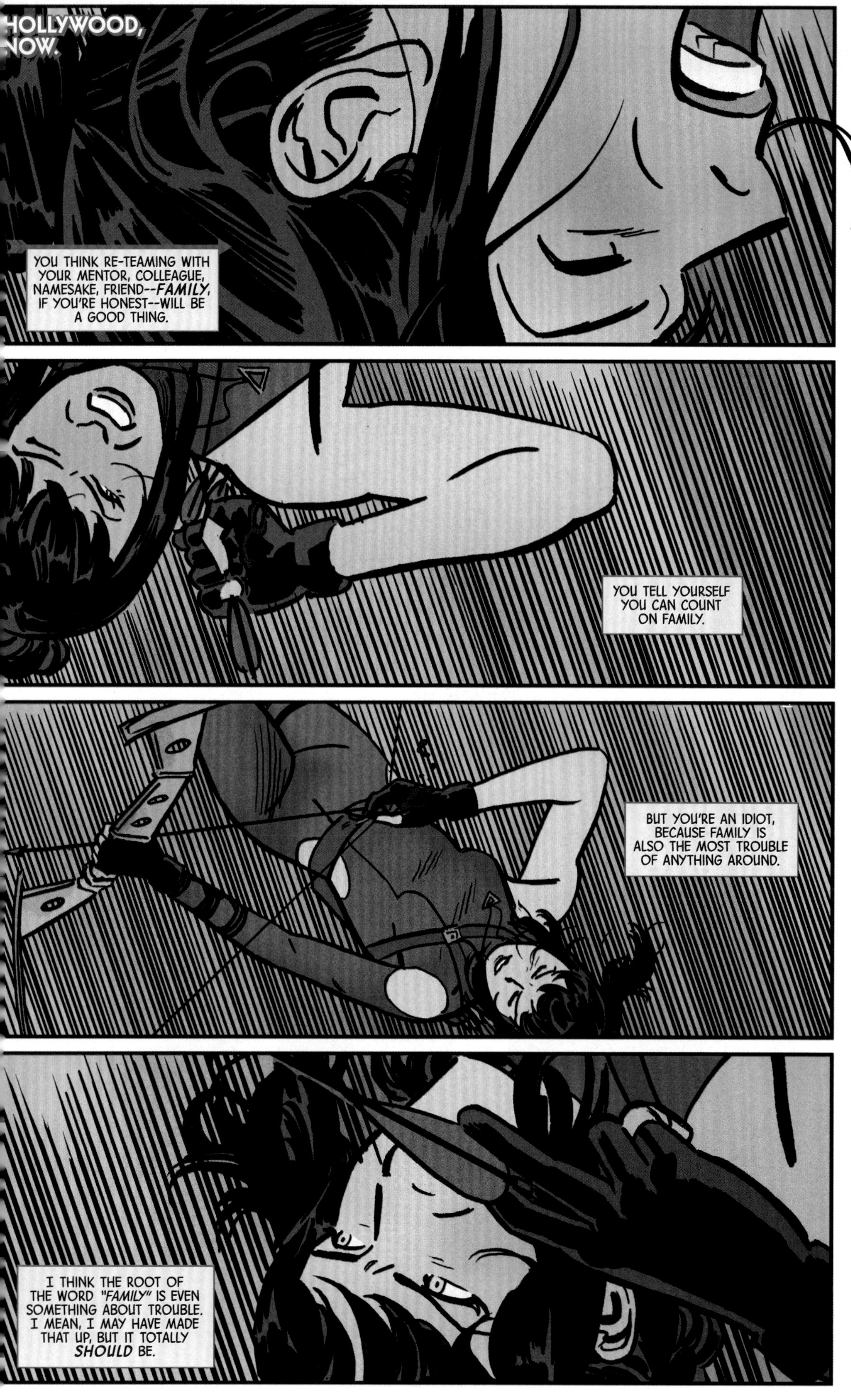
HOLLYWOOD, NOW.
YOU THINK RE-TEAMING WITH YOUR MENTOR, COLLEAGUE, NAMESAKE, FRIEND--FAMILY, IF YOU'RE HONEST--WILL BE A GOOD THING.
YOU TELL YOURSELF YOU CAN COUNT ON FAMILY.
BUT YOU'RE AN IDIOT, BECAUSE FAMILY IS ALSO THE MOST TROUBLE OF ANYTHING AROUND.
I THINK THE ROOT OF THE WORD "FAMILY" IS EVEN SOMETHING ABOUT TROUBLE. I MEAN, I MAY HAVE MADE THAT UP, BUT IT TOTALLY SHOULD BE.

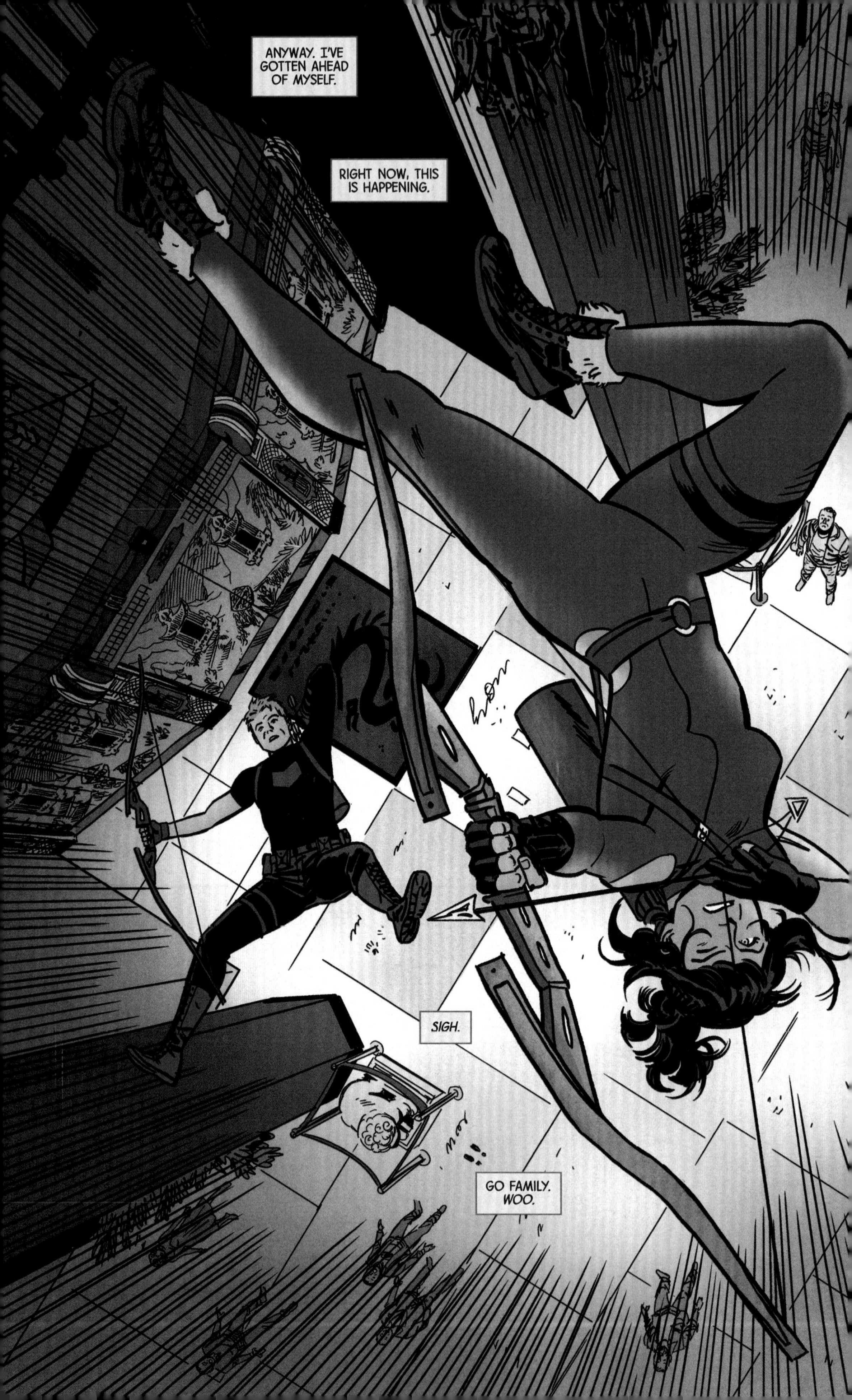
ANYWAY. I'VE GOTTEN AHEAD OF MYSELF.
RIGHT NOW, THIS IS HAPPENING.
SIGH.
GO FAMILY. WOO.

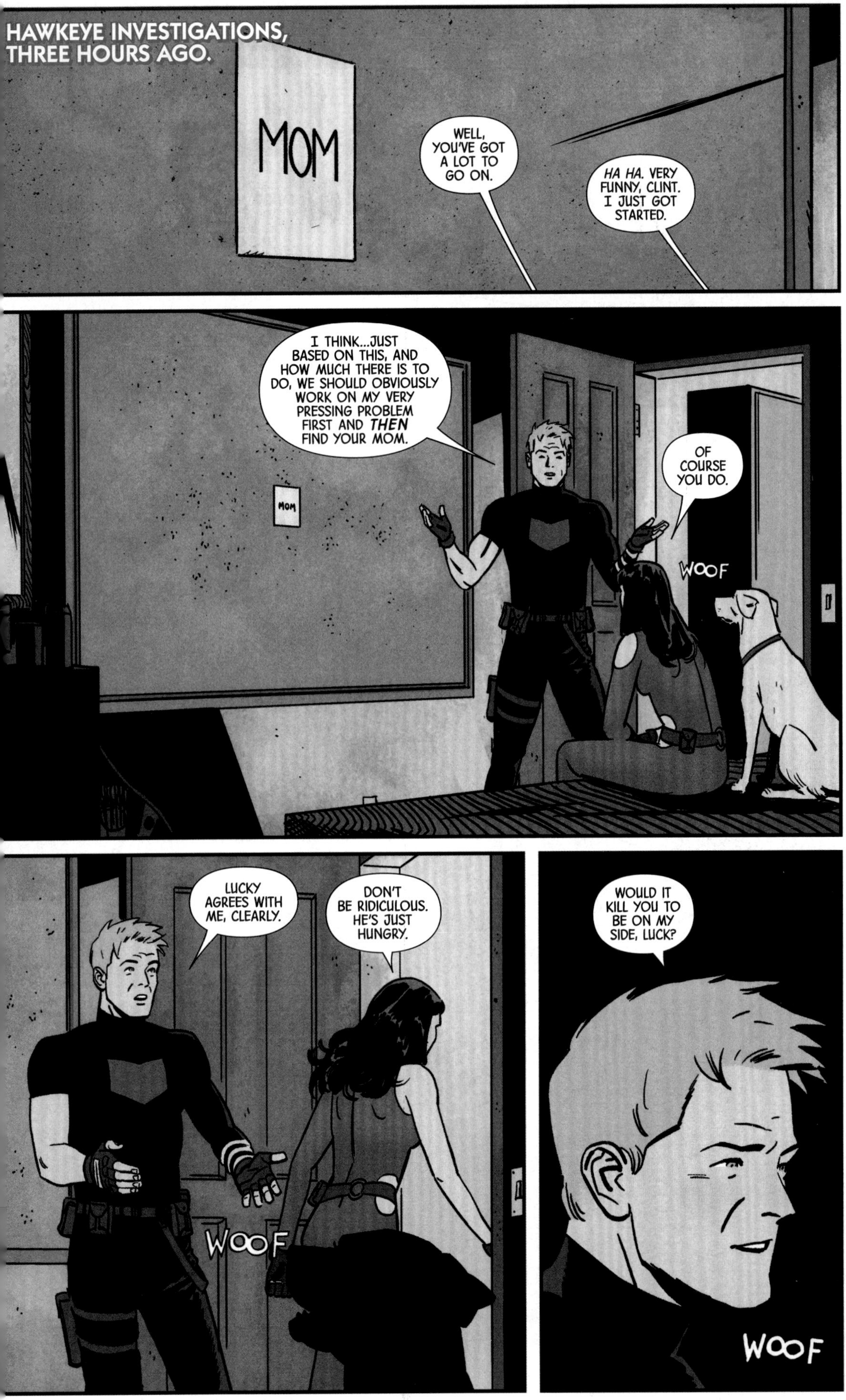
HAWKEYE INVESTIGATIONS, THREE HOURS AGO.
MOM
WELL, YOU'VE GOT A LOT TO GO ON.
HA HA. VERY FUNNY, CLINT. I JUST GOT STARTED.
I THINK...JUST BASED ON THIS, AND HOW MUCH THERE IS TO DO, WE SHOULD OBVIOUSLY WORK ON MY VERY PRESSING PROBLEM FIRST AND THEN FIND YOUR MOM.
OF COURSE YOU DO.
WOOF
MOM
LUCKY AGREES WITH ME, CLEARLY.
DON'T BE RIDICULOUS. HE'S JUST HUNGRY.
WOOF
WOULD IT KILL YOU TO BE ON MY SIDE, LUCK?
WOOF

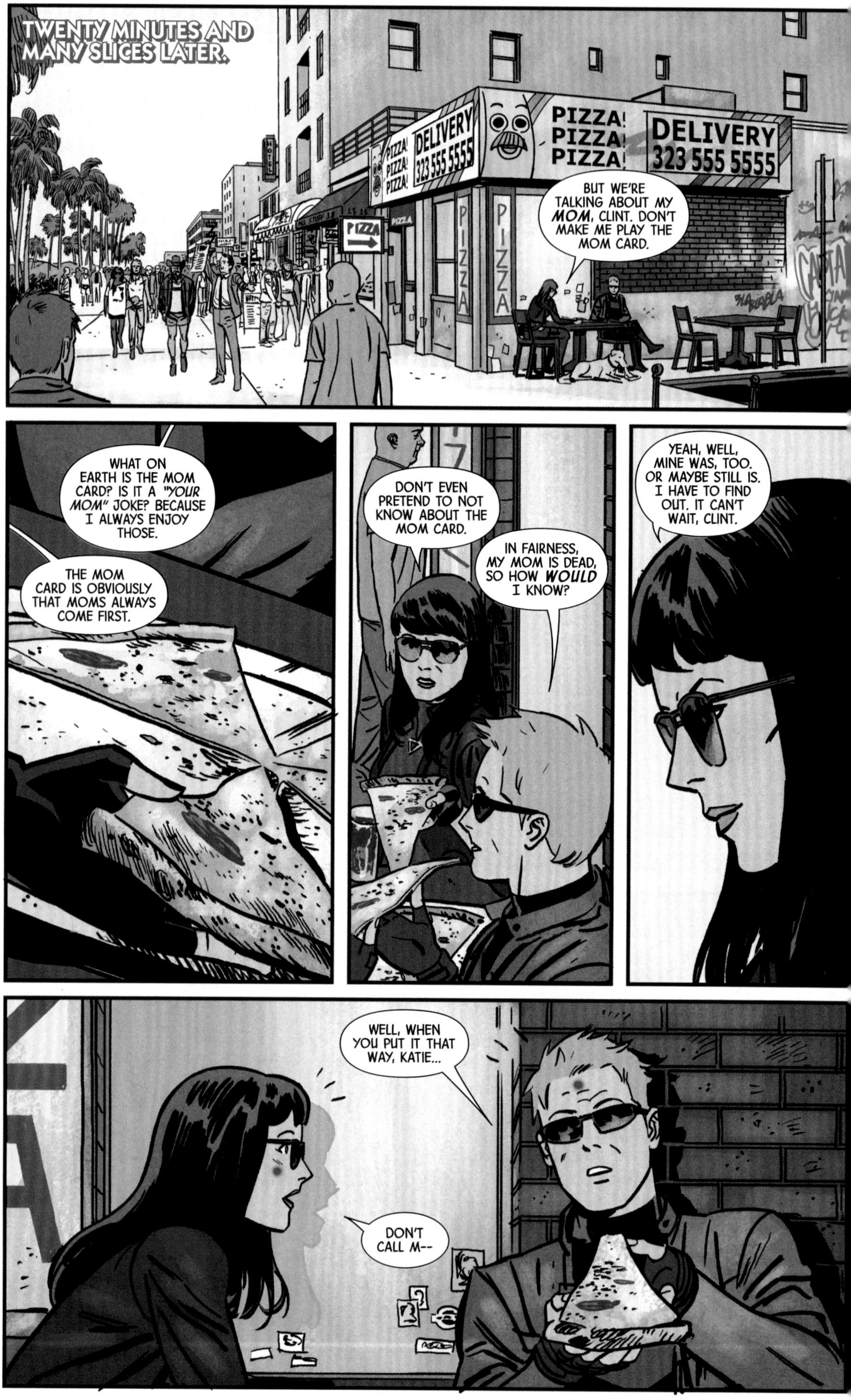
TWENTY MINUTES AND MANY SLICES LATER.
PIZZA! PIZZA! PIZZA!
DELIVERY 323 555 5555
PIZZA
BUT WE'RE TALKING ABOUT MY MOM, CLINT. DON'T MAKE ME PLAY THE MOM CARD.
WHAT ON EARTH IS THE MOM CARD? IS IT A "YOUR MOM" JOKE? BECAUSE I ALWAYS ENJOY THOSE.
THE MOM CARD IS OBVIOUSLY THAT MOMS ALWAYS COME FIRST.
DON'T EVEN PRETEND TO NOT KNOW ABOUT THE MOM CARD.
IN FAIRNESS, MY MOM IS DEAD, SO HOW WOULD I KNOW?
YEAH, WELL, MINE WAS, TOO. OR MAYBE STILL IS. I HAVE TO FIND OUT. IT CAN'T WAIT, CLINT.
WELL, WHEN YOU PUT IT THAT WAY, KATIE...
DON'T CALL M--

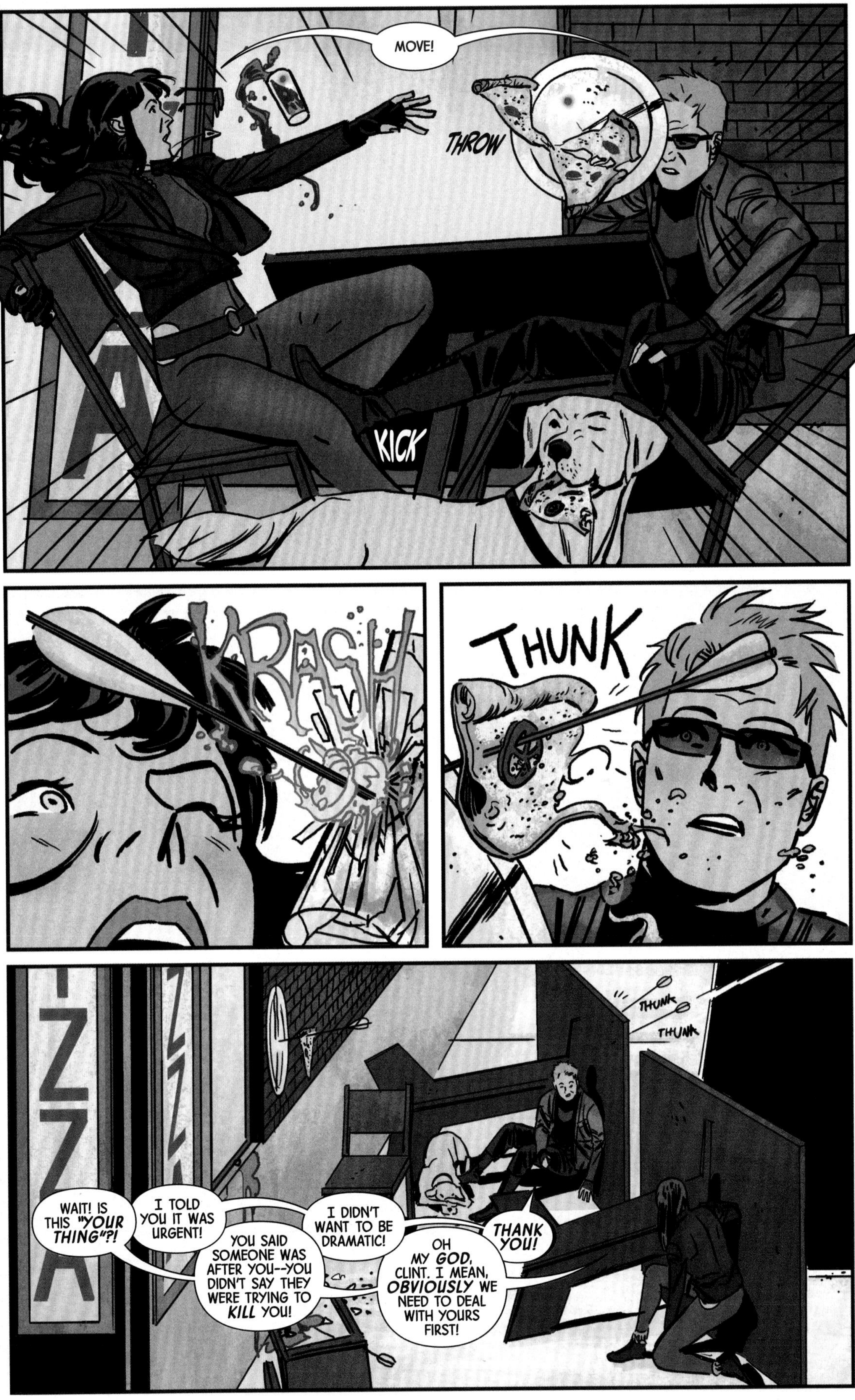
MOVE!
THROW
KICK
KRASH
THUNK
THUNK
THUNK
WAIT! IS THIS "YOUR THING"?!
I TOLD YOU IT WAS URGENT!
YOU SAID SOMEONE WAS AFTER YOU--YOU DIDN'T SAY THEY WERE TRYING TO KILL YOU!
I DIDN'T WANT TO BE DRAMATIC!
OH MY GOD, CLINT. I MEAN, OBVIOUSLY WE NEED TO DEAL WITH YOURS FIRST!
THANK YOU!

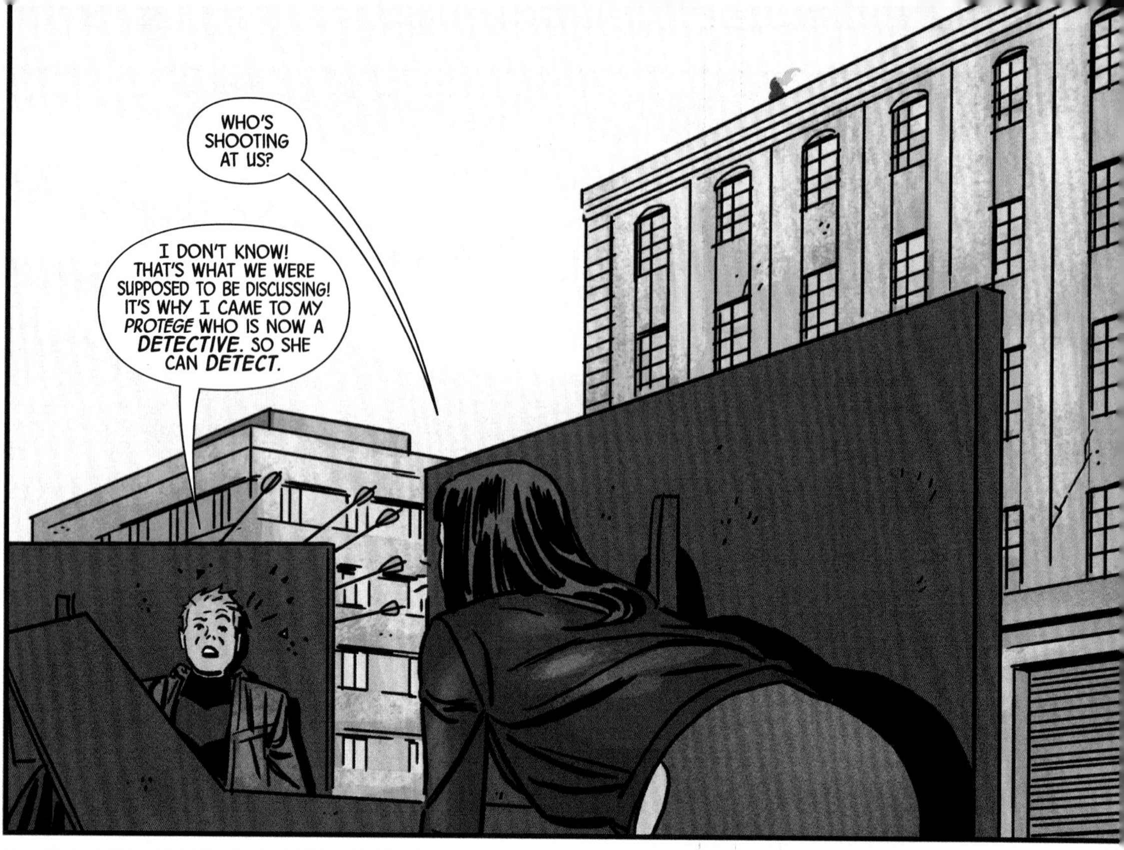
WHO'S SHOOTING AT US?
I DON'T KNOW! THAT'S WHAT WE WERE SUPPOSED TO BE DISCUSSING! IT'S WHY I CAME TO MY *PROTEGE* WHO IS NOW A ***DETECTIVE***. SO SHE CAN ***DETECT***.

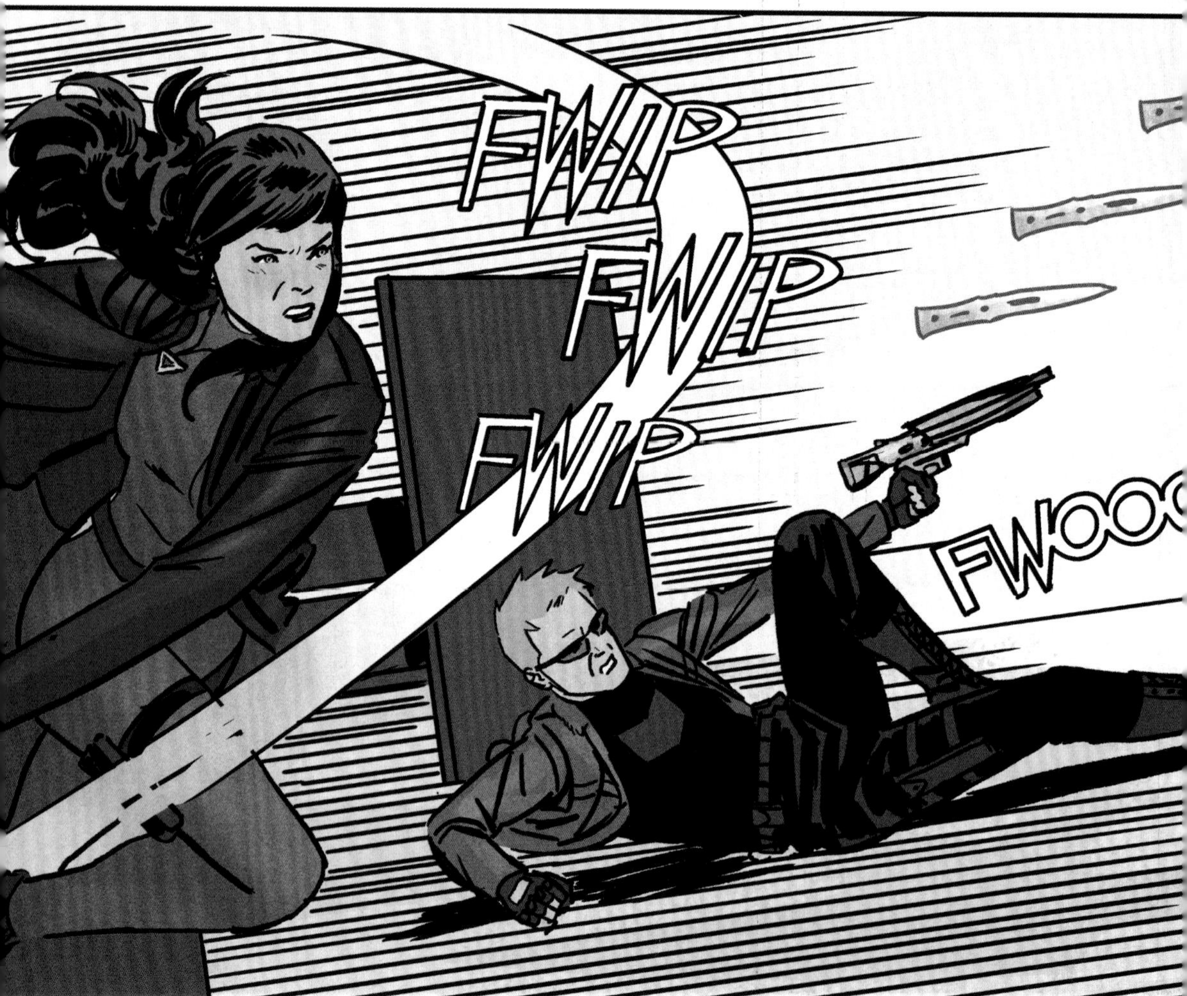
FWIP
FWIP
FWIP
FWOOO

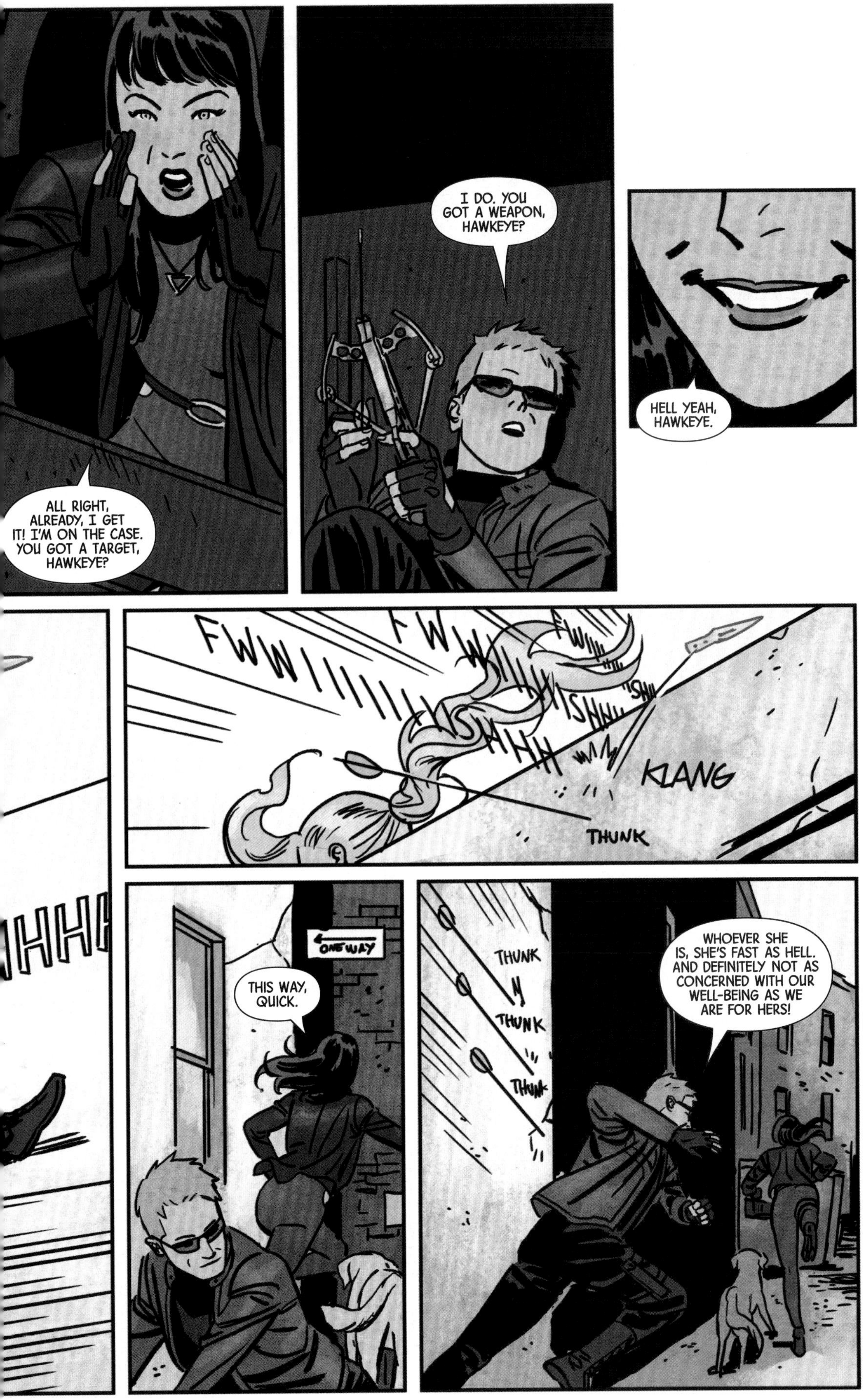

ALL RIGHT, ALREADY, I GET IT! I'M ON THE CASE. YOU GOT A TARGET, HAWKEYE?
I DO. YOU GOT A WEAPON, HAWKEYE?
HELL YEAH, HAWKEYE.
FWWIIIII
FWWIIII
FWIII
SHHHH
SHHH
SHHHH
KLANG
THUNK
THIS WAY, QUICK.
ONE WAY
THUNK
THUNK
THUNK
WHOEVER SHE IS, SHE'S FAST AS HELL. AND DEFINITELY NOT AS CONCERNED WITH OUR WELL-BEING AS WE ARE FOR HERS!

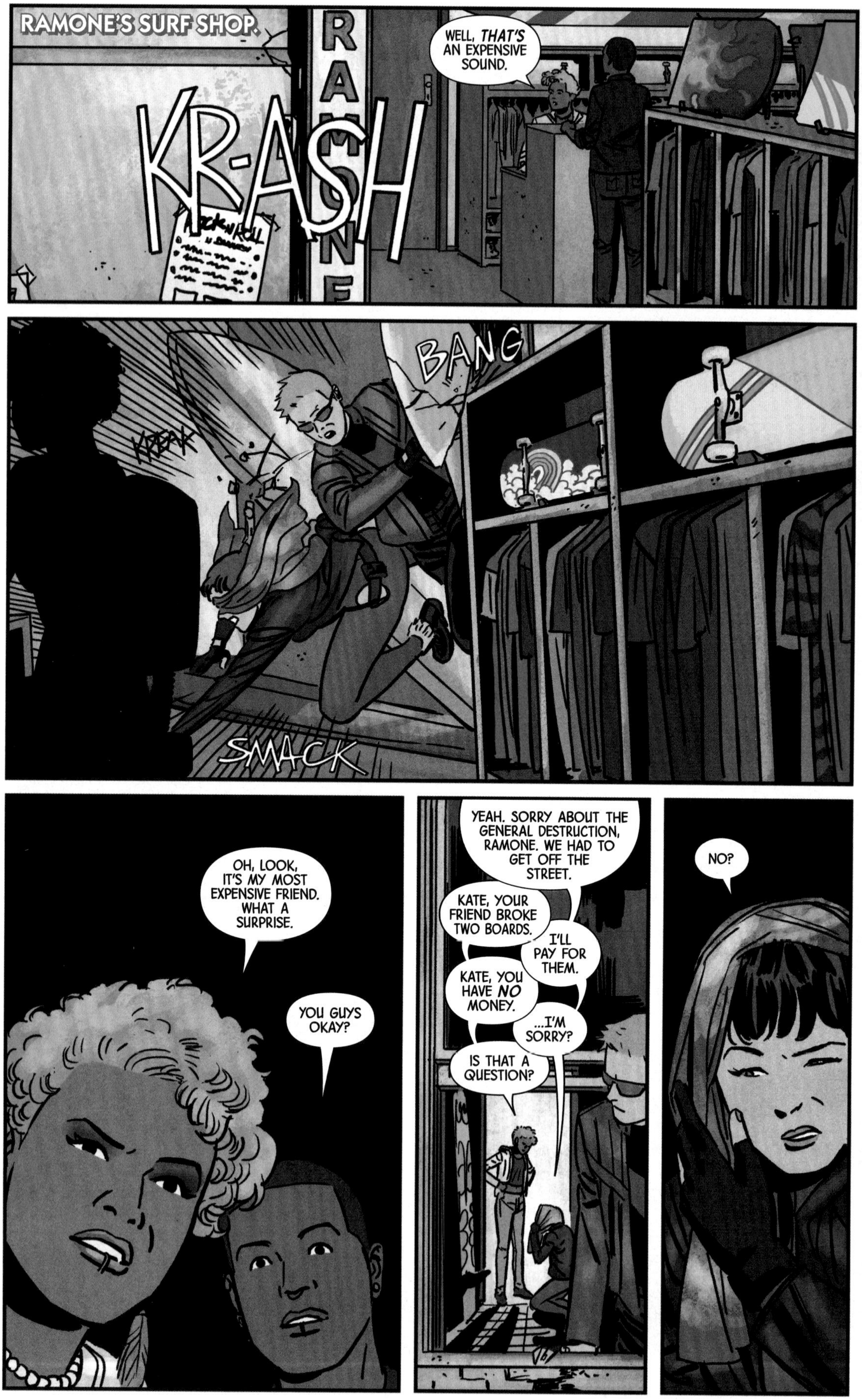
RAMONE'S SURF SHOP.
KR-ASH
WELL, THAT'S AN EXPENSIVE SOUND.
BANG
KRRAK
SMACK
OH, LOOK, IT'S MY MOST EXPENSIVE FRIEND. WHAT A SURPRISE.
YOU GUYS OKAY?
YEAH. SORRY ABOUT THE GENERAL DESTRUCTION, RAMONE. WE HAD TO GET OFF THE STREET.
KATE, YOUR FRIEND BROKE TWO BOARDS.
I'LL PAY FOR THEM.
KATE, YOU HAVE NO MONEY.
...I'M SORRY?
IS THAT A QUESTION?
NO?

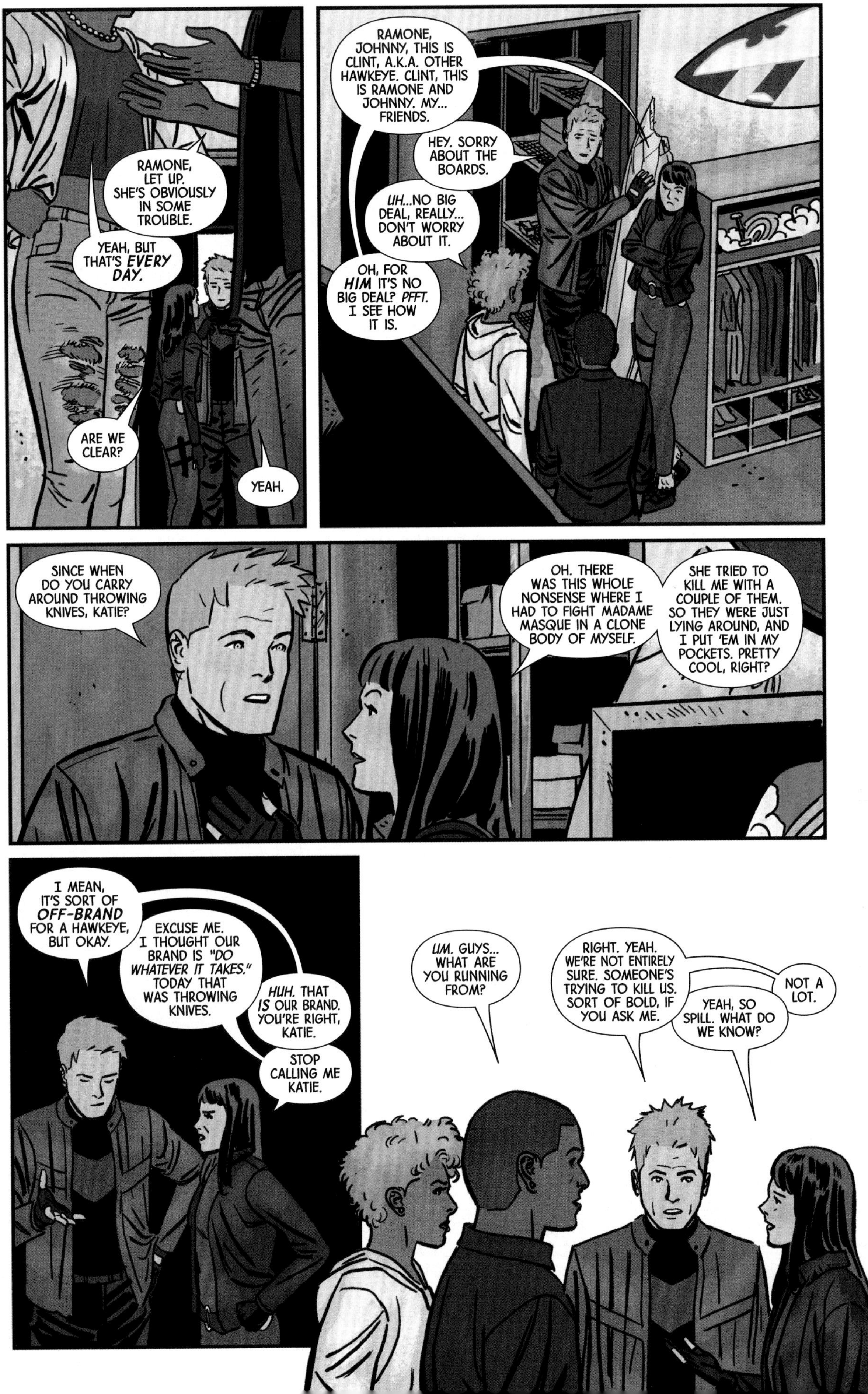
RAMONE, LET UP. SHE'S OBVIOUSLY IN SOME TROUBLE.
YEAH, BUT THAT'S EVERY DAY.
ARE WE CLEAR?
YEAH.
RAMONE, JOHNNY, THIS IS CLINT, A.K.A. OTHER HAWKEYE. CLINT, THIS IS RAMONE AND JOHNNY. MY... FRIENDS.
HEY. SORRY ABOUT THE BOARDS.
UH...NO BIG DEAL, REALLY... DON'T WORRY ABOUT IT.
OH, FOR HIM IT'S NO BIG DEAL? PFFT. I SEE HOW IT IS.
SINCE WHEN DO YOU CARRY AROUND THROWING KNIVES, KATIE?
OH. THERE WAS THIS WHOLE NONSENSE WHERE I HAD TO FIGHT MADAME MASQUE IN A CLONE BODY OF MYSELF.
SHE TRIED TO KILL ME WITH A COUPLE OF THEM. SO THEY WERE JUST LYING AROUND, AND I PUT 'EM IN MY POCKETS. PRETTY COOL, RIGHT?
I MEAN, IT'S SORT OF OFF-BRAND FOR A HAWKEYE, BUT OKAY.
EXCUSE ME. I THOUGHT OUR BRAND IS "DO WHATEVER IT TAKES." TODAY THAT WAS THROWING KNIVES.
HUH. THAT IS OUR BRAND. YOU'RE RIGHT, KATIE.
STOP CALLING ME KATIE.
UM. GUYS... WHAT ARE YOU RUNNING FROM?
RIGHT. YEAH. WE'RE NOT ENTIRELY SURE. SOMEONE'S TRYING TO KILL US. SORT OF BOLD, IF YOU ASK ME.
NOT A LOT.
YEAH, SO SPILL. WHAT DO WE KNOW?

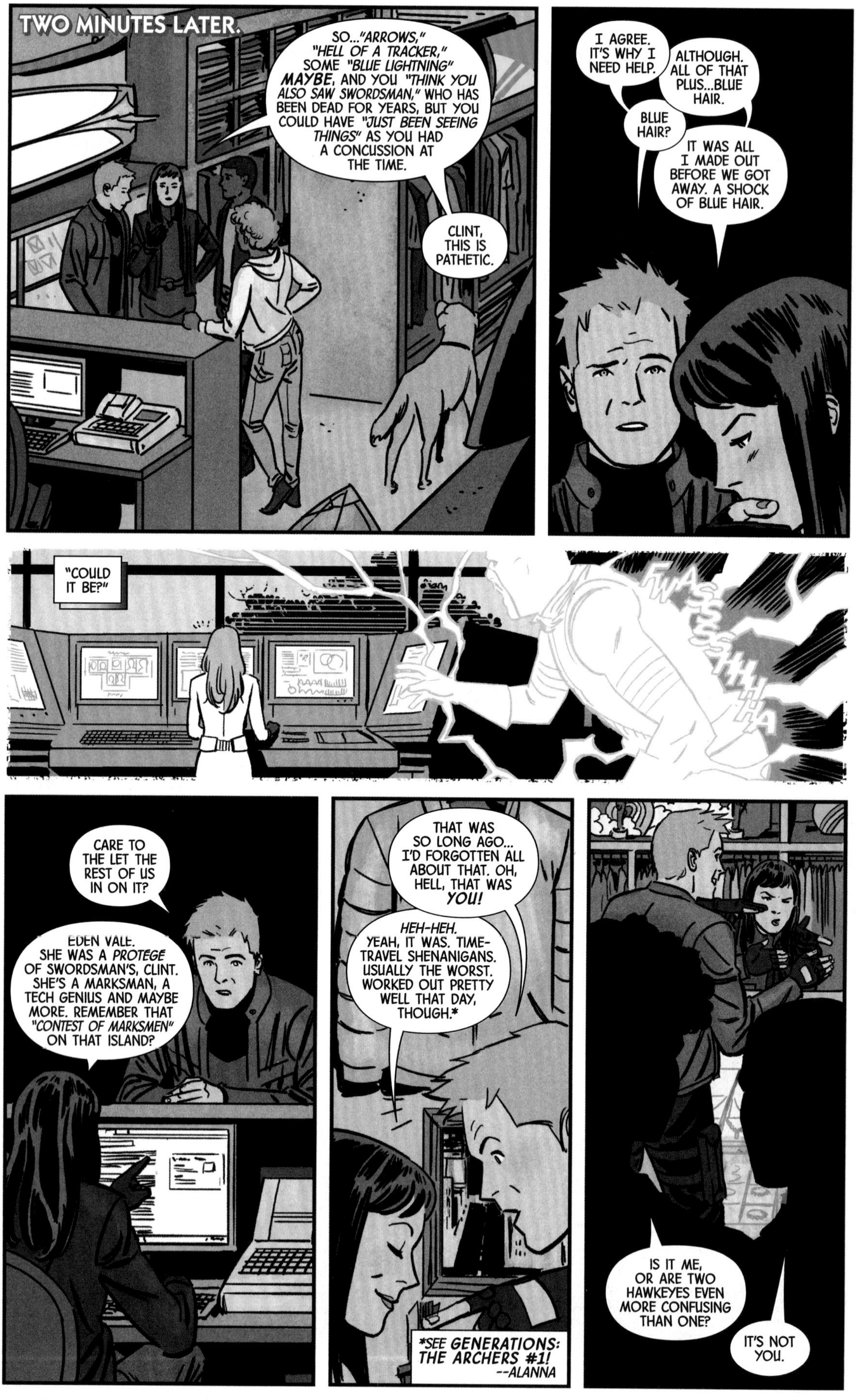
TWO MINUTES LATER.
SO..."ARROWS," "HELL OF A TRACKER," SOME "BLUE LIGHTNING" MAYBE, AND YOU "THINK YOU ALSO SAW SWORDSMAN," WHO HAS BEEN DEAD FOR YEARS, BUT YOU COULD HAVE "JUST BEEN SEEING THINGS" AS YOU HAD A CONCUSSION AT THE TIME.
CLINT, THIS IS PATHETIC.
I AGREE. IT'S WHY I NEED HELP.
ALTHOUGH. ALL OF THAT PLUS...BLUE HAIR.
BLUE HAIR?
IT WAS ALL I MADE OUT BEFORE WE GOT AWAY. A SHOCK OF BLUE HAIR.
"COULD IT BE?"
FWASSSHHHA
CARE TO THE LET THE REST OF US IN ON IT?
EDEN VALE. SHE WAS A PROTEGE OF SWORDSMAN'S, CLINT. SHE'S A MARKSMAN, A TECH GENIUS AND MAYBE MORE. REMEMBER THAT "CONTEST OF MARKSMEN" ON THAT ISLAND?
THAT WAS SO LONG AGO... I'D FORGOTTEN ALL ABOUT THAT. OH, HELL, THAT WAS YOU!
HEH-HEH. YEAH, IT WAS. TIME-TRAVEL SHENANIGANS. USUALLY THE WORST. WORKED OUT PRETTY WELL THAT DAY, THOUGH.*
*SEE GENERATIONS: THE ARCHERS #1! --ALANNA
IS IT ME, OR ARE TWO HAWKEYES EVEN MORE CONFUSING THAN ONE?
IT'S NOT YOU.

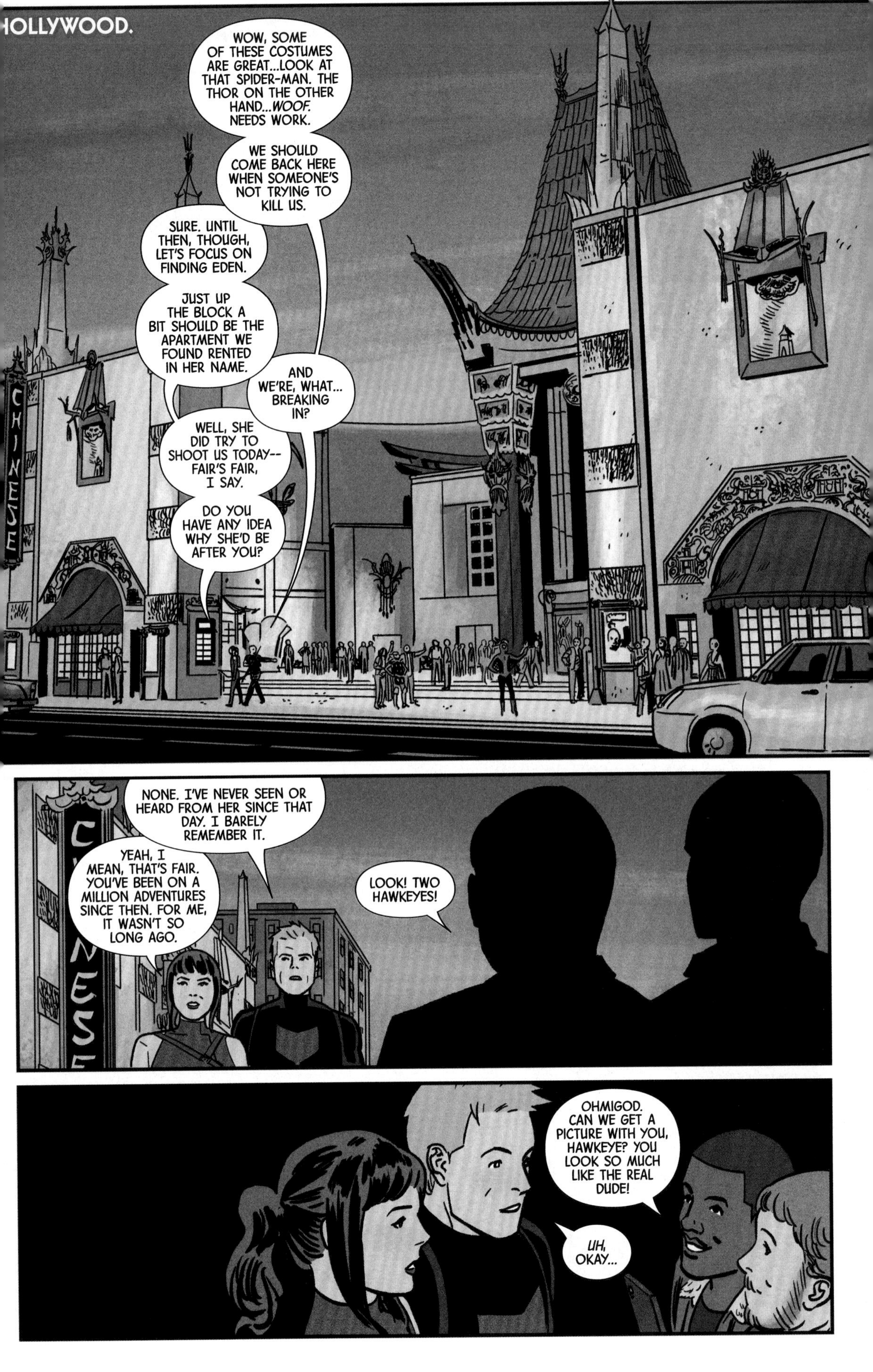
HOLLYWOOD.
WOW, SOME OF THESE COSTUMES ARE GREAT...LOOK AT THAT SPIDER-MAN. THE THOR ON THE OTHER HAND...WOOF. NEEDS WORK.
WE SHOULD COME BACK HERE WHEN SOMEONE'S NOT TRYING TO KILL US.
SURE. UNTIL THEN, THOUGH, LET'S FOCUS ON FINDING EDEN.
JUST UP THE BLOCK A BIT SHOULD BE THE APARTMENT WE FOUND RENTED IN HER NAME.
AND WE'RE, WHAT... BREAKING IN?
WELL, SHE DID TRY TO SHOOT US TODAY-- FAIR'S FAIR, I SAY.
DO YOU HAVE ANY IDEA WHY SHE'D BE AFTER YOU?
NONE. I'VE NEVER SEEN OR HEARD FROM HER SINCE THAT DAY. I BARELY REMEMBER IT.
YEAH, I MEAN, THAT'S FAIR. YOU'VE BEEN ON A MILLION ADVENTURES SINCE THEN. FOR ME, IT WASN'T SO LONG AGO.
LOOK! TWO HAWKEYES!
OHMIGOD. CAN WE GET A PICTURE WITH YOU, HAWKEYE? YOU LOOK SO MUCH LIKE THE REAL DUDE!
UH, OKAY...

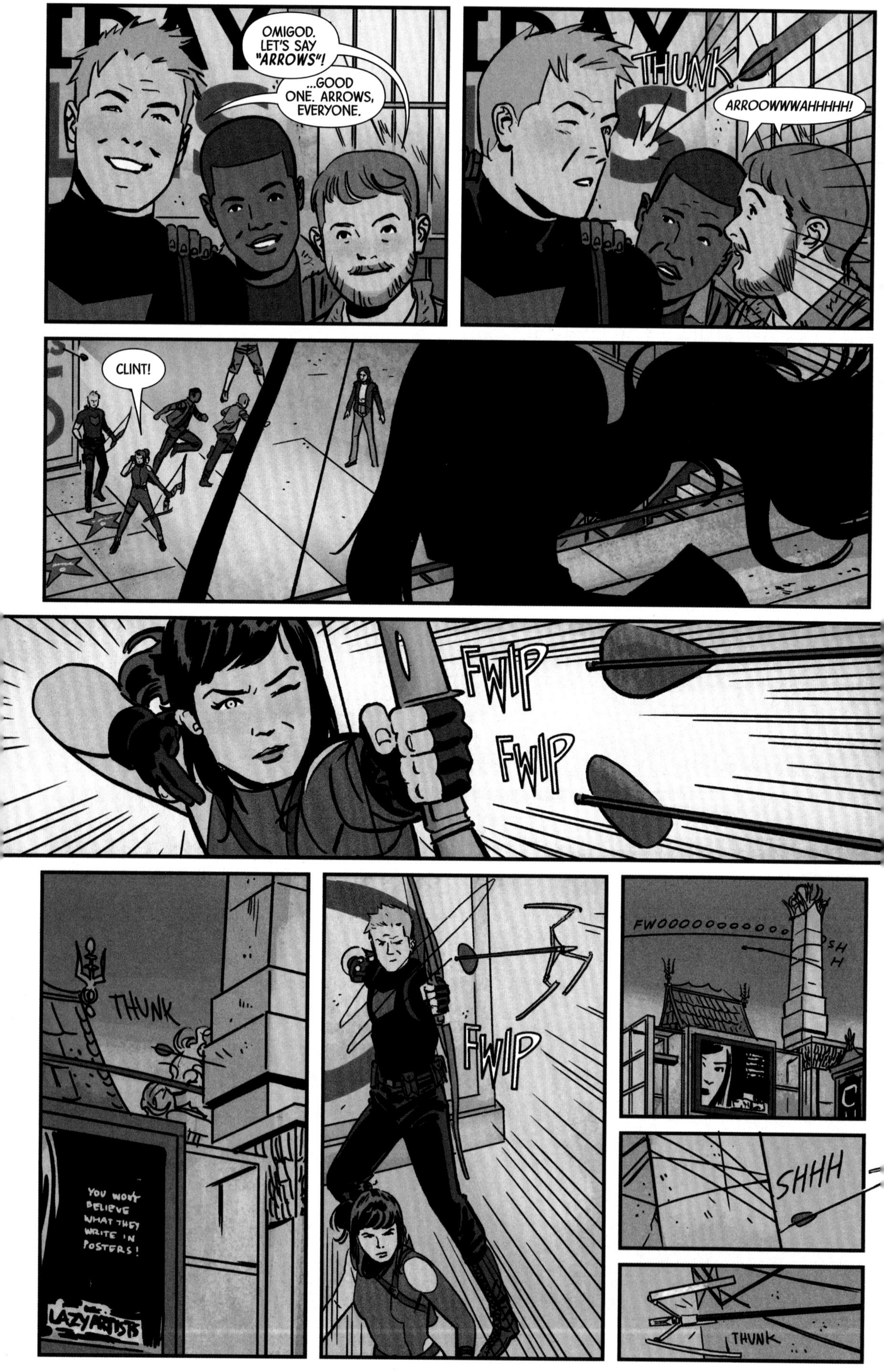

OMIGOD. LET'S SAY "ARROWS"!
...GOOD ONE. ARROWS, EVERYONE.
THUNK
ARROOWWWAHHHHH!
CLINT!
FWIP
FWIP
THUNK
YOU WON'T BELIEVE WHAT THEY WRITE IN POSTERS!
LAZY ARTISTS
FWIP
FWOOOOOOOOOOOSHH
SHHH
THUNK

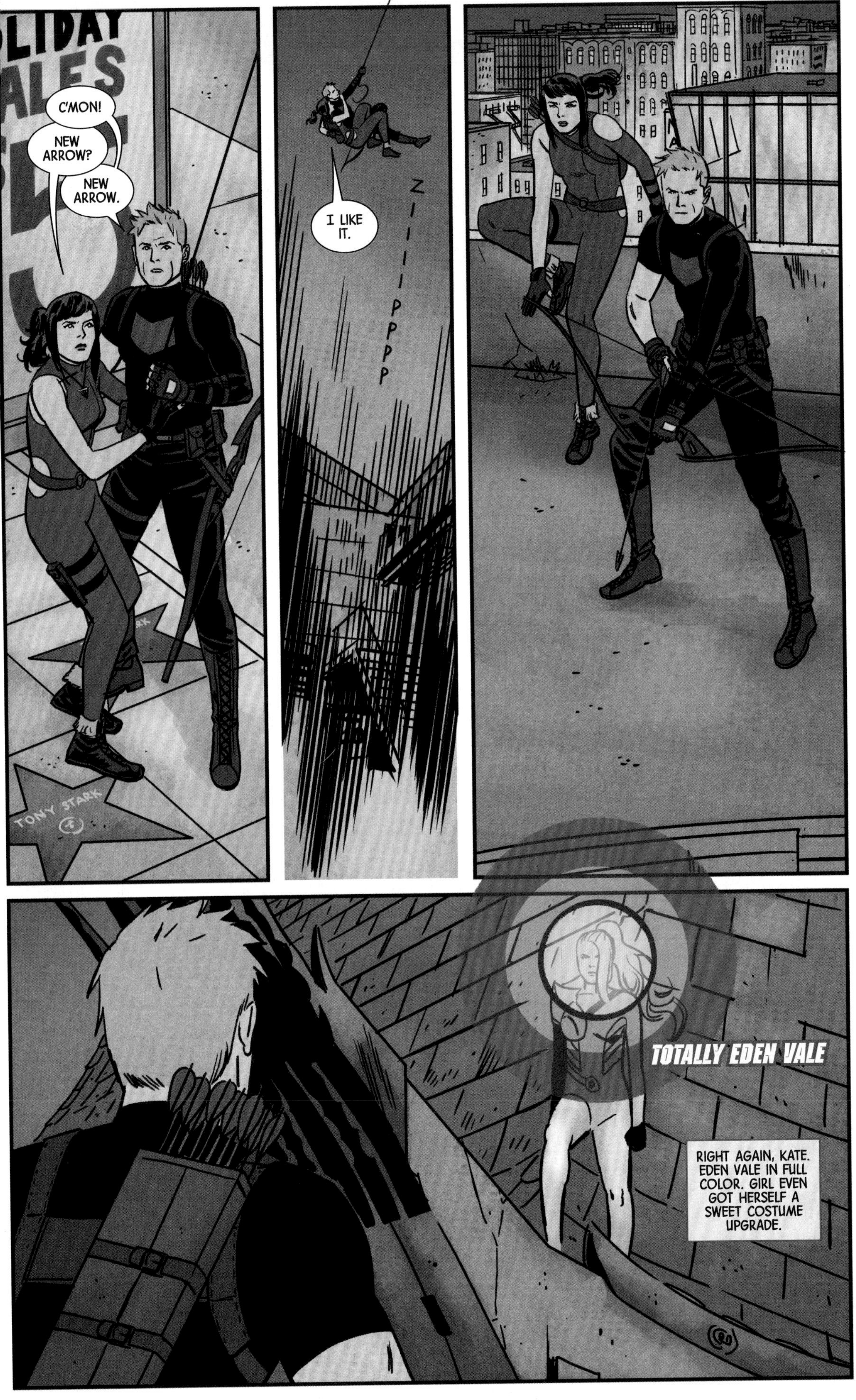
C'MON!
NEW ARROW?
NEW ARROW.
TONY STARK
I LIKE IT.
ZIIIPPPP
TOTALLY EDEN VALE
RIGHT AGAIN, KATE. EDEN VALE IN FULL COLOR. GIRL EVEN GOT HERSELF A SWEET COSTUME UPGRADE.

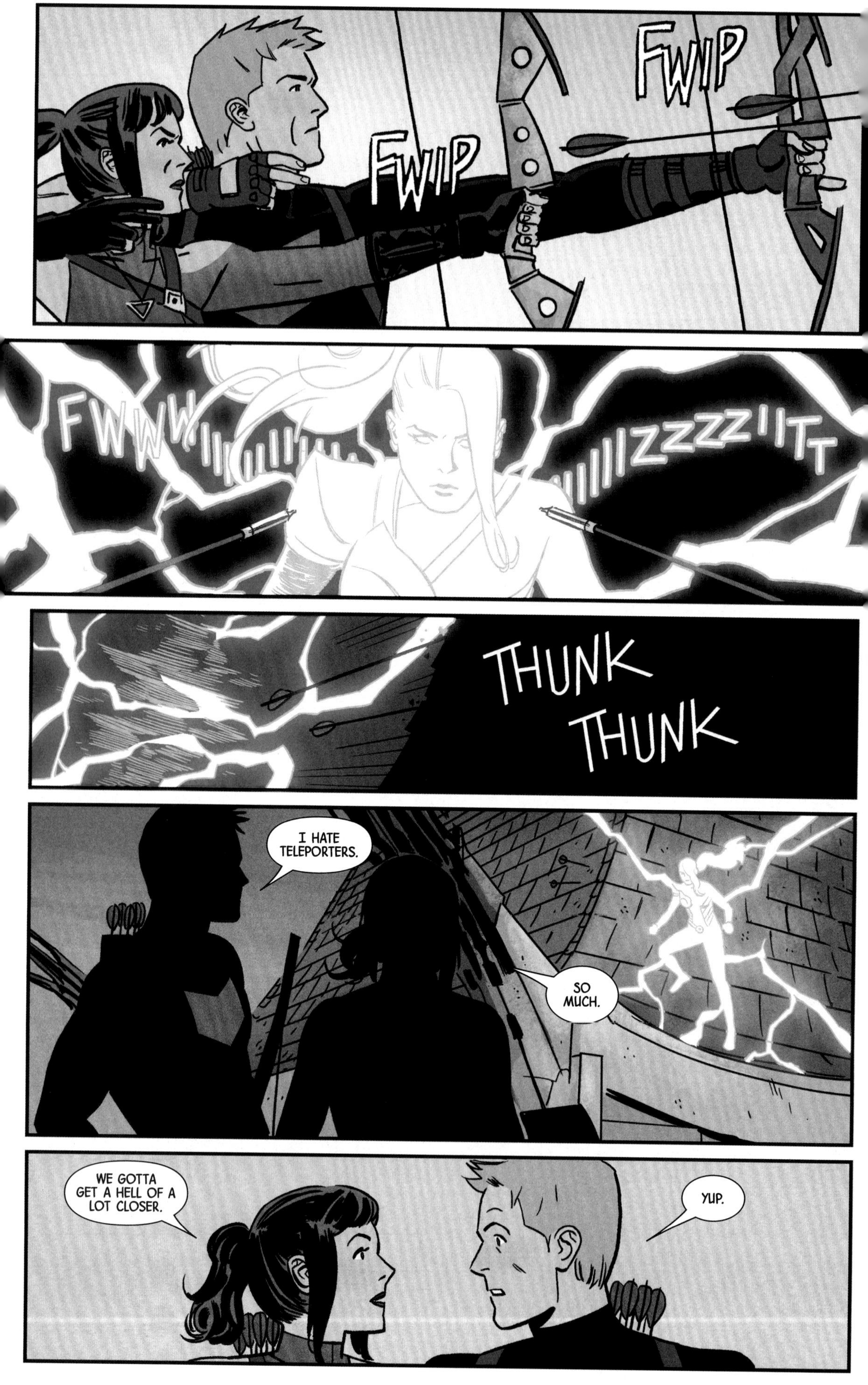
FWIP
FWIP
FWWW
IZZZZITT
THUNK
THUNK
I HATE TELEPORTERS.
SO MUCH.
WE GOTTA GET A HELL OF A LOT CLOSER.
YUP.

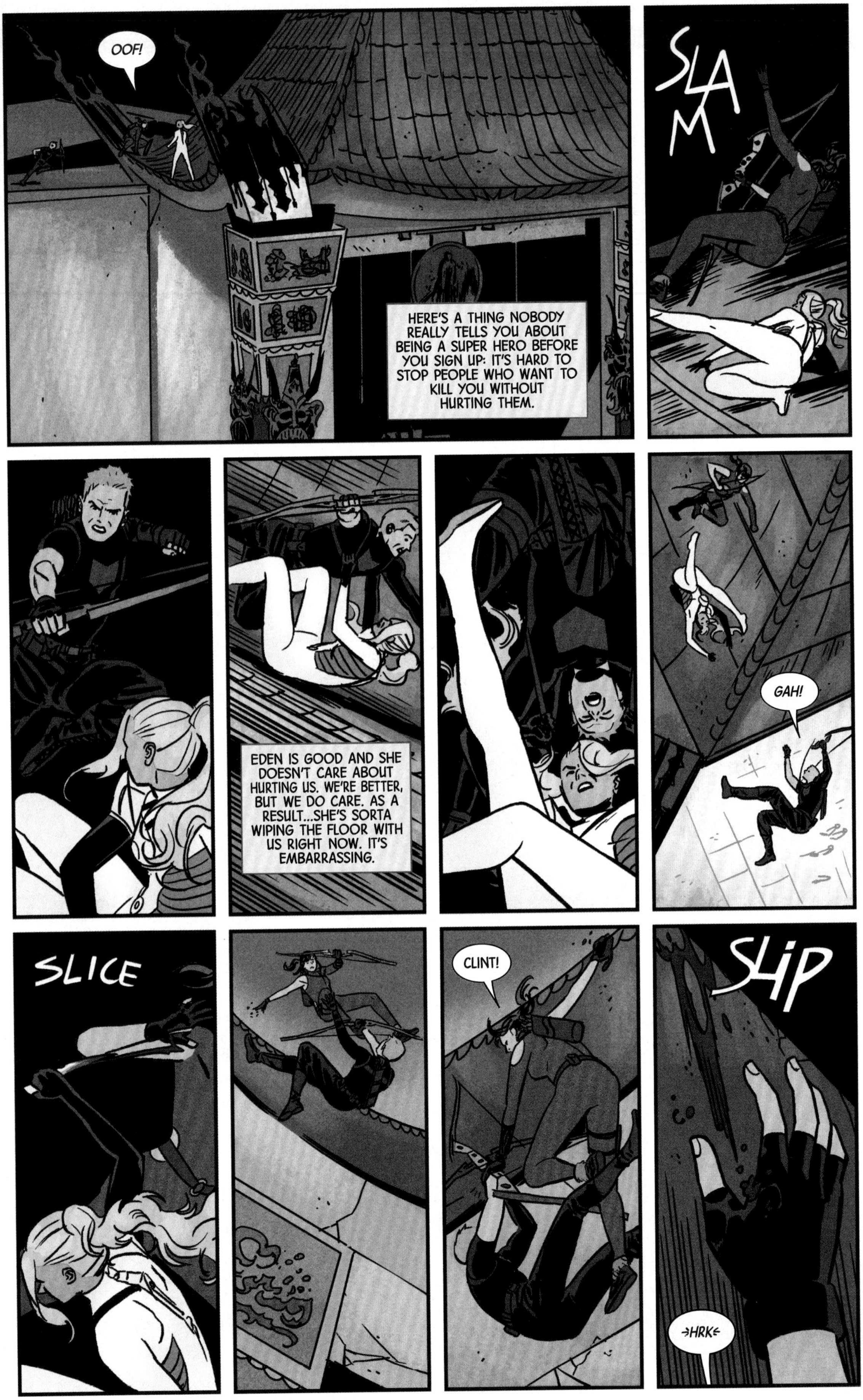
OOF!
HERE'S A THING NOBODY REALLY TELLS YOU ABOUT BEING A SUPER HERO BEFORE YOU SIGN UP: IT'S HARD TO STOP PEOPLE WHO WANT TO KILL YOU WITHOUT HURTING THEM.
SLAM
EDEN IS GOOD AND SHE DOESN'T CARE ABOUT HURTING US. WE'RE BETTER, BUT WE DO CARE. AS A RESULT...SHE'S SORTA WIPING THE FLOOR WITH US RIGHT NOW. IT'S EMBARRASSING.
GAH!
SLICE
CLINT!
SLIP
HRK

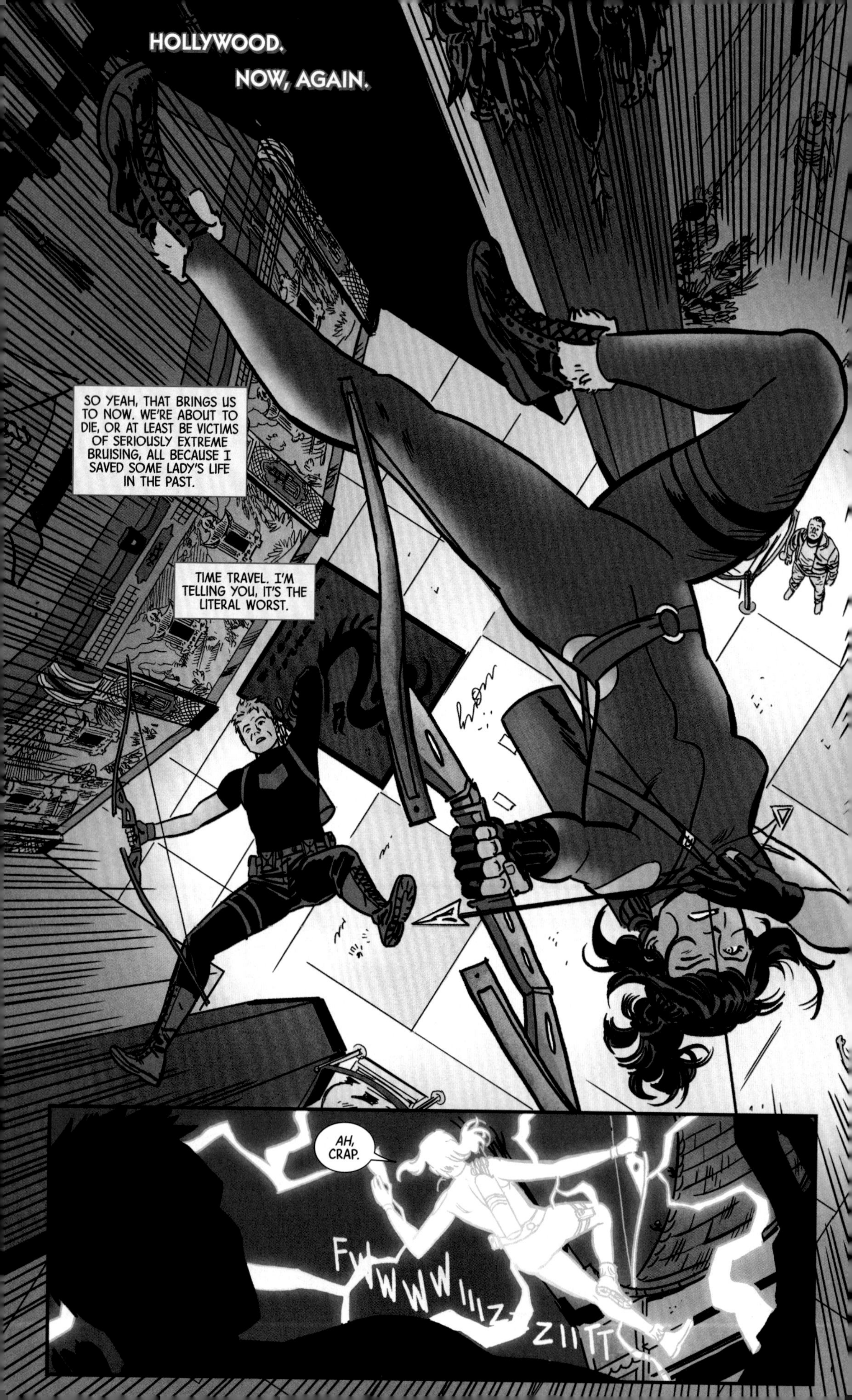
HOLLYWOOD.
NOW, AGAIN.
SO YEAH, THAT BRINGS US TO NOW. WE'RE ABOUT TO DIE, OR AT LEAST BE VICTIMS OF SERIOUSLY EXTREME BRUISING, ALL BECAUSE I SAVED SOME LADY'S LIFE IN THE PAST.
TIME TRAVEL. I'M TELLING YOU, IT'S THE LITERAL WORST.
AH, CRAP.
FWWWWIIIZZZIITT

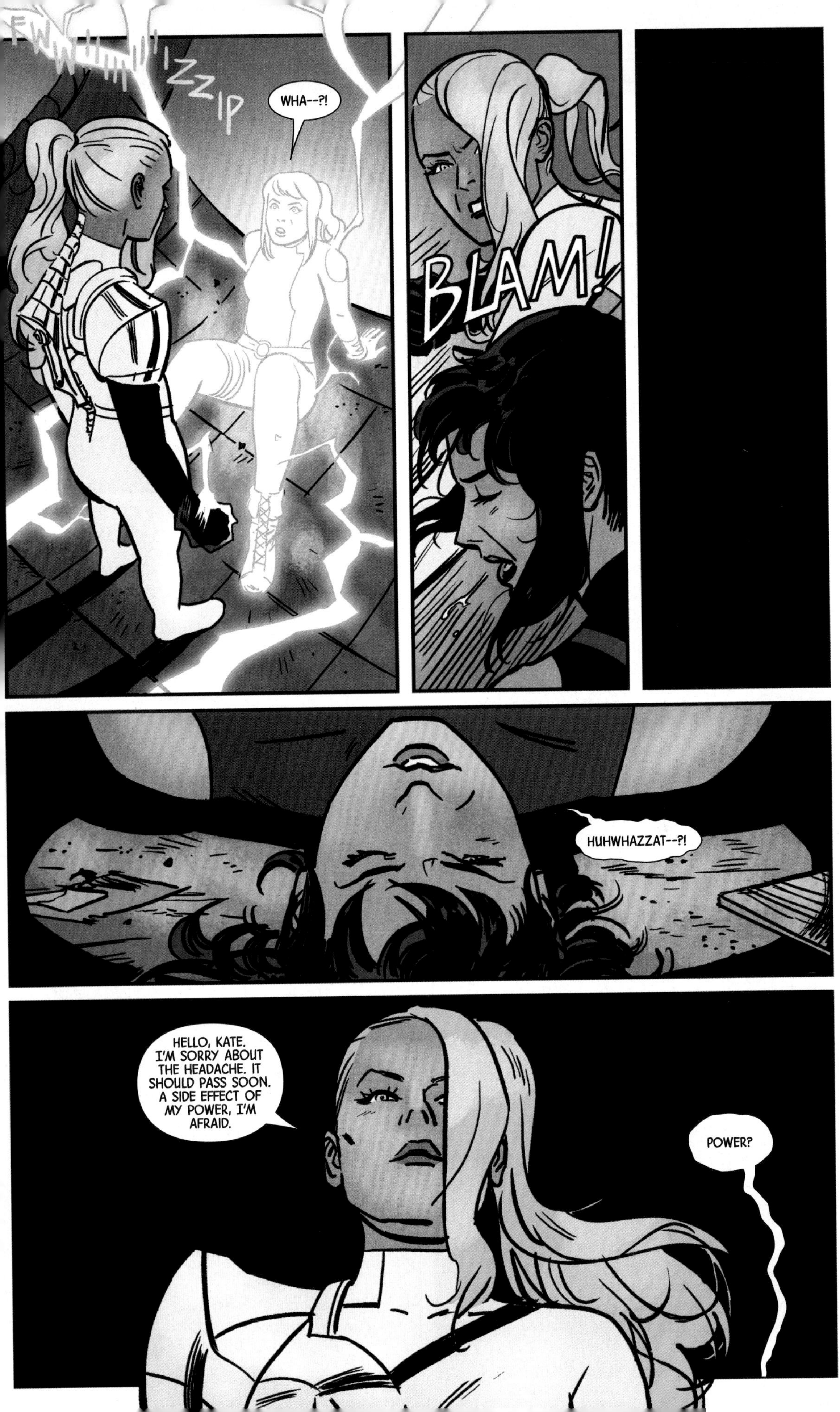
FWWHIIIIIIIZZZIP
WHA--?!
BLAM!
HUHWHAZZAT--?!
HELLO, KATE. I'M SORRY ABOUT THE HEADACHE. IT SHOULD PASS SOON. A SIDE EFFECT OF MY POWER, I'M AFRAID.
POWER?

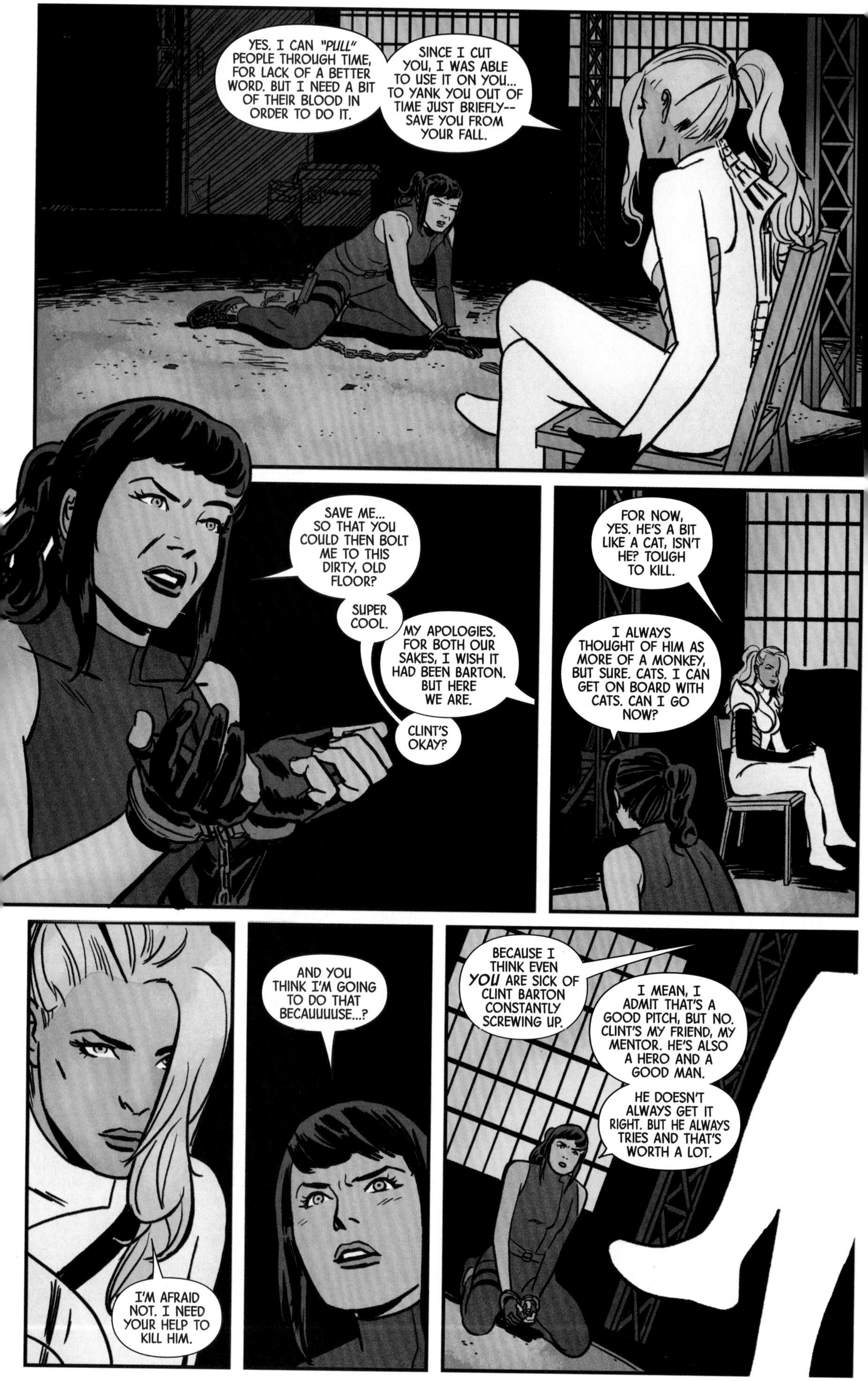
YES. I CAN "PULL" PEOPLE THROUGH TIME, FOR LACK OF A BETTER WORD. BUT I NEED A BIT OF THEIR BLOOD IN ORDER TO DO IT.
SINCE I CUT YOU, I WAS ABLE TO USE IT ON YOU... TO YANK YOU OUT OF TIME JUST BRIEFLY-- SAVE YOU FROM YOUR FALL.
SAVE ME... SO THAT YOU COULD THEN BOLT ME TO THIS DIRTY, OLD FLOOR?
SUPER COOL.
MY APOLOGIES. FOR BOTH OUR SAKES, I WISH IT HAD BEEN BARTON. BUT HERE WE ARE.
CLINT'S OKAY?
FOR NOW, YES. HE'S A BIT LIKE A CAT, ISN'T HE? TOUGH TO KILL.
I ALWAYS THOUGHT OF HIM AS MORE OF A MONKEY, BUT SURE. CATS. I CAN GET ON BOARD WITH CATS. CAN I GO NOW?
I'M AFRAID NOT. I NEED YOUR HELP TO KILL HIM.
AND YOU THINK I'M GOING TO DO THAT BECAUUUUSE...?
BECAUSE I THINK EVEN YOU ARE SICK OF CLINT BARTON CONSTANTLY SCREWING UP.
I MEAN, I ADMIT THAT'S A GOOD PITCH, BUT NO. CLINT'S MY FRIEND, MY MENTOR. HE'S ALSO A HERO AND A GOOD MAN.
HE DOESN'T ALWAYS GET IT RIGHT. BUT HE ALWAYS TRIES AND THAT'S WORTH A LOT.

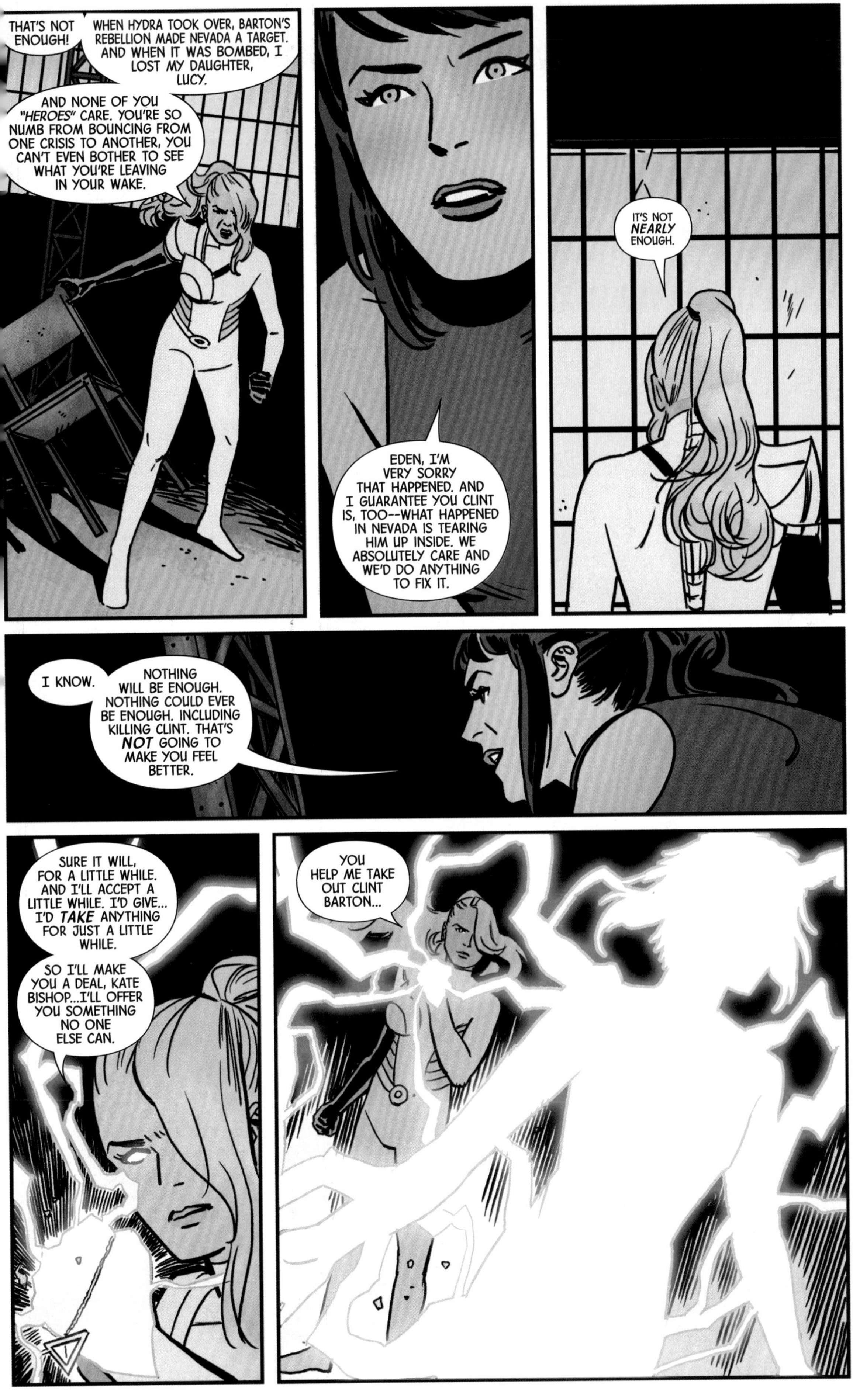
THAT'S NOT ENOUGH!
WHEN HYDRA TOOK OVER, BARTON'S REBELLION MADE NEVADA A TARGET. AND WHEN IT WAS BOMBED, I LOST MY DAUGHTER, LUCY.
AND NONE OF YOU "HEROES" CARE. YOU'RE SO NUMB FROM BOUNCING FROM ONE CRISIS TO ANOTHER, YOU CAN'T EVEN BOTHER TO SEE WHAT YOU'RE LEAVING IN YOUR WAKE.
EDEN, I'M VERY SORRY THAT HAPPENED. AND I GUARANTEE YOU CLINT IS, TOO--WHAT HAPPENED IN NEVADA IS TEARING HIM UP INSIDE. WE ABSOLUTELY CARE AND WE'D DO ANYTHING TO FIX IT.
IT'S NOT NEARLY ENOUGH.
I KNOW.
NOTHING WILL BE ENOUGH. NOTHING COULD EVER BE ENOUGH. INCLUDING KILLING CLINT. THAT'S NOT GOING TO MAKE YOU FEEL BETTER.
SURE IT WILL, FOR A LITTLE WHILE. AND I'LL ACCEPT A LITTLE WHILE. I'D GIVE... I'D TAKE ANYTHING FOR JUST A LITTLE WHILE.
SO I'LL MAKE YOU A DEAL, KATE BISHOP...I'LL OFFER YOU SOMETHING NO ONE ELSE CAN.
YOU HELP ME TAKE OUT CLINT BARTON...

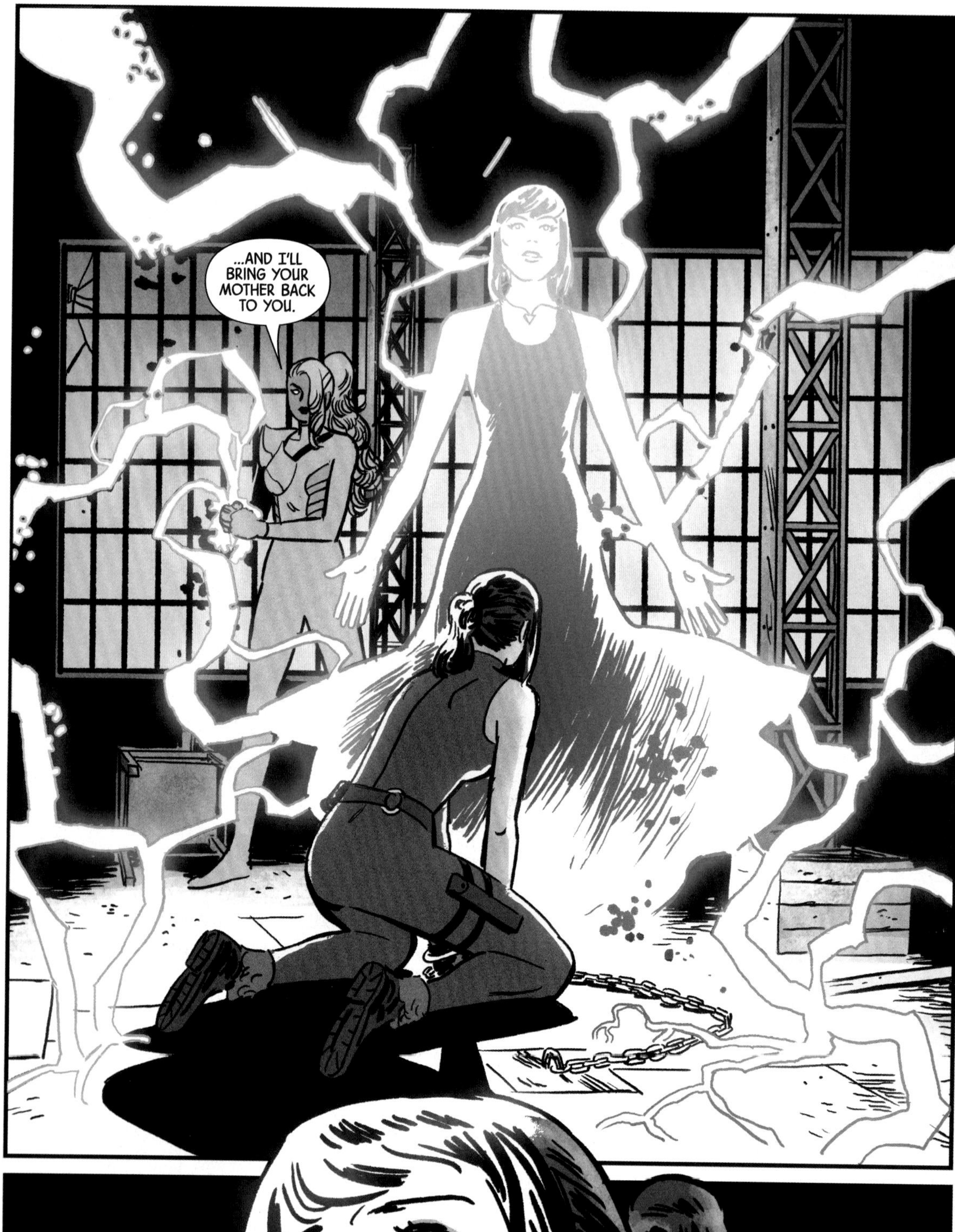
...AND I'LL BRING YOUR MOTHER BACK TO YOU.

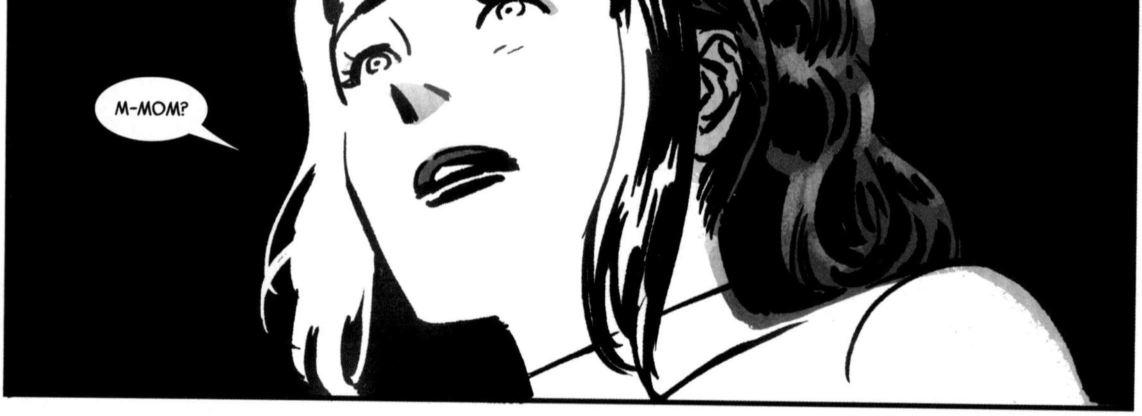
M-MOM?

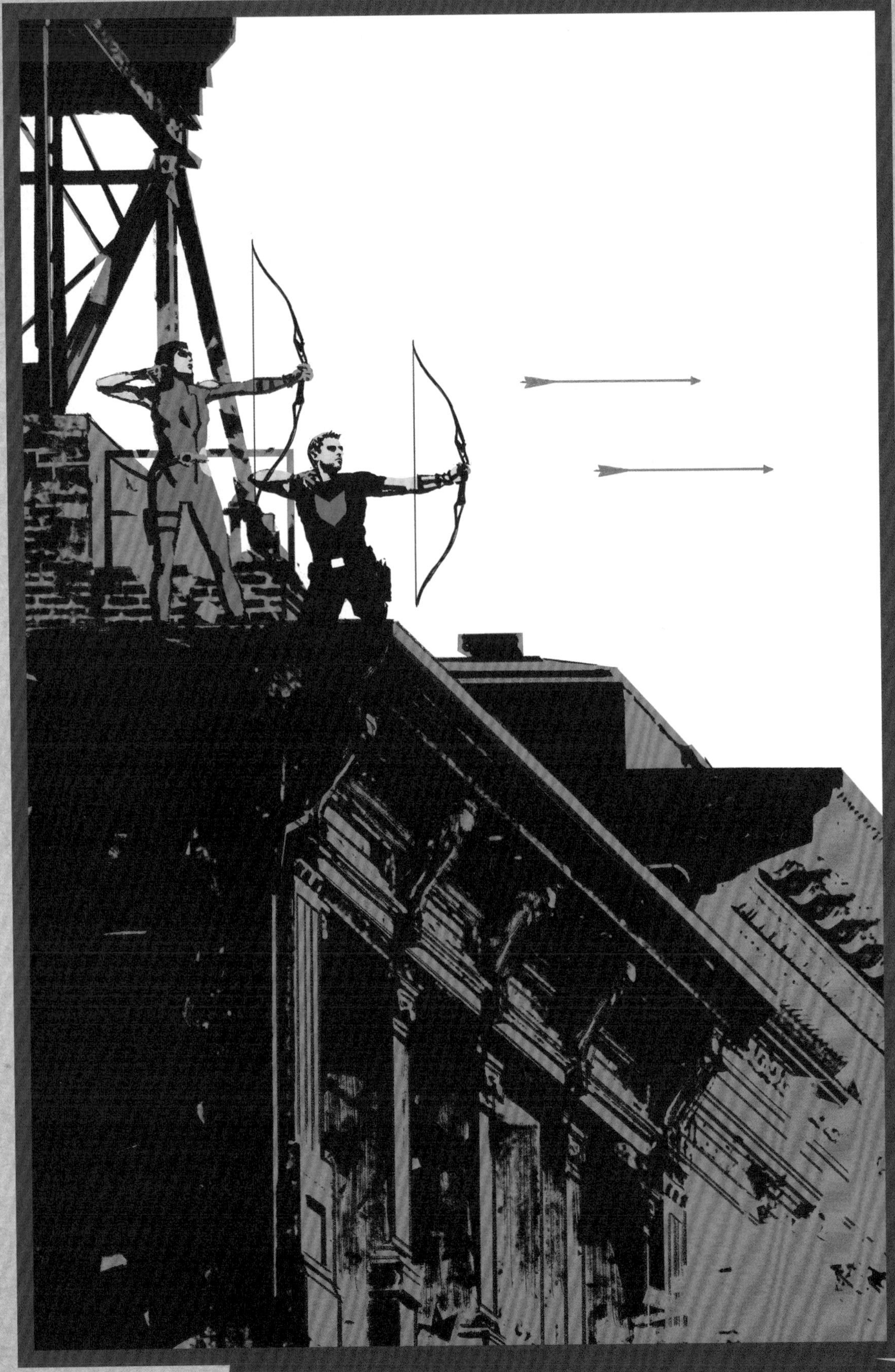

#13 homage variant
by **Greg Smallwood**

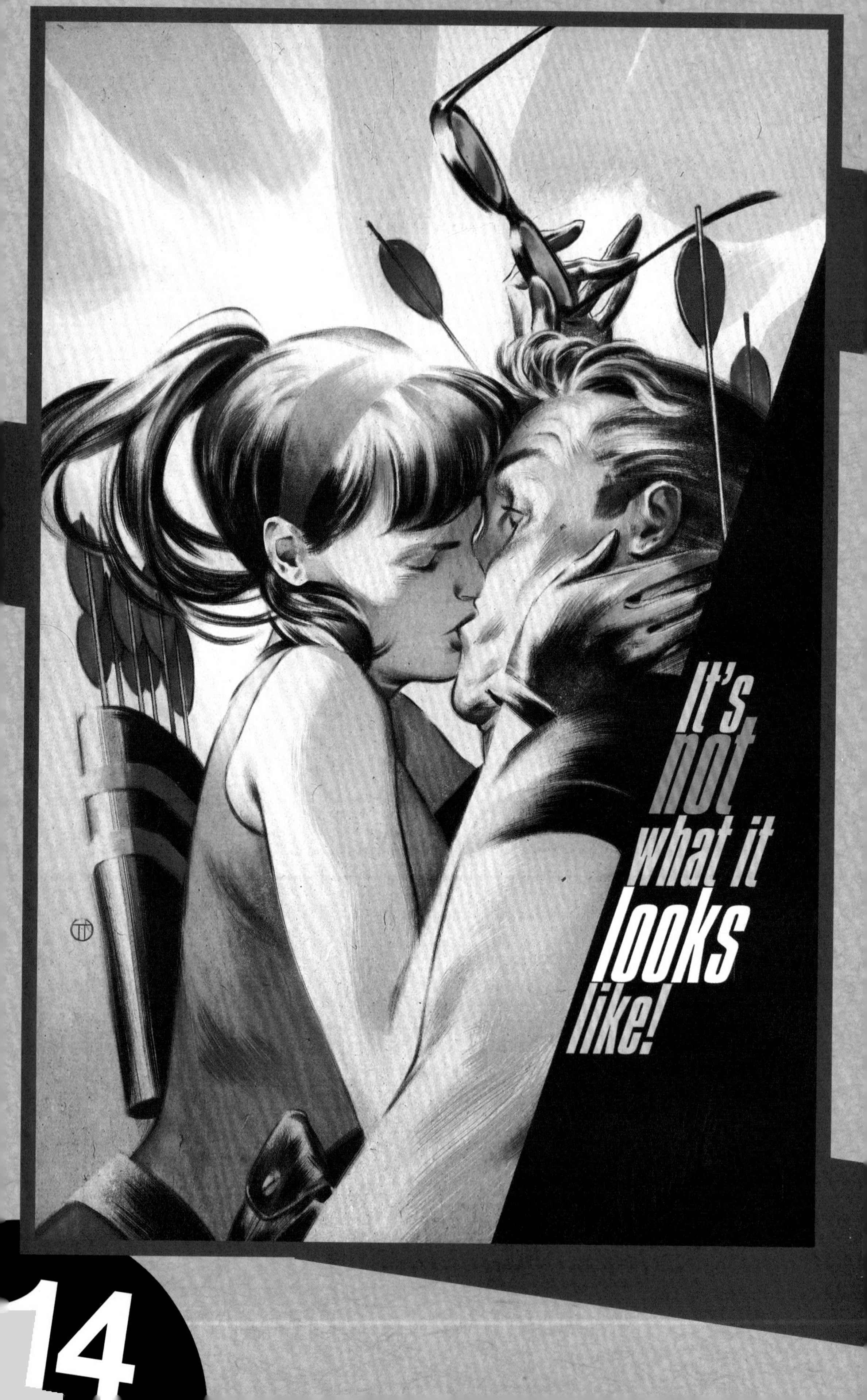
It's not what it looks like!
14

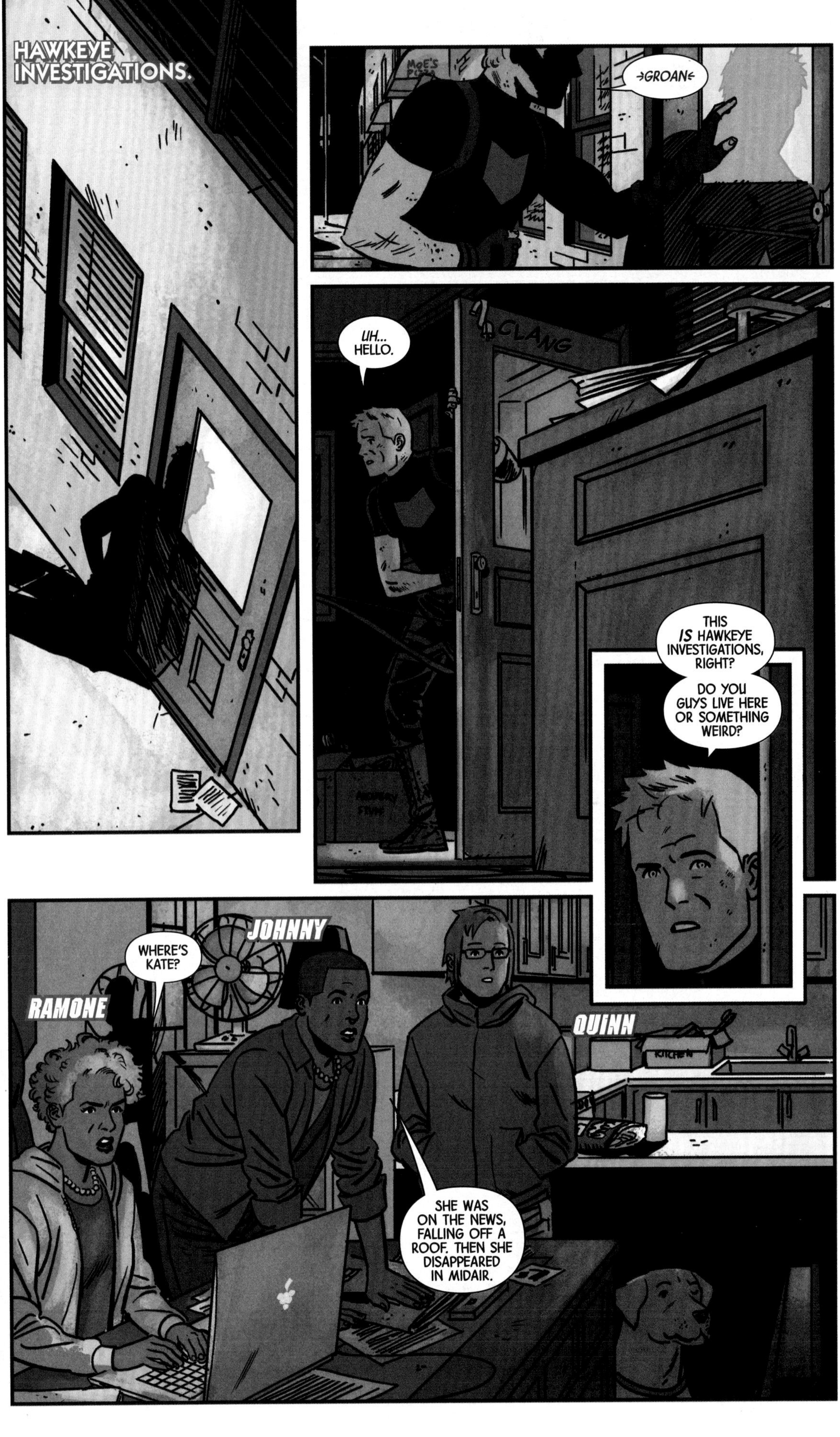
HAWKEYE INVESTIGATIONS.
MOE'S PIZZA
GROAN
CLANG
UH... HELLO.
THIS IS HAWKEYE INVESTIGATIONS, RIGHT?
DO YOU GUYS LIVE HERE OR SOMETHING WEIRD?
JOHNNY
RAMONE
WHERE'S KATE?
QUINN
KITCHEN
SHE WAS ON THE NEWS, FALLING OFF A ROOF. THEN SHE DISAPPEARED IN MIDAIR.

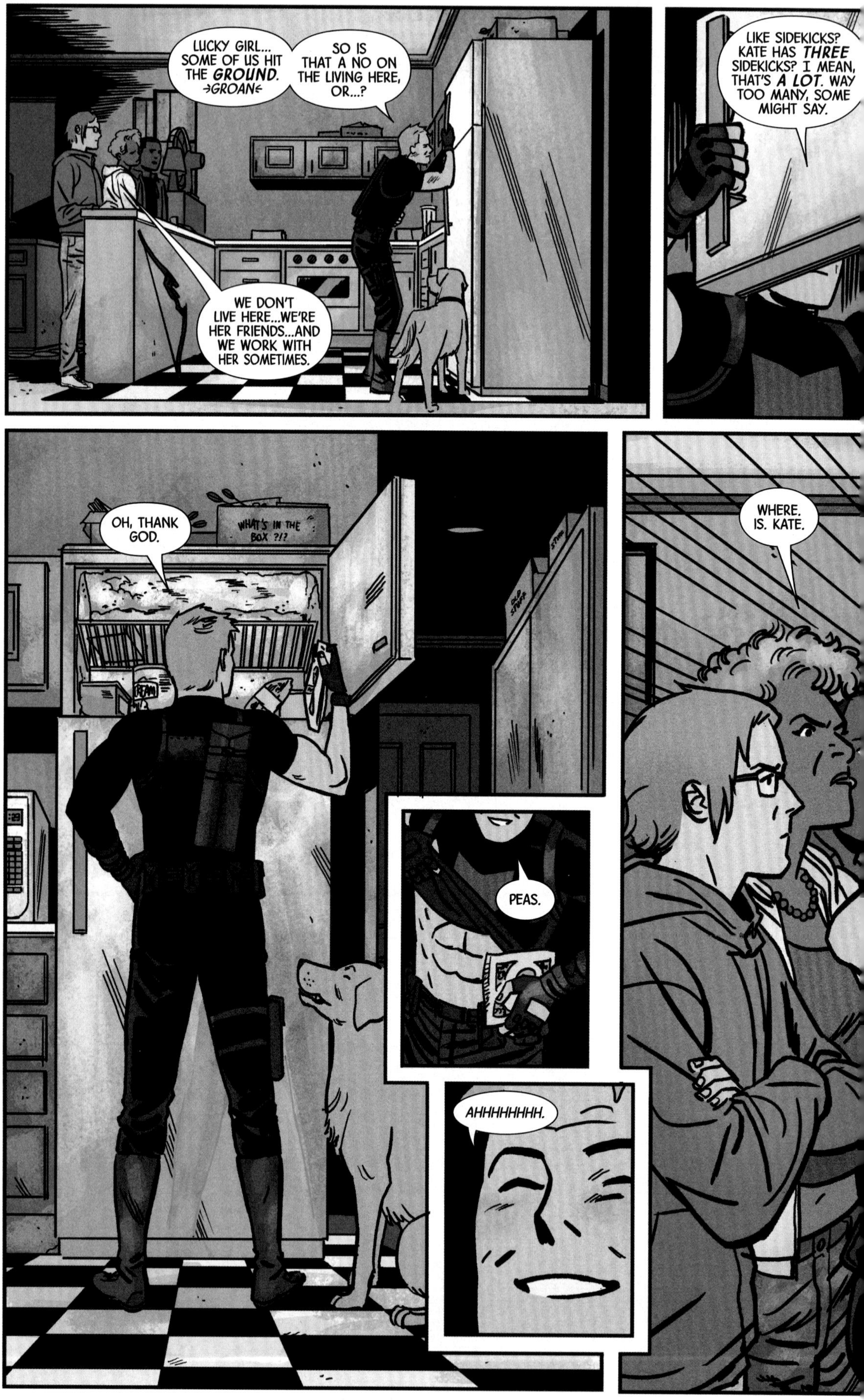
LUCKY GIRL... SOME OF US HIT THE GROUND. →GROAN←
SO IS THAT A NO ON THE LIVING HERE, OR...?
WE DON'T LIVE HERE...WE'RE HER FRIENDS...AND WE WORK WITH HER SOMETIMES.
LIKE SIDEKICKS? KATE HAS THREE SIDEKICKS? I MEAN, THAT'S A LOT. WAY TOO MANY, SOME MIGHT SAY.
OH, THANK GOD.
WHAT'S IN THE BOX ?!?
PEAS.
AHHHHHHHH.
WHERE. IS. KATE.

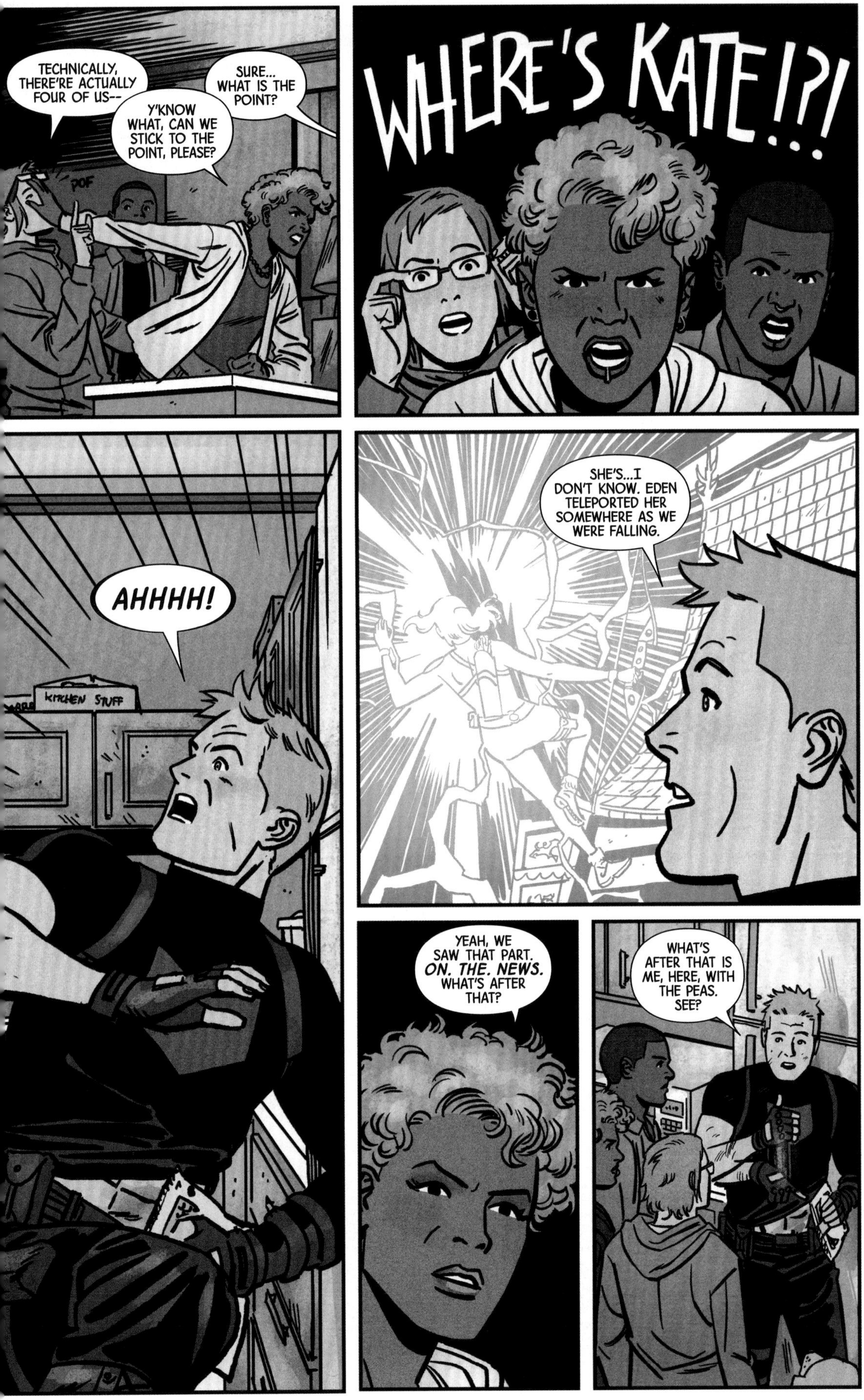
TECHNICALLY, THERE'RE ACTUALLY FOUR OF US--
SURE... WHAT IS THE POINT?
Y'KNOW WHAT, CAN WE STICK TO THE POINT, PLEASE?
POF
WHERE'S KATE!?!
AHHHH!
KITCHEN STUFF
SHE'S...I DON'T KNOW. EDEN TELEPORTED HER SOMEWHERE AS WE WERE FALLING.
YEAH, WE SAW THAT PART. ON. THE. NEWS. WHAT'S AFTER THAT?
WHAT'S AFTER THAT IS ME, HERE, WITH THE PEAS. SEE?

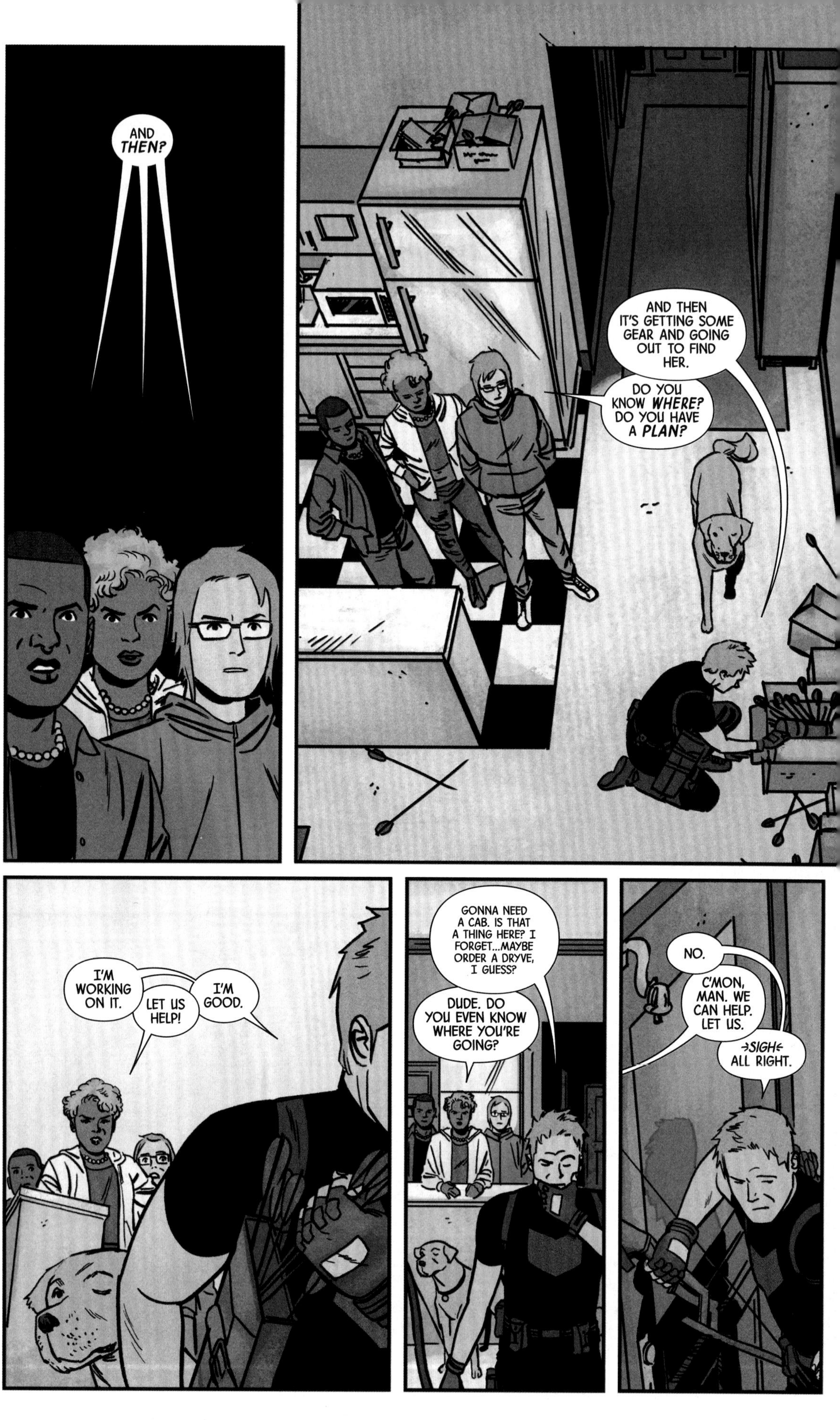
AND *THEN?*
AND THEN IT'S GETTING SOME GEAR AND GOING OUT TO FIND HER.
DO YOU KNOW *WHERE?* DO YOU HAVE A *PLAN?*
I'M WORKING ON IT.
LET US HELP!
I'M GOOD.
GONNA NEED A CAB. IS THAT A THING HERE? I FORGET...MAYBE ORDER A DRYVE, I GUESS?
DUDE. DO YOU EVEN KNOW WHERE YOU'RE GOING?
NO.
C'MON, MAN. WE CAN HELP. LET US.
→SIGH← ALL RIGHT.

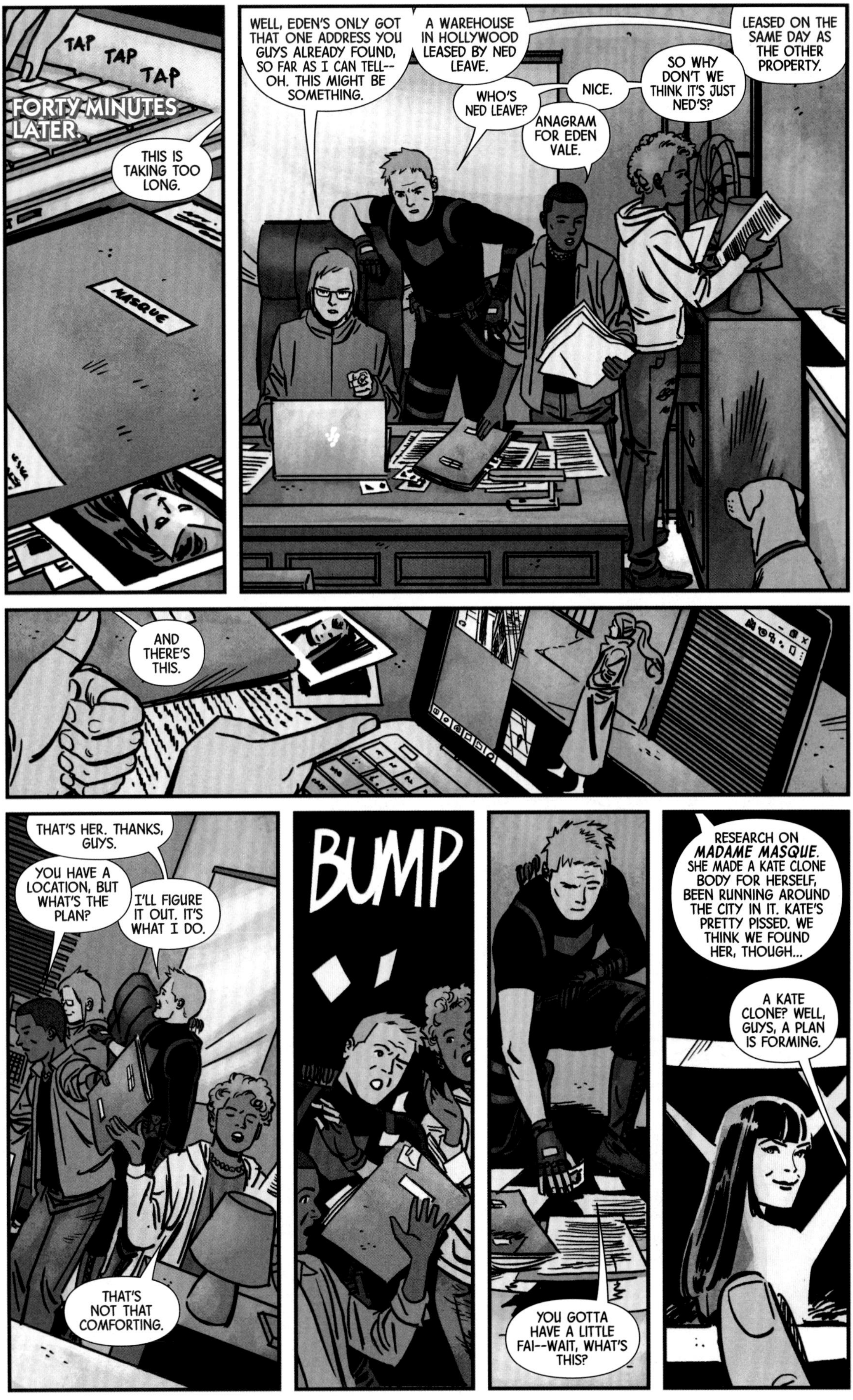
TAP TAP TAP
FORTY MINUTES LATER.
THIS IS TAKING TOO LONG.
MASQUE
WELL, EDEN'S ONLY GOT THAT ONE ADDRESS YOU GUYS ALREADY FOUND, SO FAR AS I CAN TELL-- OH. THIS MIGHT BE SOMETHING.
A WAREHOUSE IN HOLLYWOOD LEASED BY NED LEAVE.
WHO'S NED LEAVE?
NICE.
ANAGRAM FOR EDEN VALE.
SO WHY DON'T WE THINK IT'S JUST NED'S?
LEASED ON THE SAME DAY AS THE OTHER PROPERTY.
AND THERE'S THIS.
THAT'S HER. THANKS, GUYS.
YOU HAVE A LOCATION, BUT WHAT'S THE PLAN?
I'LL FIGURE IT OUT. IT'S WHAT I DO.
THAT'S NOT THAT COMFORTING.
BUMP
YOU GOTTA HAVE A LITTLE FAI--WAIT, WHAT'S THIS?
RESEARCH ON *MADAME MASQUE*. SHE MADE A KATE CLONE BODY FOR HERSELF, BEEN RUNNING AROUND THE CITY IN IT. KATE'S PRETTY PISSED. WE THINK WE FOUND HER, THOUGH...
A KATE CLONE? WELL, GUYS, A PLAN IS FORMING.

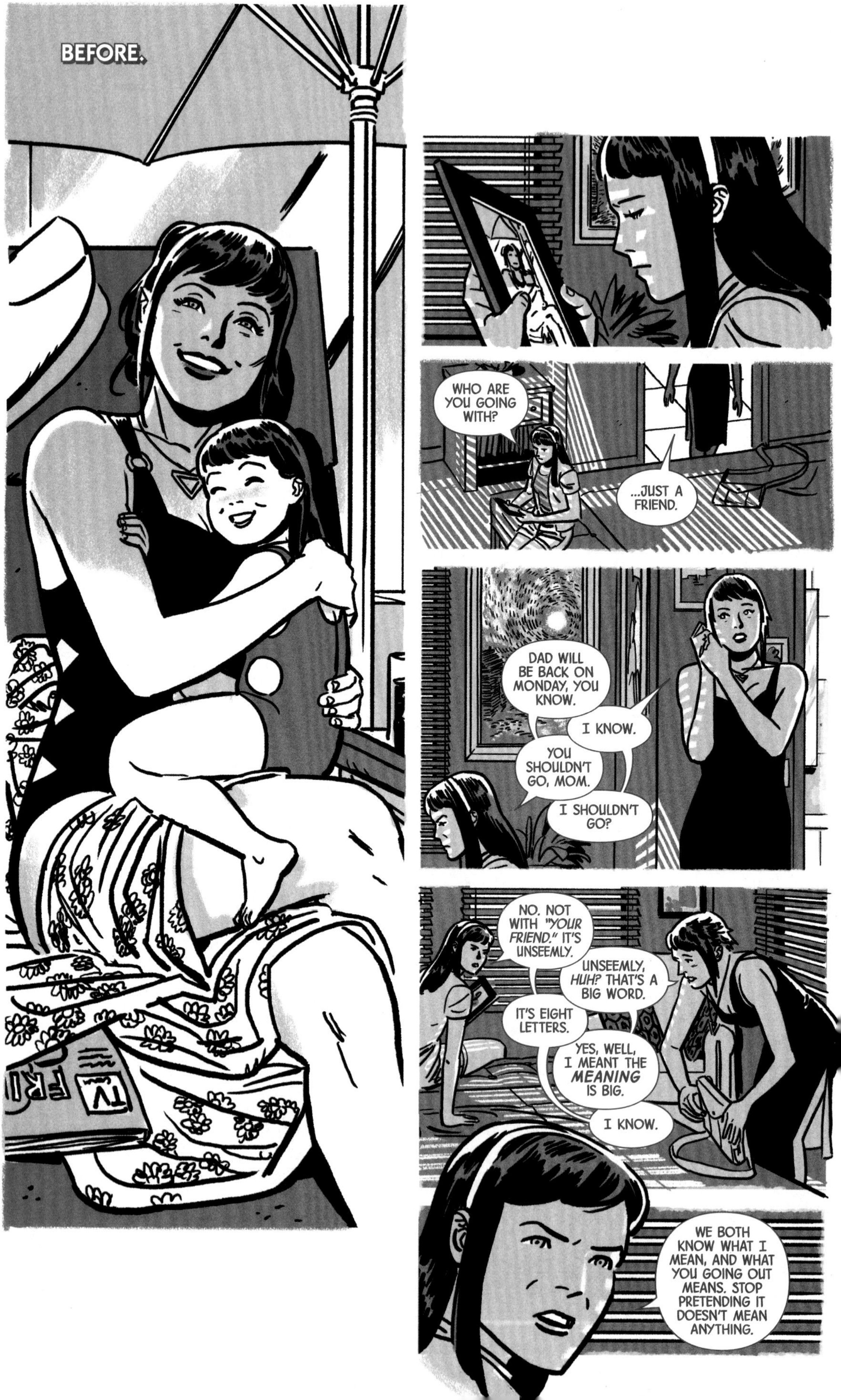
BEFORE.
WHO ARE YOU GOING WITH?
...JUST A FRIEND.
DAD WILL BE BACK ON MONDAY, YOU KNOW.
I KNOW.
YOU SHOULDN'T GO, MOM.
I SHOULDN'T GO?
NO. NOT WITH "YOUR FRIEND." IT'S UNSEEMLY.
UNSEEMLY, HUH? THAT'S A BIG WORD.
IT'S EIGHT LETTERS.
YES, WELL, I MEANT THE MEANING IS BIG.
I KNOW.
WE BOTH KNOW WHAT I MEAN, AND WHAT YOU GOING OUT MEANS. STOP PRETENDING IT DOESN'T MEAN ANYTHING.

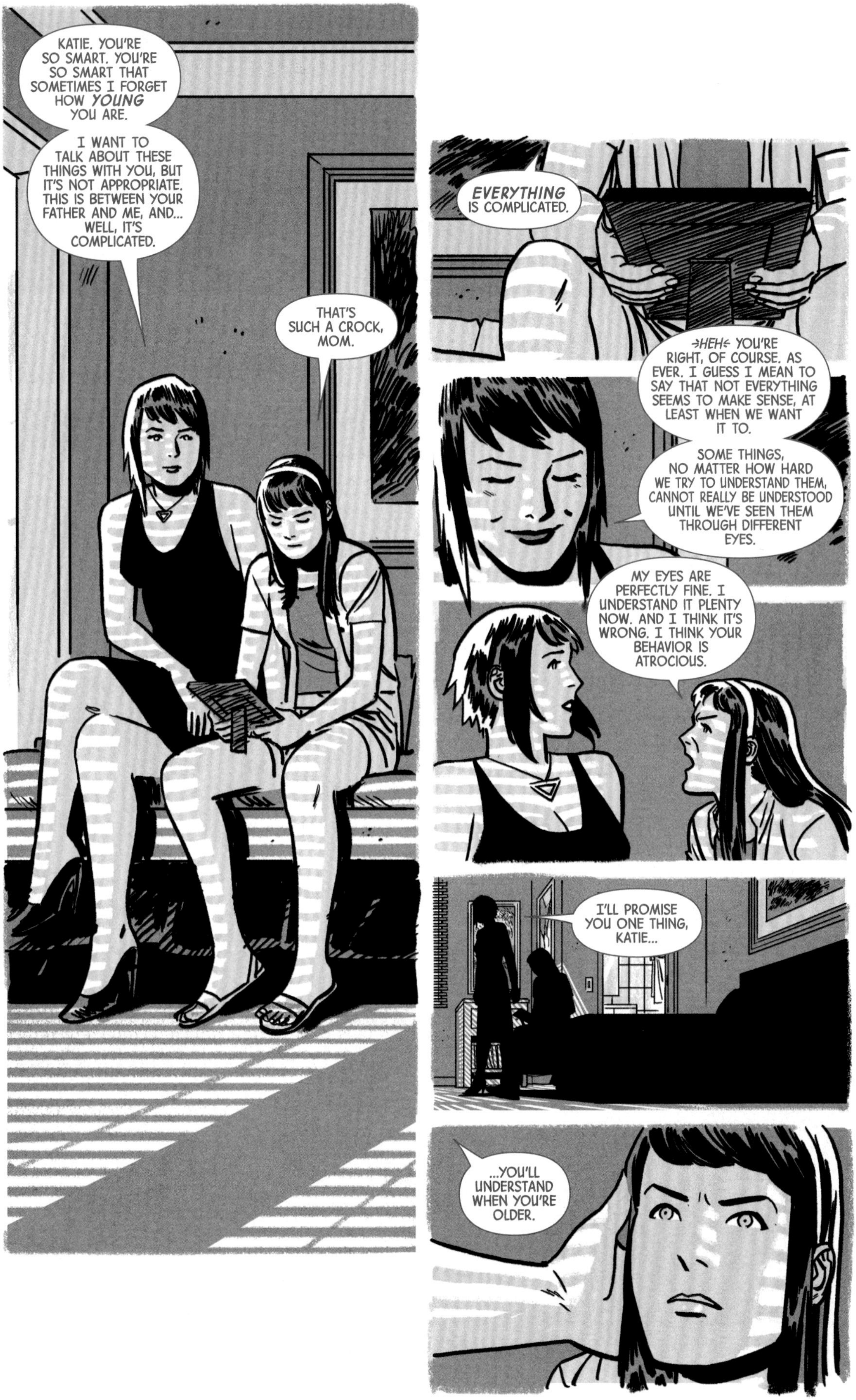
KATIE. YOU'RE SO SMART. YOU'RE SO SMART THAT SOMETIMES I FORGET HOW *YOUNG* YOU ARE.
I WANT TO TALK ABOUT THESE THINGS WITH YOU, BUT IT'S NOT APPROPRIATE. THIS IS BETWEEN YOUR FATHER AND ME, AND... WELL, IT'S COMPLICATED.
THAT'S SUCH A CROCK, MOM.
EVERYTHING IS COMPLICATED.
HEH YOU'RE RIGHT, OF COURSE. AS EVER. I GUESS I MEAN TO SAY THAT NOT EVERYTHING SEEMS TO MAKE SENSE, AT LEAST WHEN WE WANT IT TO.
SOME THINGS, NO MATTER HOW HARD WE TRY TO UNDERSTAND THEM, CANNOT REALLY BE UNDERSTOOD UNTIL WE'VE SEEN THEM THROUGH DIFFERENT EYES.
MY EYES ARE PERFECTLY FINE. I UNDERSTAND IT PLENTY NOW. AND I THINK IT'S WRONG. I THINK YOUR BEHAVIOR IS ATROCIOUS.
I'LL PROMISE YOU ONE THING, KATIE...
...YOU'LL UNDERSTAND WHEN YOU'RE OLDER.

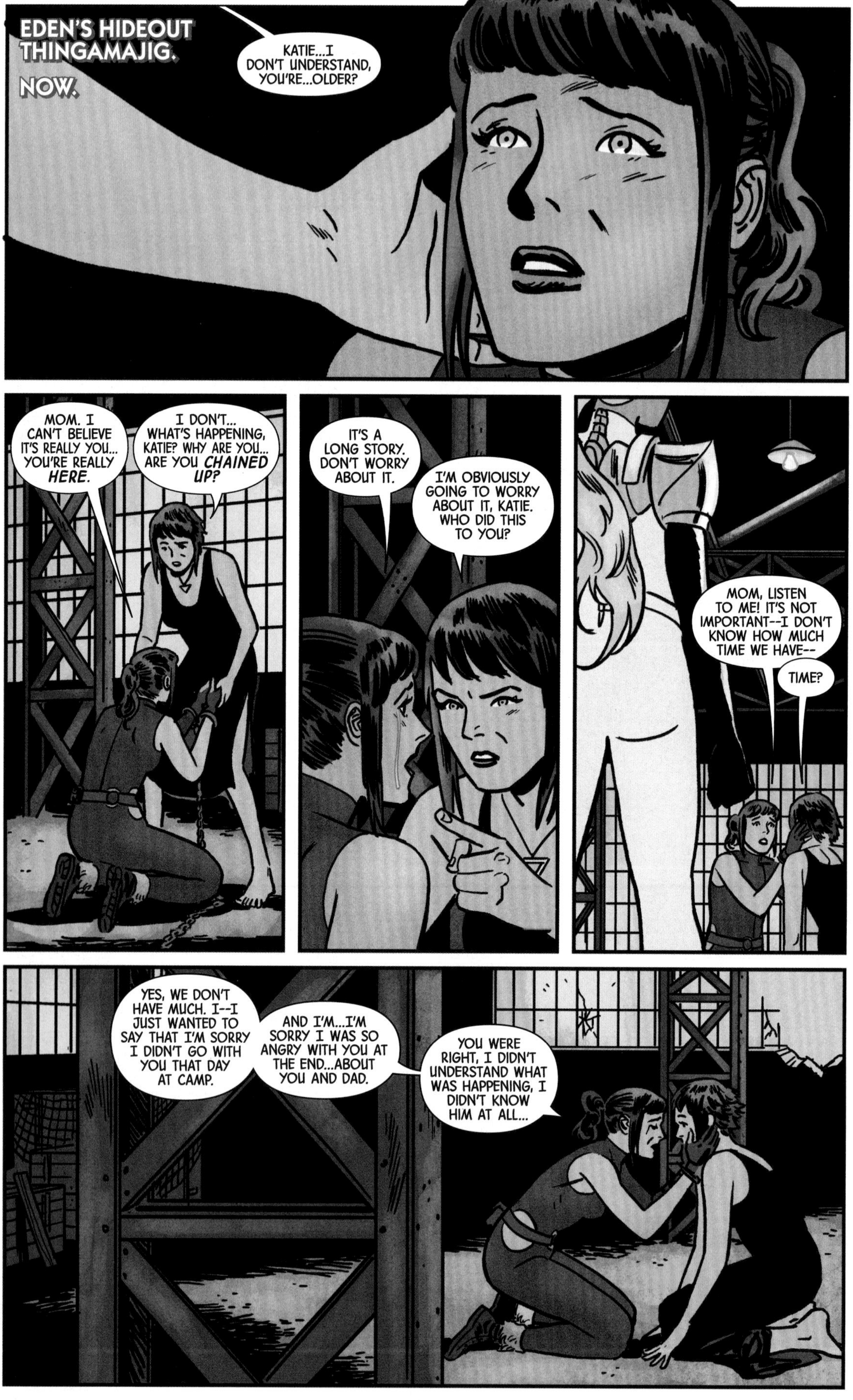
EDEN'S HIDEOUT THINGAMAJIG.
NOW.
KATIE...I DON'T UNDERSTAND, YOU'RE...OLDER?
MOM. I CAN'T BELIEVE IT'S REALLY YOU... YOU'RE REALLY *HERE*.
I DON'T... WHAT'S HAPPENING, KATIE? WHY ARE YOU... ARE YOU *CHAINED UP*?
IT'S A LONG STORY. DON'T WORRY ABOUT IT.
I'M OBVIOUSLY GOING TO WORRY ABOUT IT, KATIE. WHO DID THIS TO YOU?
MOM, LISTEN TO ME! IT'S NOT IMPORTANT--I DON'T KNOW HOW MUCH TIME WE HAVE--
TIME?
YES, WE DON'T HAVE MUCH. I--I JUST WANTED TO SAY THAT I'M SORRY I DIDN'T GO WITH YOU THAT DAY AT CAMP.
AND I'M...I'M SORRY I WAS SO ANGRY WITH YOU AT THE END...ABOUT YOU AND DAD.
YOU WERE RIGHT, I DIDN'T UNDERSTAND WHAT WAS HAPPENING, I DIDN'T KNOW HIM AT ALL...

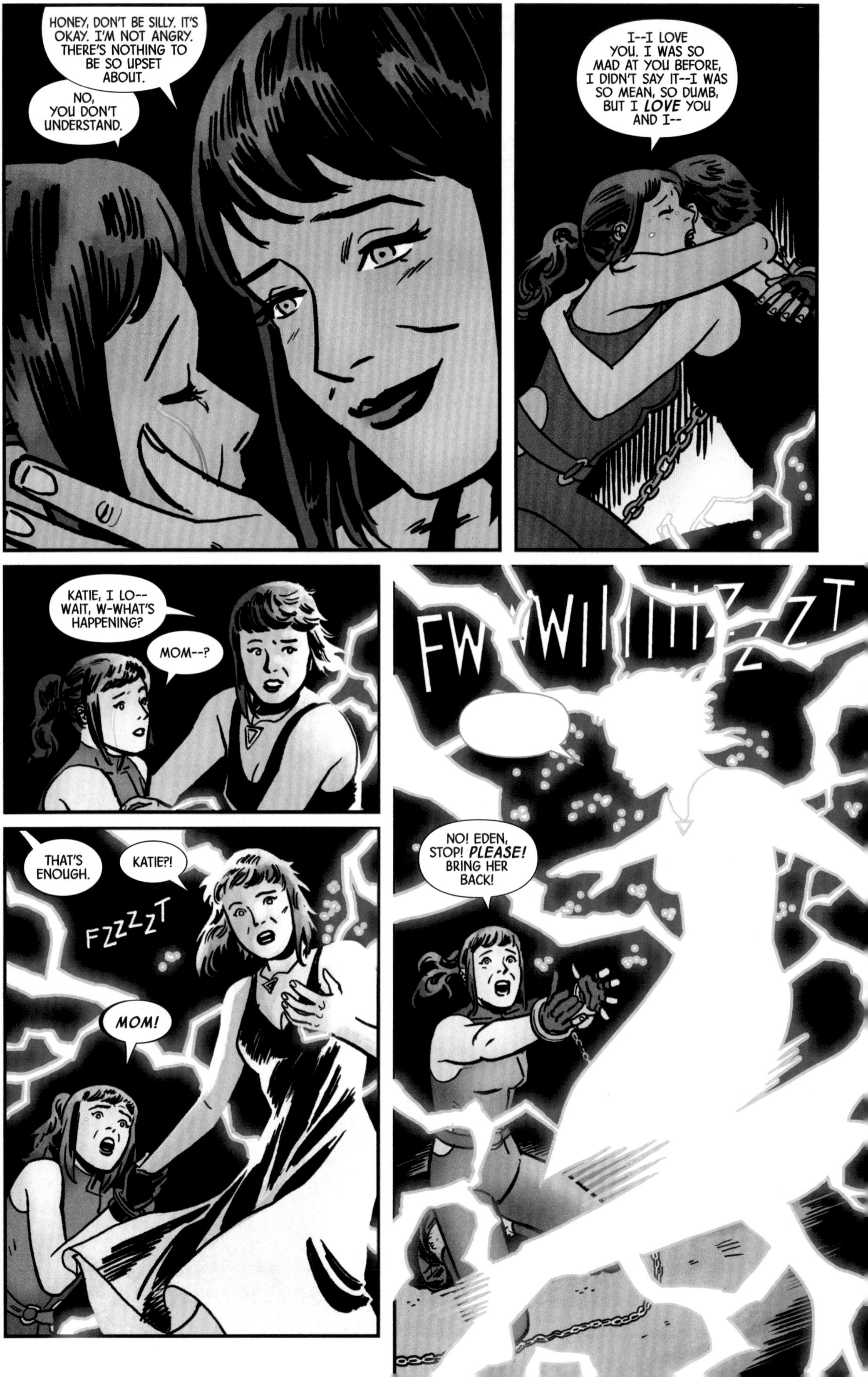

HONEY, DON'T BE SILLY. IT'S OKAY. I'M NOT ANGRY. THERE'S NOTHING TO BE SO UPSET ABOUT.
NO, YOU DON'T UNDERSTAND.
I--I LOVE YOU. I WAS SO MAD AT YOU BEFORE, I DIDN'T SAY IT--I WAS SO MEAN, SO DUMB, BUT I *LOVE* YOU AND I--
KATIE, I LO-- WAIT, W-WHAT'S HAPPENING?
MOM--?
THAT'S ENOUGH.
KATIE?!
FZZZZT
MOM!
FWWIIIIIZZZT
NO! EDEN, STOP! *PLEASE!* BRING HER BACK!

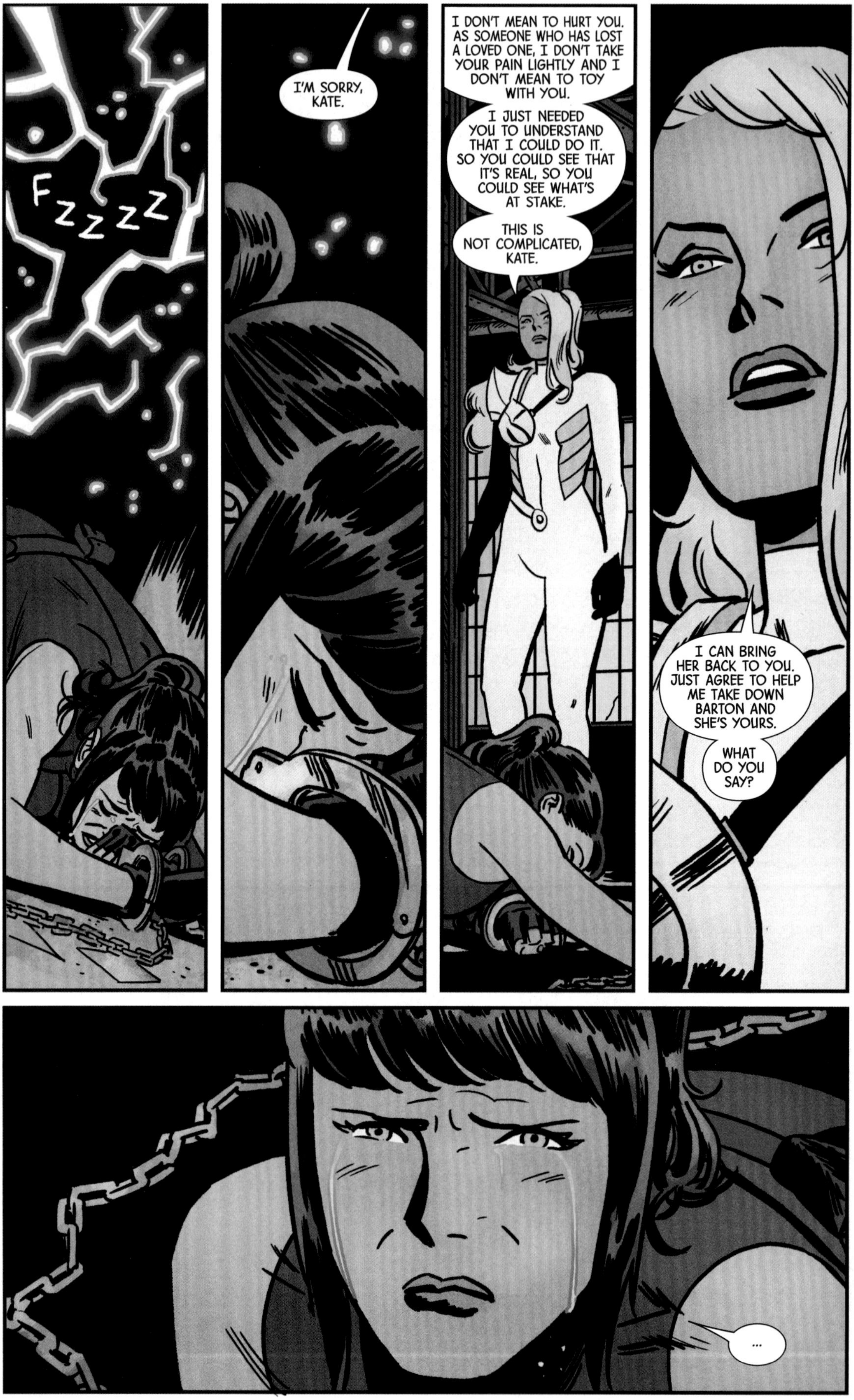
FZZZZZ
I'M SORRY, KATE.
I DON'T MEAN TO HURT YOU. AS SOMEONE WHO HAS LOST A LOVED ONE, I DON'T TAKE YOUR PAIN LIGHTLY AND I DON'T MEAN TO TOY WITH YOU.
I JUST NEEDED YOU TO UNDERSTAND THAT I COULD DO IT. SO YOU COULD SEE THAT IT'S REAL, SO YOU COULD SEE WHAT'S AT STAKE.
THIS IS NOT COMPLICATED, KATE.
I CAN BRING HER BACK TO YOU. JUST AGREE TO HELP ME TAKE DOWN BARTON AND SHE'S YOURS.
WHAT DO YOU SAY?
...

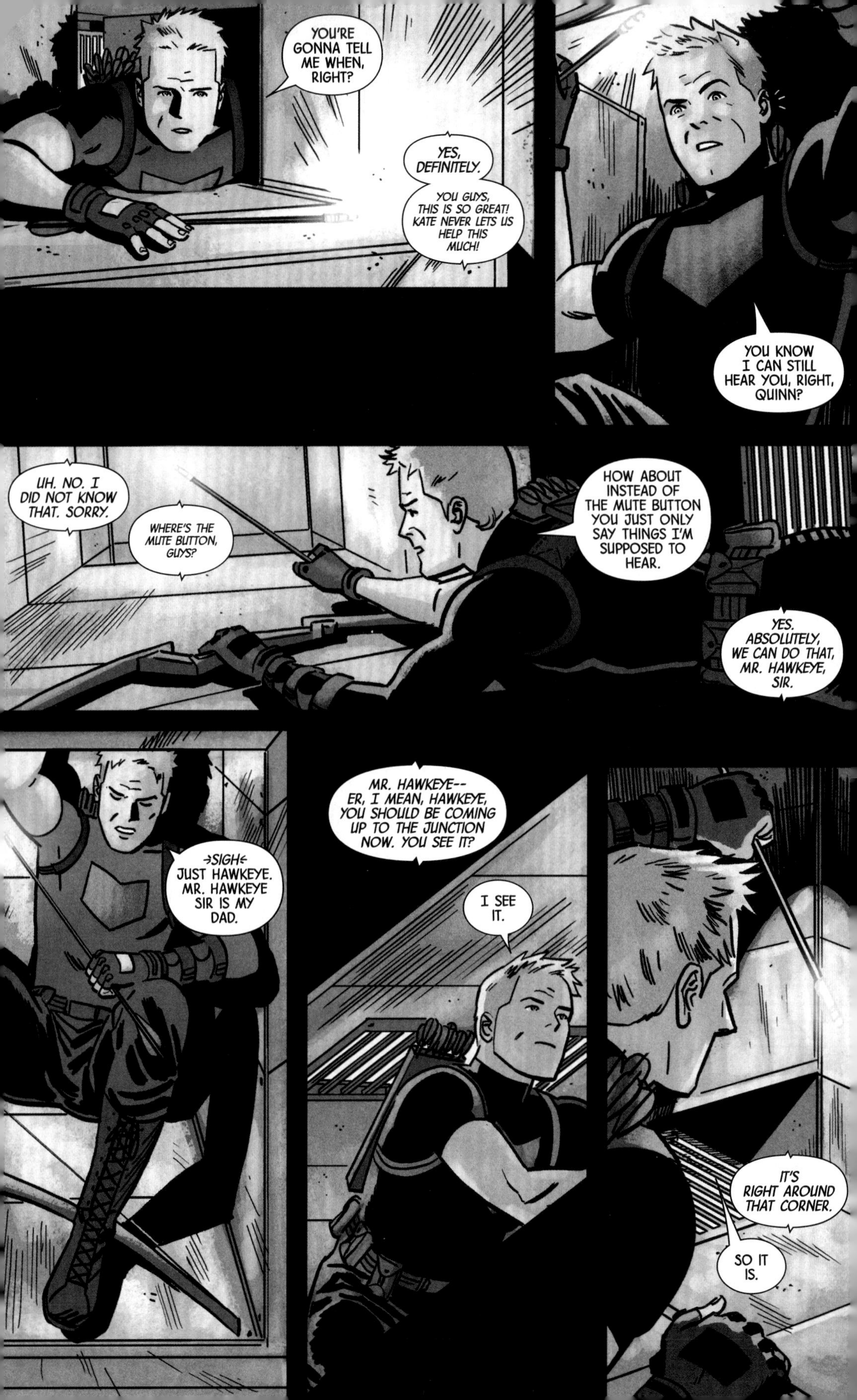
YOU'RE GONNA TELL ME WHEN, RIGHT?
YES, DEFINITELY.
YOU GUYS, THIS IS SO GREAT! KATE NEVER LETS US HELP THIS MUCH!
YOU KNOW I CAN STILL HEAR YOU, RIGHT, QUINN?
UH. NO. I DID NOT KNOW THAT. SORRY.
WHERE'S THE MUTE BUTTON, GUYS?
HOW ABOUT INSTEAD OF THE MUTE BUTTON YOU JUST ONLY SAY THINGS I'M SUPPOSED TO HEAR.
YES. ABSOLUTELY, WE CAN DO THAT, MR. HAWKEYE, SIR.
→SIGH← JUST HAWKEYE. MR. HAWKEYE SIR IS MY DAD.
MR. HAWKEYE-- ER, I MEAN, HAWKEYE, YOU SHOULD BE COMING UP TO THE JUNCTION NOW. YOU SEE IT?
I SEE IT.
IT'S RIGHT AROUND THAT CORNER.
SO IT IS.

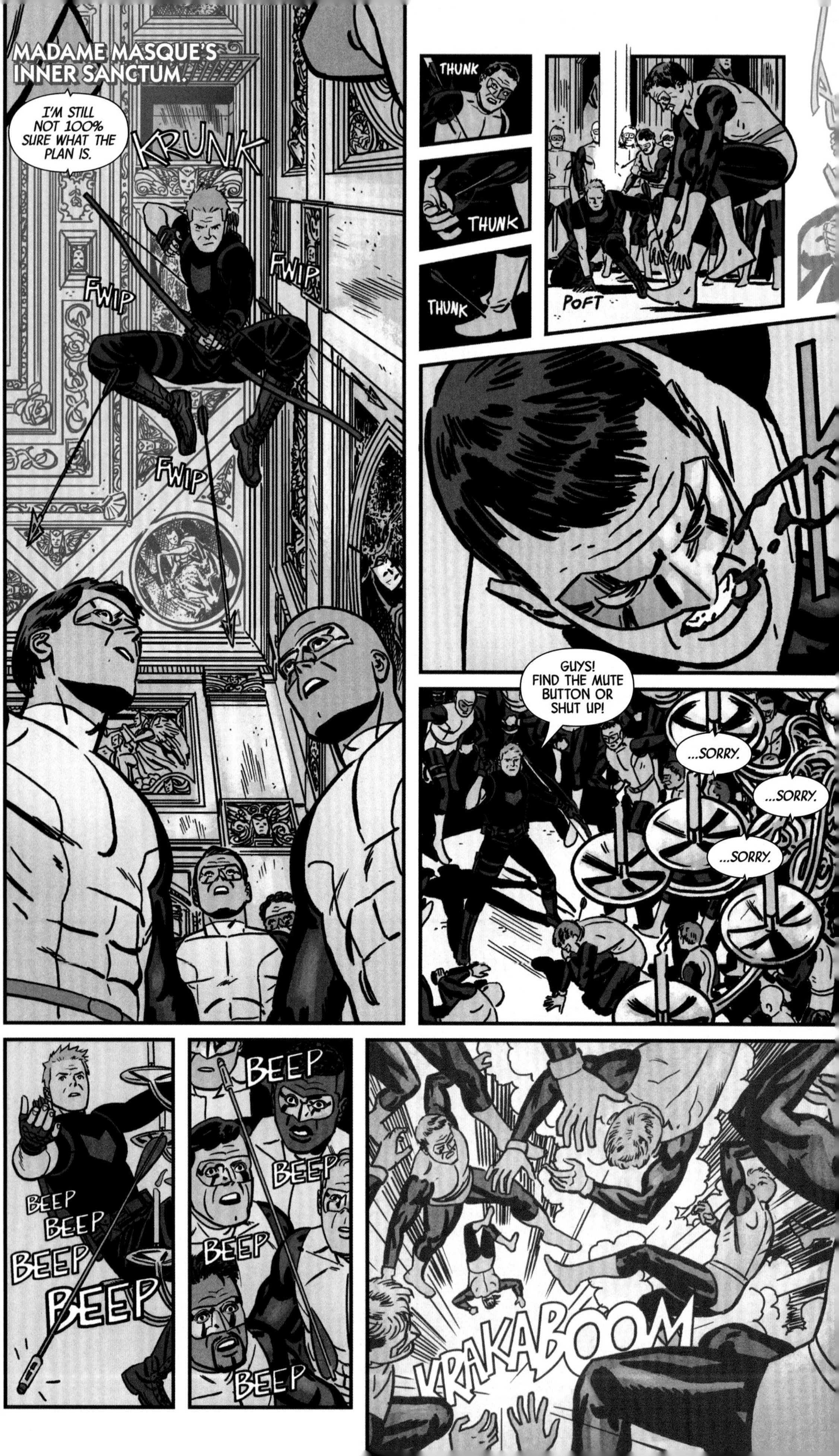

MADAME MASQUE'S INNER SANCTUM.
I'M STILL NOT 100% SURE WHAT THE PLAN IS.
KRUNK
FWIP
FWIP
FWIP
THUNK
THUNK
THUNK
POFT
GUYS! FIND THE MUTE BUTTON OR SHUT UP!
...SORRY.
...SORRY.
...SORRY.
BEEP
BEEP
BEEP
BEEP
BEEP
BEEP
BEEP
BEEP
VRAKABOOM

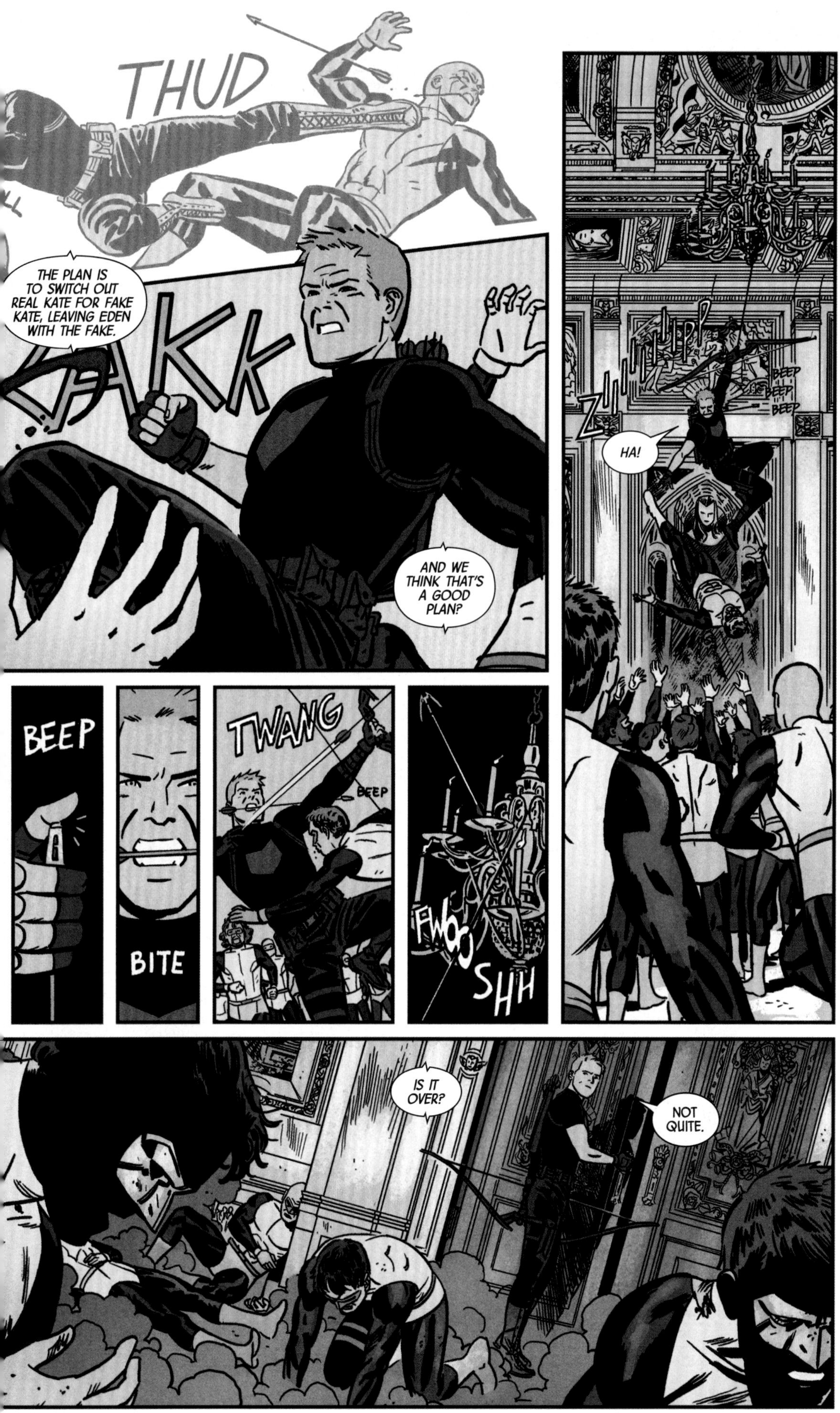
THUD
THE PLAN IS TO SWITCH OUT REAL KATE FOR FAKE KATE, LEAVING EDEN WITH THE FAKE.
AND WE THINK THAT'S A GOOD PLAN?
ZIIIIIIIPP
BEEP BEEP BEEP
HA!
BEEP
BITE
TWANG
BEEP
FWOOSHH
IS IT OVER?
NOT QUITE.

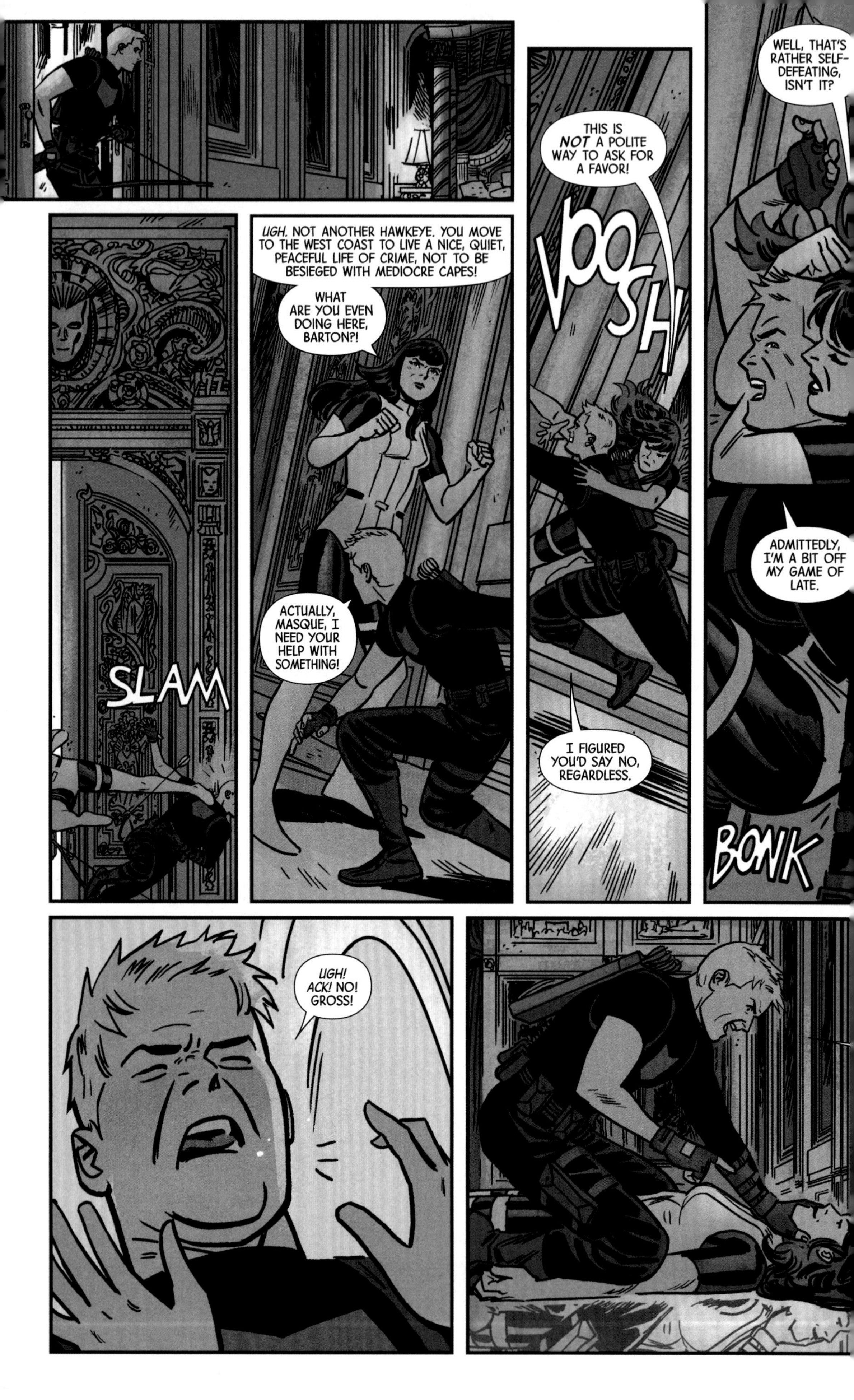
UGH. NOT ANOTHER HAWKEYE. YOU MOVE TO THE WEST COAST TO LIVE A NICE, QUIET, PEACEFUL LIFE OF CRIME, NOT TO BE BESIEGED WITH MEDIOCRE CAPES!
WHAT ARE YOU EVEN DOING HERE, BARTON?!
ACTUALLY, MASQUE, I NEED YOUR HELP WITH SOMETHING!
SLAM
THIS IS NOT A POLITE WAY TO ASK FOR A FAVOR!
VOOSH
I FIGURED YOU'D SAY NO, REGARDLESS.
WELL, THAT'S RATHER SELF-DEFEATING, ISN'T IT?
ADMITTEDLY, I'M A BIT OFF MY GAME OF LATE.
BONK
UGH! ACK! NO! GROSS!

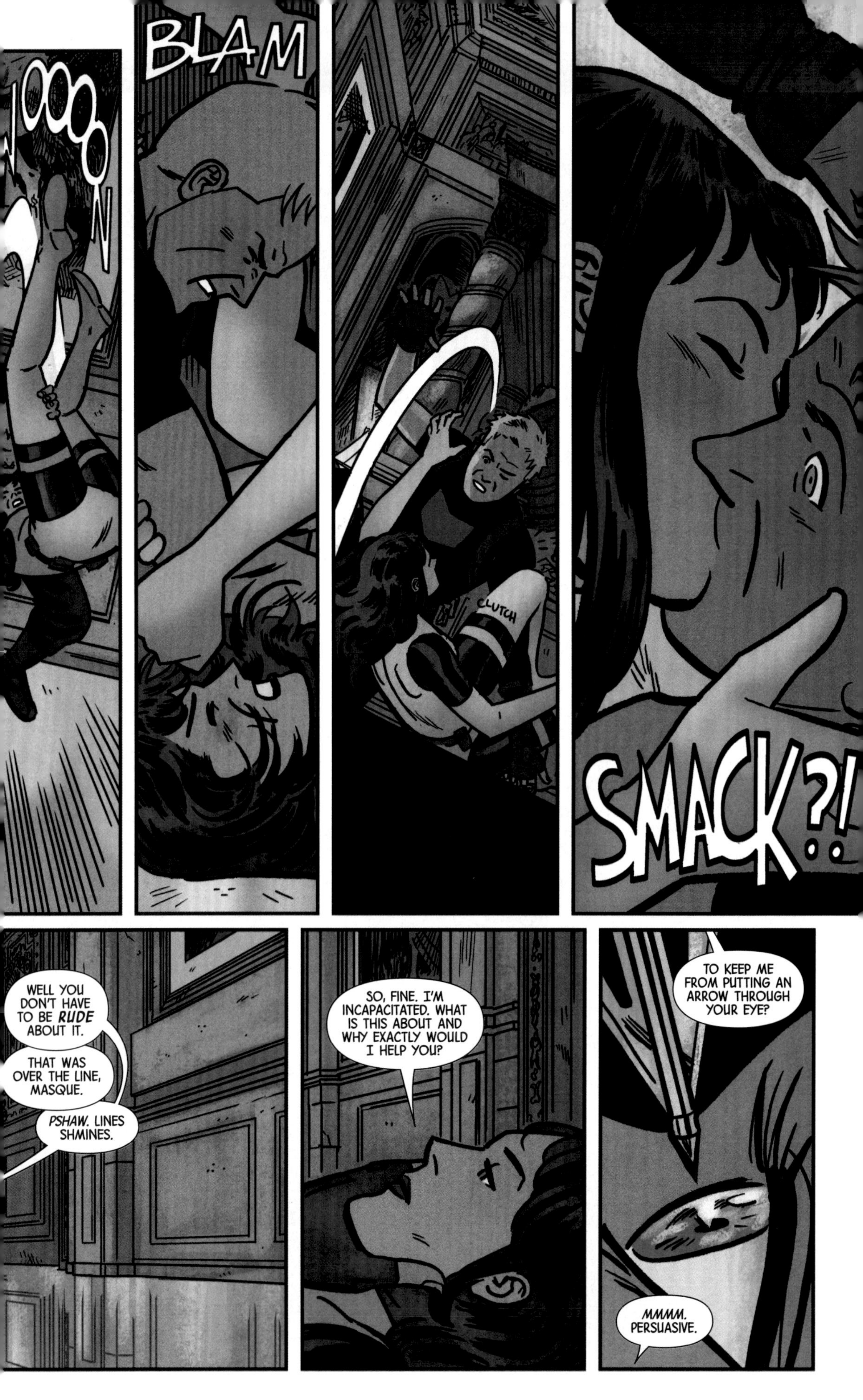
WOOOOON
BLAM
CLUTCH
SMACK?!
WELL YOU DON'T HAVE TO BE *RUDE* ABOUT IT.
THAT WAS OVER THE LINE, MASQUE.
PSHAW. LINES SHMINES.
SO, FINE. I'M INCAPACITATED. WHAT IS THIS ABOUT AND WHY EXACTLY WOULD I HELP YOU?
TO KEEP ME FROM PUTTING AN ARROW THROUGH YOUR EYE?
MMMM. PERSUASIVE.

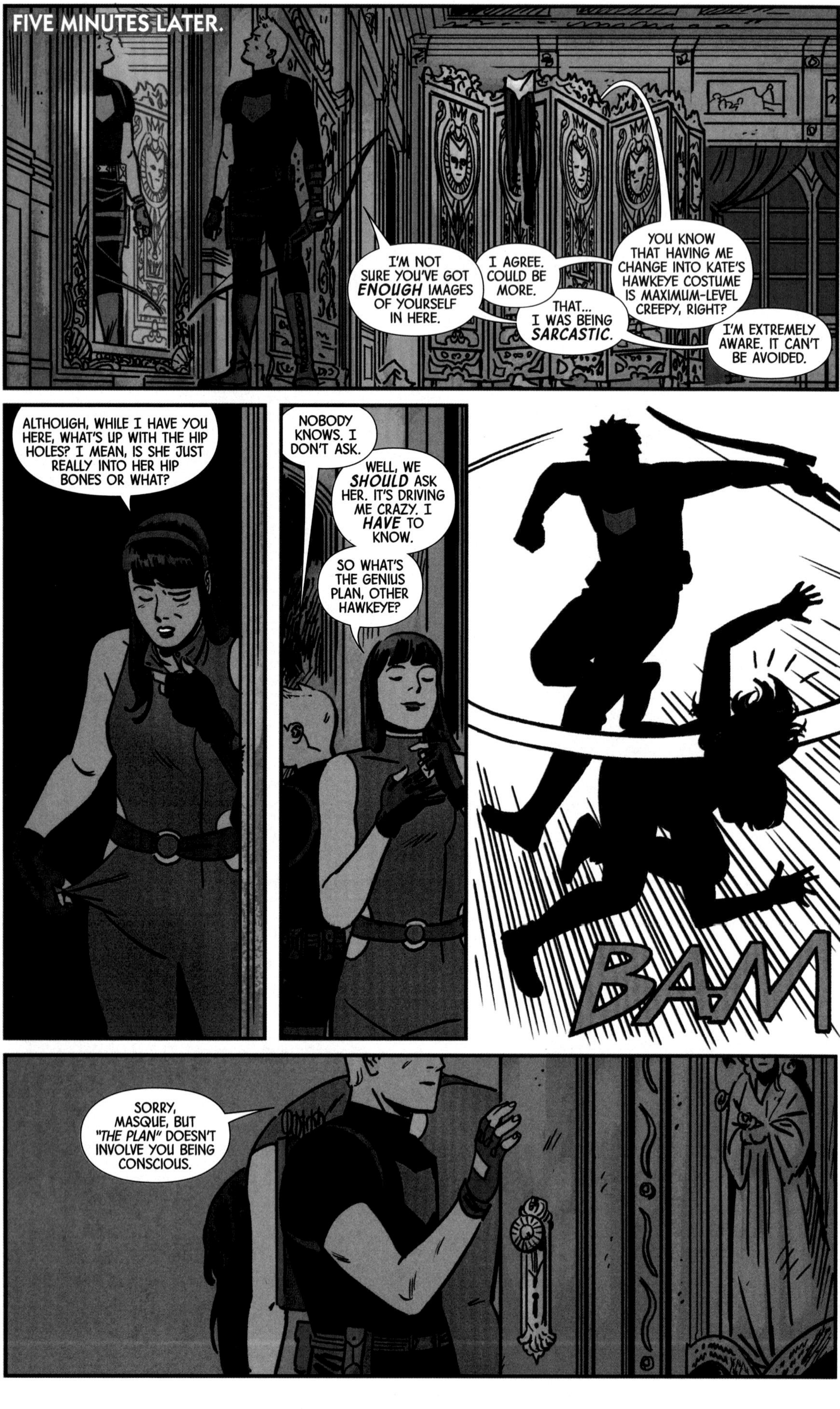
FIVE MINUTES LATER.
I'M NOT SURE YOU'VE GOT ENOUGH IMAGES OF YOURSELF IN HERE.
I AGREE. COULD BE MORE.
THAT... I WAS BEING SARCASTIC.
YOU KNOW THAT HAVING ME CHANGE INTO KATE'S HAWKEYE COSTUME IS MAXIMUM-LEVEL CREEPY, RIGHT?
I'M EXTREMELY AWARE. IT CAN'T BE AVOIDED.
ALTHOUGH, WHILE I HAVE YOU HERE, WHAT'S UP WITH THE HIP HOLES? I MEAN, IS SHE JUST REALLY INTO HER HIP BONES OR WHAT?
NOBODY KNOWS. I DON'T ASK.
WELL, WE SHOULD ASK HER. IT'S DRIVING ME CRAZY. I HAVE TO KNOW.
SO WHAT'S THE GENIUS PLAN, OTHER HAWKEYE?
BAM
SORRY, MASQUE, BUT "THE PLAN" DOESN'T INVOLVE YOU BEING CONSCIOUS.

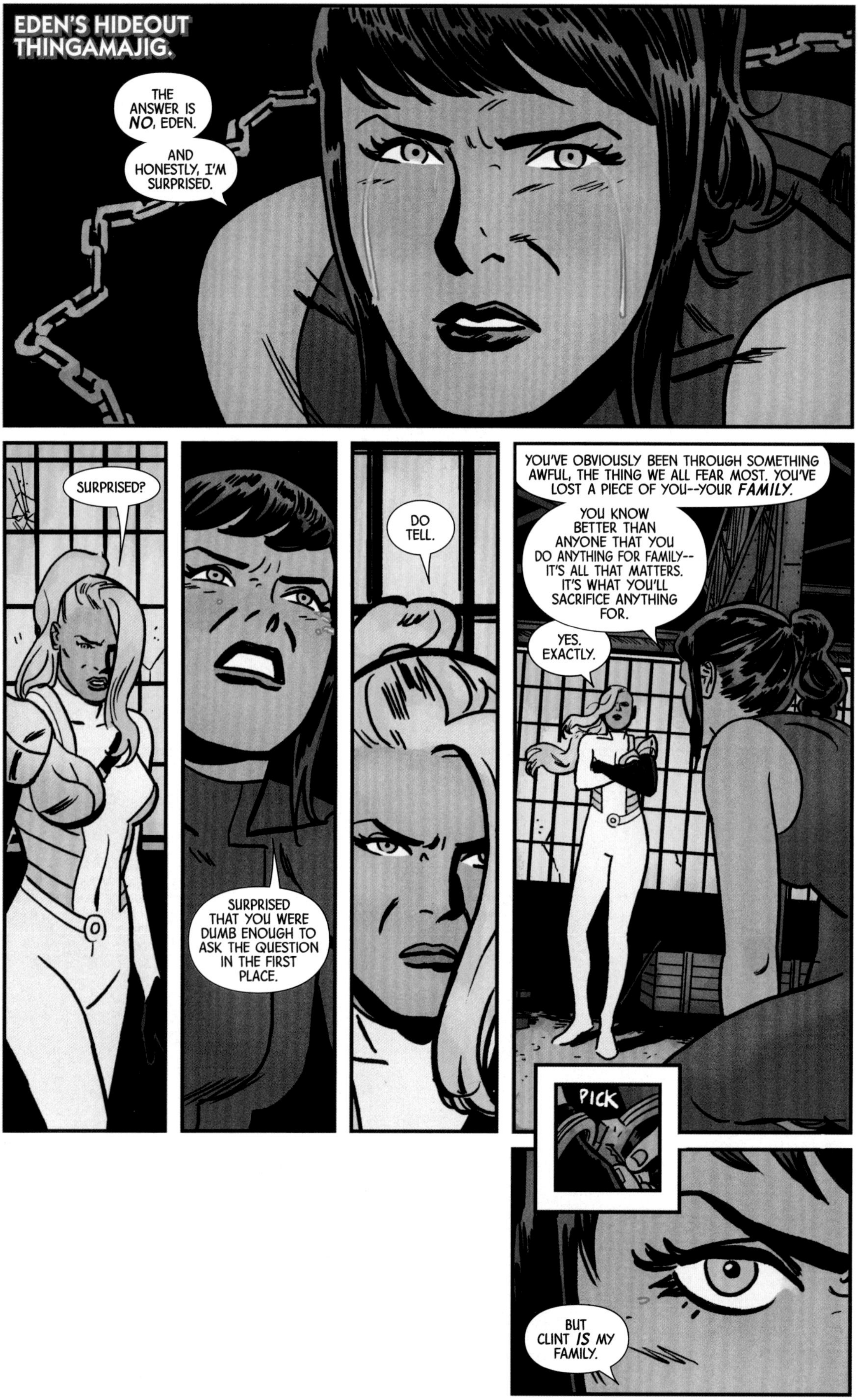
EDEN'S HIDEOUT THINGAMAJIG.
THE ANSWER IS *NO*, EDEN.
AND HONESTLY, I'M SURPRISED.
SURPRISED?
SURPRISED THAT YOU WERE DUMB ENOUGH TO ASK THE QUESTION IN THE FIRST PLACE.
DO TELL.
YOU'VE OBVIOUSLY BEEN THROUGH SOMETHING AWFUL, THE THING WE ALL FEAR MOST. YOU'VE LOST A PIECE OF YOU--YOUR *FAMILY*.
YOU KNOW BETTER THAN ANYONE THAT YOU DO ANYTHING FOR FAMILY-- IT'S ALL THAT MATTERS. IT'S WHAT YOU'LL SACRIFICE ANYTHING FOR.
YES. EXACTLY.
PICK
BUT CLINT *IS* MY FAMILY.

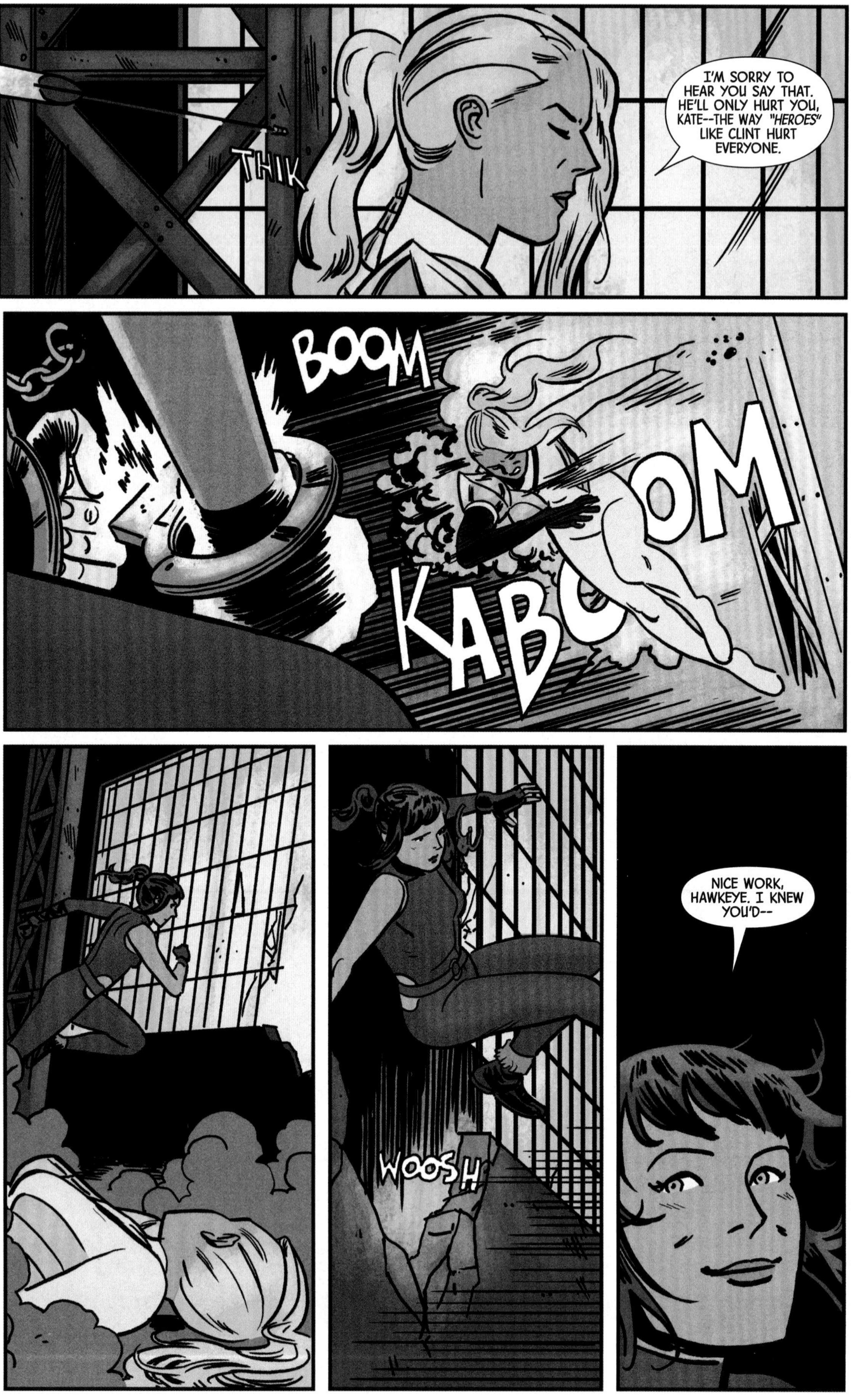
THIK
I'M SORRY TO HEAR YOU SAY THAT. HE'LL ONLY HURT YOU, KATE--THE WAY "HEROES" LIKE CLINT HURT EVERYONE.
BOOM
KABOOM
WOOSH
NICE WORK, HAWKEYE. I KNEW YOU'D--

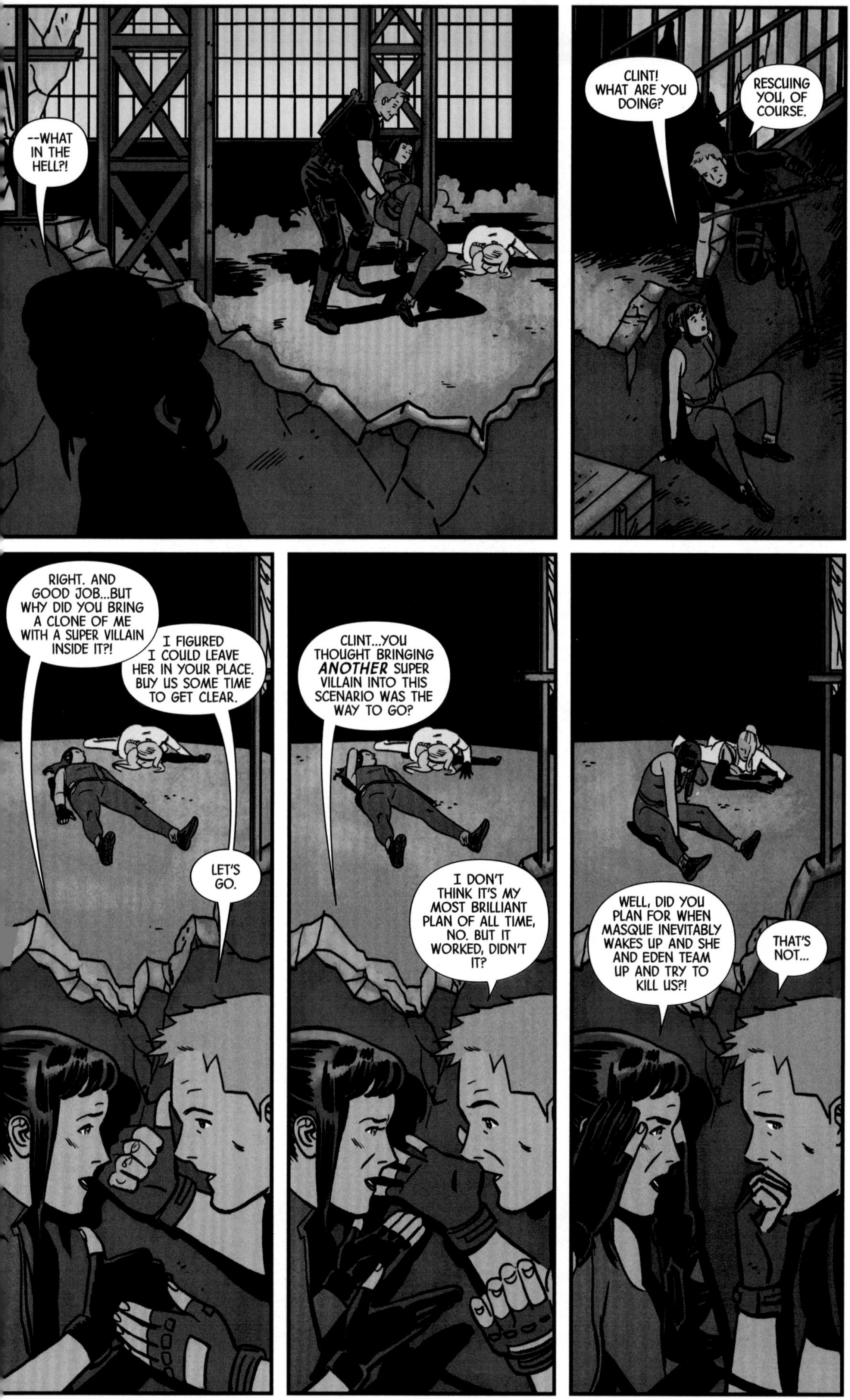
--WHAT IN THE HELL?!
CLINT! WHAT ARE YOU DOING?
RESCUING YOU, OF COURSE.
RIGHT. AND GOOD JOB...BUT WHY DID YOU BRING A CLONE OF ME WITH A SUPER VILLAIN INSIDE IT?!
I FIGURED I COULD LEAVE HER IN YOUR PLACE. BUY US SOME TIME TO GET CLEAR.
LET'S GO.
CLINT...YOU THOUGHT BRINGING ANOTHER SUPER VILLAIN INTO THIS SCENARIO WAS THE WAY TO GO?
I DON'T THINK IT'S MY MOST BRILLIANT PLAN OF ALL TIME, NO. BUT IT WORKED, DIDN'T IT?
WELL, DID YOU PLAN FOR WHEN MASQUE INEVITABLY WAKES UP AND SHE AND EDEN TEAM UP AND TRY TO KILL US?!
THAT'S NOT...

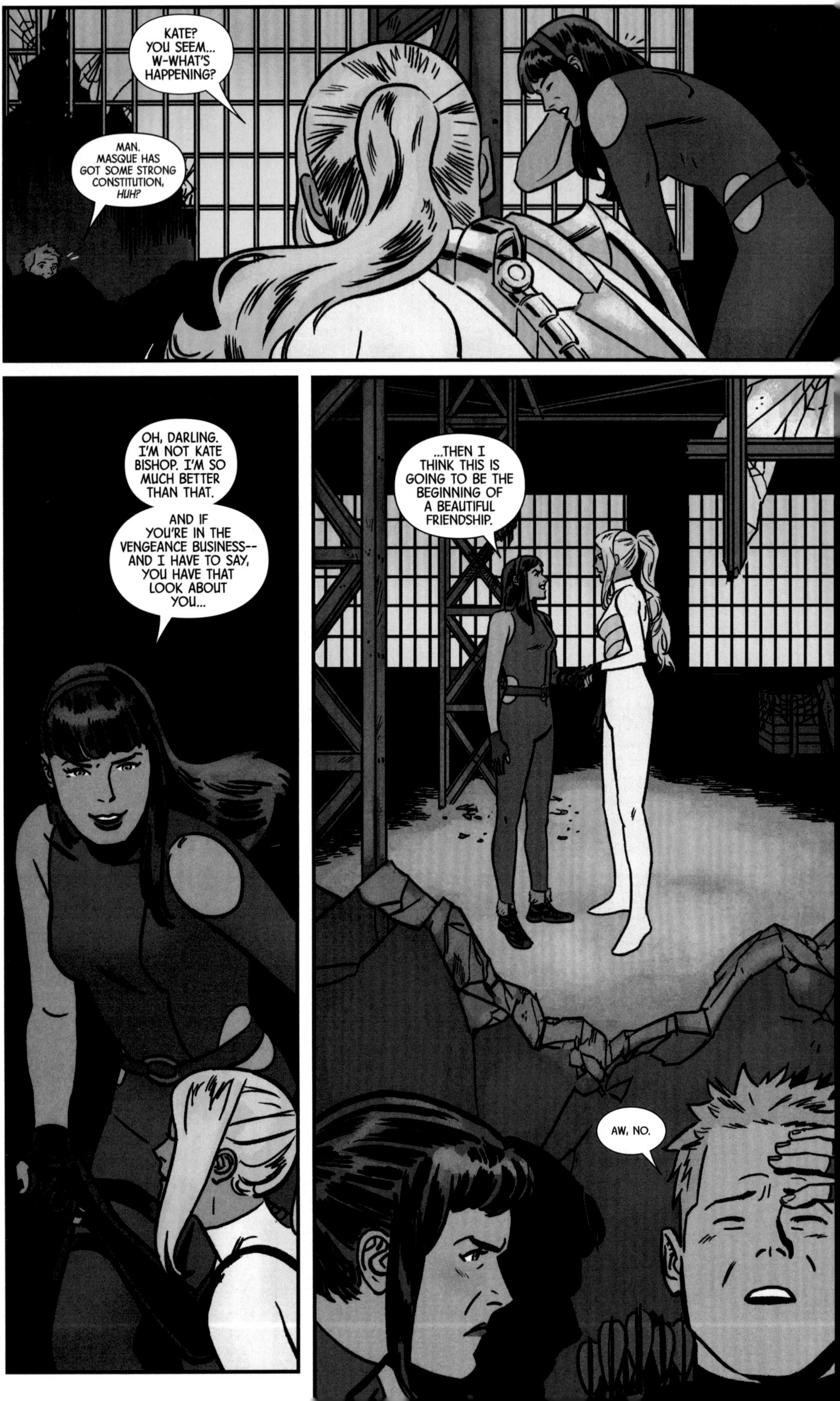
KATE? YOU SEEM... W-WHAT'S HAPPENING?
MAN. MASQUE HAS GOT SOME STRONG CONSTITUTION, HUH?
OH, DARLING. I'M NOT KATE BISHOP. I'M SO MUCH BETTER THAN THAT.
AND IF YOU'RE IN THE VENGEANCE BUSINESS-- AND I HAVE TO SAY, YOU HAVE THAT LOOK ABOUT YOU...
...THEN I THINK THIS IS GOING TO BE THE BEGINNING OF A BEAUTIFUL FRIENDSHIP.
AW, NO.

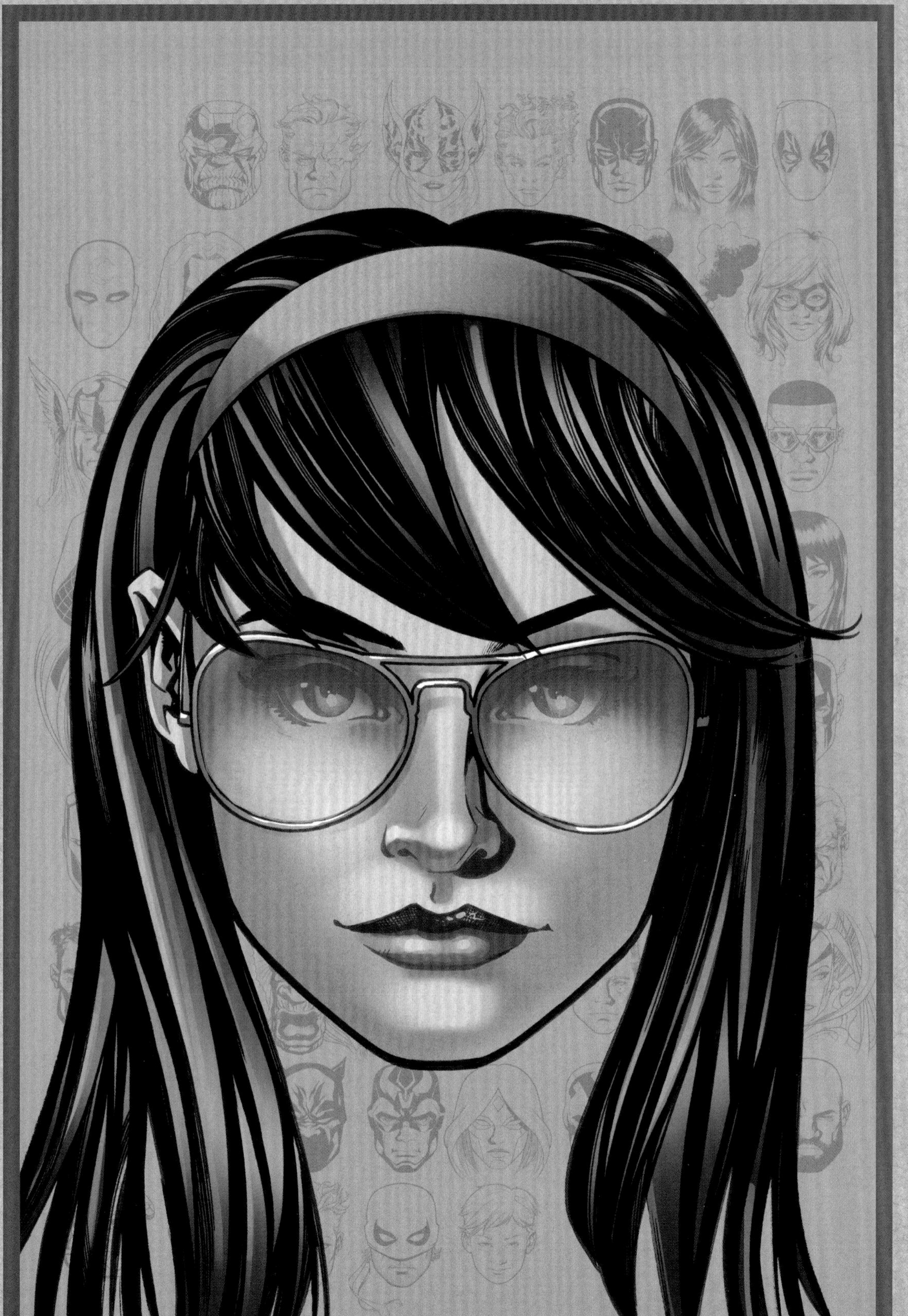

#13 legacy headshot variant
by Mike McKone & Rachelle Rosenberg

15

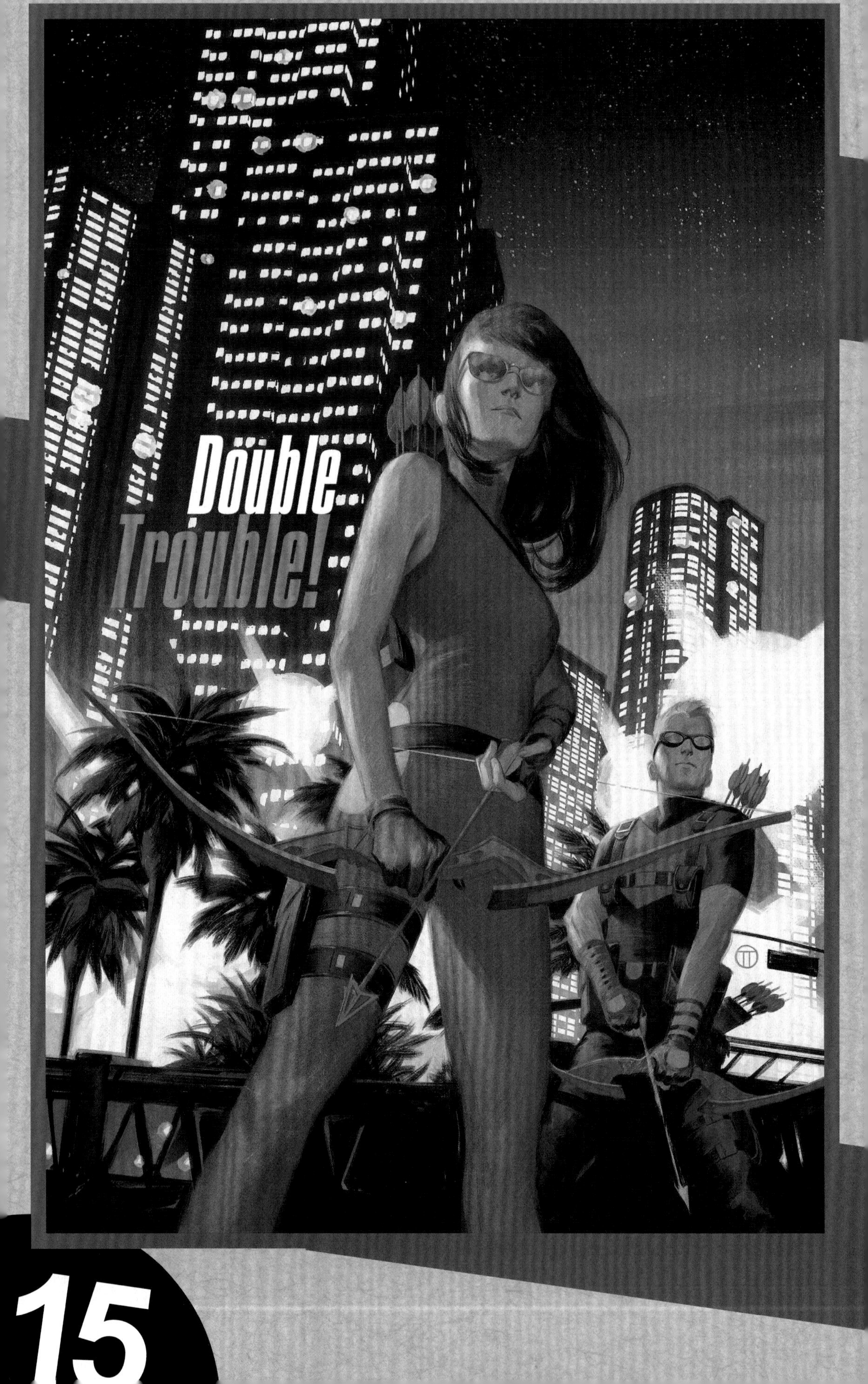
Double
Trouble!

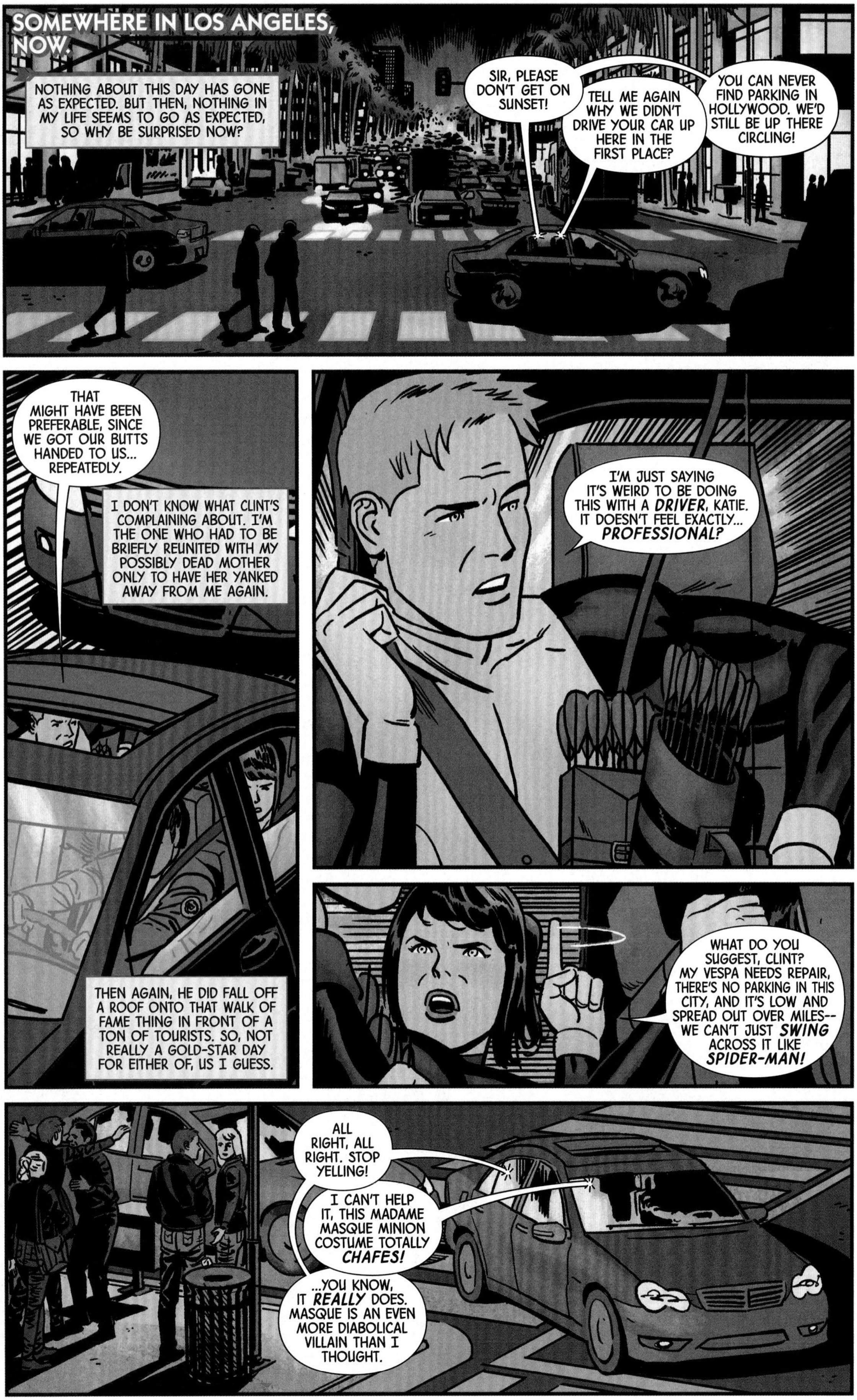
SOMEWHERE IN LOS ANGELES, NOW.
NOTHING ABOUT THIS DAY HAS GONE AS EXPECTED. BUT THEN, NOTHING IN MY LIFE SEEMS TO GO AS EXPECTED, SO WHY BE SURPRISED NOW?
SIR, PLEASE DON'T GET ON SUNSET!
TELL ME AGAIN WHY WE DIDN'T DRIVE YOUR CAR UP HERE IN THE FIRST PLACE?
YOU CAN NEVER FIND PARKING IN HOLLYWOOD. WE'D STILL BE UP THERE CIRCLING!
THAT MIGHT HAVE BEEN PREFERABLE, SINCE WE GOT OUR BUTTS HANDED TO US... REPEATEDLY.
I DON'T KNOW WHAT CLINT'S COMPLAINING ABOUT. I'M THE ONE WHO HAD TO BE BRIEFLY REUNITED WITH MY POSSIBLY DEAD MOTHER ONLY TO HAVE HER YANKED AWAY FROM ME AGAIN.
THEN AGAIN, HE DID FALL OFF A ROOF ONTO THAT WALK OF FAME THING IN FRONT OF A TON OF TOURISTS. SO, NOT REALLY A GOLD-STAR DAY FOR EITHER OF, US I GUESS.
I'M JUST SAYING IT'S WEIRD TO BE DOING THIS WITH A DRIVER, KATIE. IT DOESN'T FEEL EXACTLY... PROFESSIONAL?
WHAT DO YOU SUGGEST, CLINT? MY VESPA NEEDS REPAIR, THERE'S NO PARKING IN THIS CITY, AND IT'S LOW AND SPREAD OUT OVER MILES-- WE CAN'T JUST SWING ACROSS IT LIKE SPIDER-MAN!
ALL RIGHT, ALL RIGHT. STOP YELLING!
I CAN'T HELP IT, THIS MADAME MASQUE MINION COSTUME TOTALLY CHAFES!
...YOU KNOW, IT REALLY DOES. MASQUE IS AN EVEN MORE DIABOLICAL VILLAIN THAN I THOUGHT.

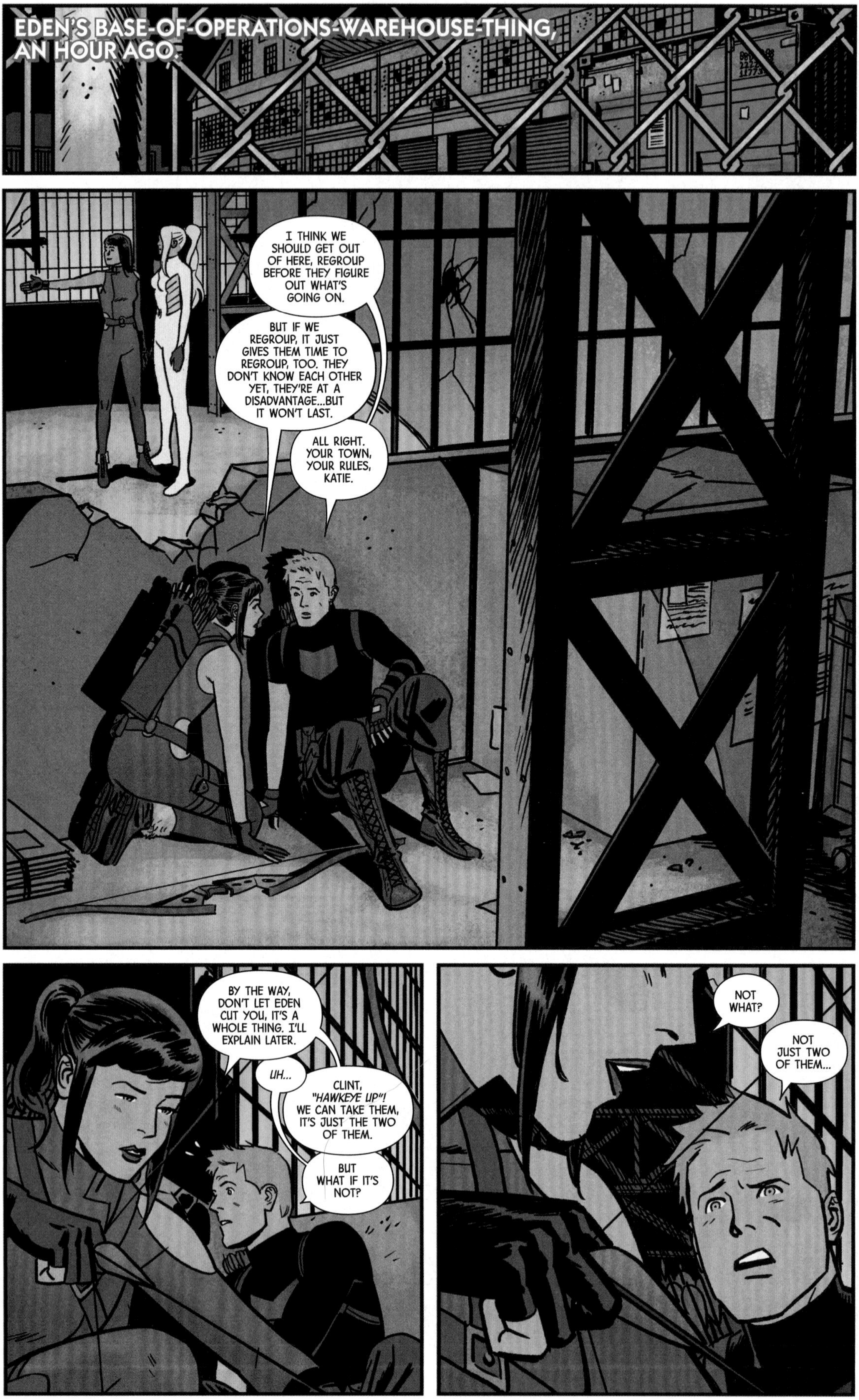
EDEN'S BASE-OF-OPERATIONS-WAREHOUSE-THING, AN HOUR AGO.
I THINK WE SHOULD GET OUT OF HERE, REGROUP BEFORE THEY FIGURE OUT WHAT'S GOING ON.
BUT IF WE REGROUP, IT JUST GIVES THEM TIME TO REGROUP, TOO. THEY DON'T KNOW EACH OTHER YET, THEY'RE AT A DISADVANTAGE...BUT IT WON'T LAST.
ALL RIGHT. YOUR TOWN, YOUR RULES, KATIE.
BY THE WAY, DON'T LET EDEN CUT YOU, IT'S A WHOLE THING. I'LL EXPLAIN LATER.
UH...
CLINT, "HAWKEYE UP"! WE CAN TAKE THEM, IT'S JUST THE TWO OF THEM.
BUT WHAT IF IT'S NOT?
NOT WHAT?
NOT JUST TWO OF THEM...

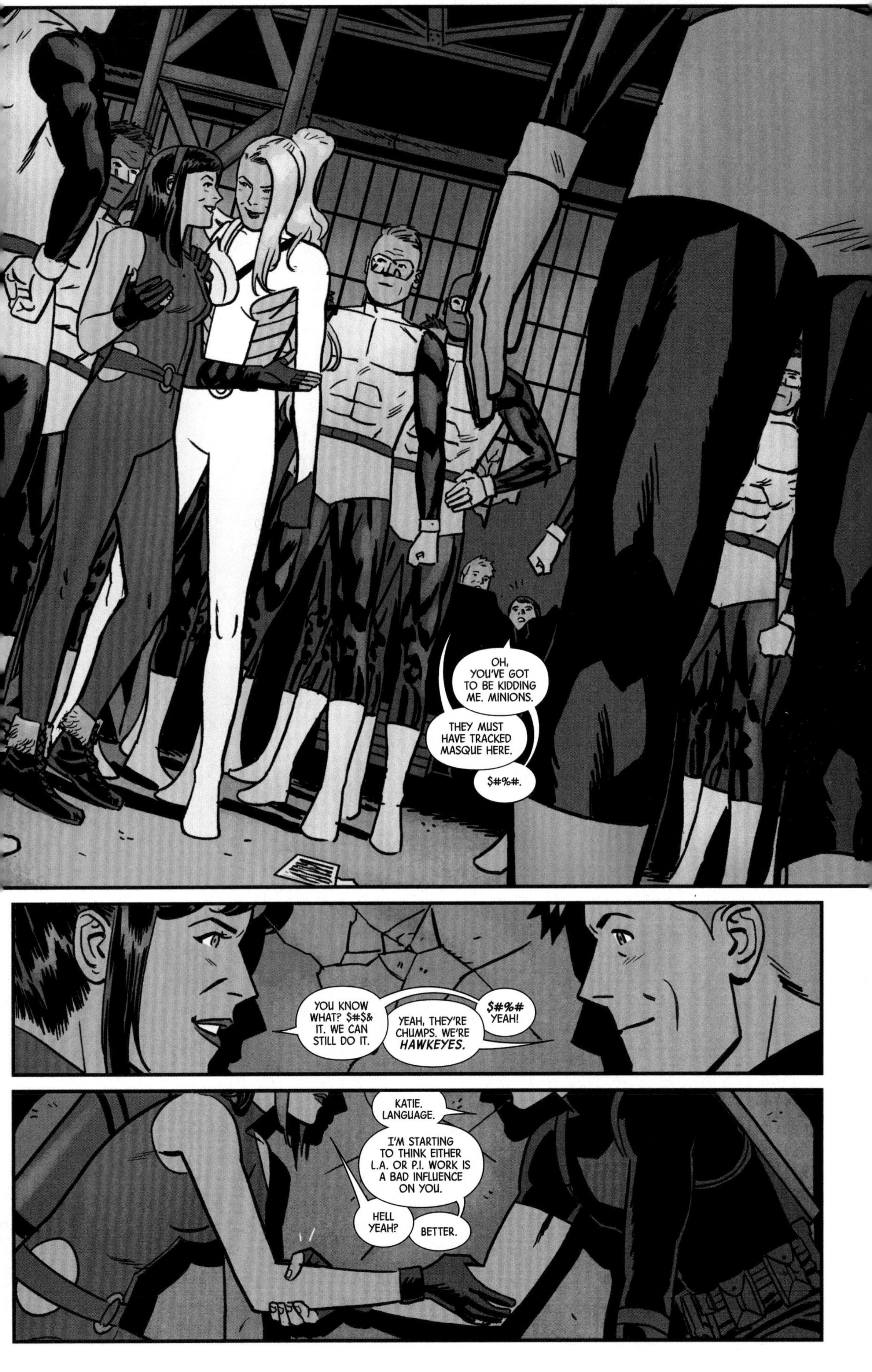
OH, YOU'VE GOT TO BE KIDDING ME. MINIONS.
THEY MUST HAVE TRACKED MASQUE HERE.
$#%#.
YOU KNOW WHAT? $#$& IT. WE CAN STILL DO IT.
YEAH, THEY'RE CHUMPS. WE'RE *HAWKEYES.*
$#%# YEAH!
KATIE. LANGUAGE.
I'M STARTING TO THINK EITHER L.A. OR P.I. WORK IS A BAD INFLUENCE ON YOU.
HELL YEAH?
BETTER.

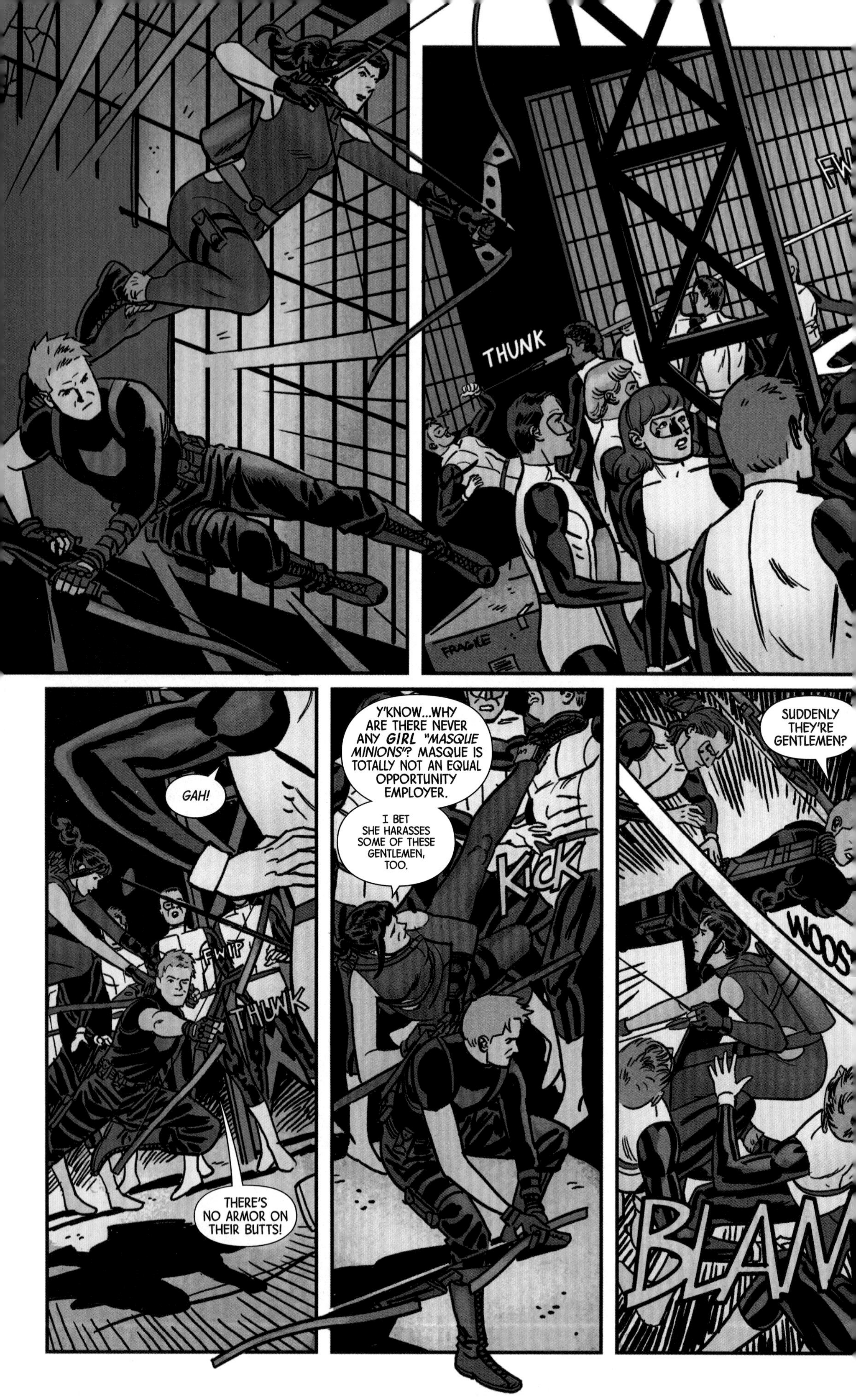

THUNK
FRAGILE
GAH!
FWIP
THUNK
THERE'S NO ARMOR ON THEIR BUTTS!
Y'KNOW...WHY ARE THERE NEVER ANY GIRL "MASQUE MINIONS"? MASQUE IS TOTALLY NOT AN EQUAL OPPORTUNITY EMPLOYER.
I BET SHE HARASSES SOME OF THESE GENTLEMEN, TOO.
KICK
SUDDENLY THEY'RE GENTLEMEN?

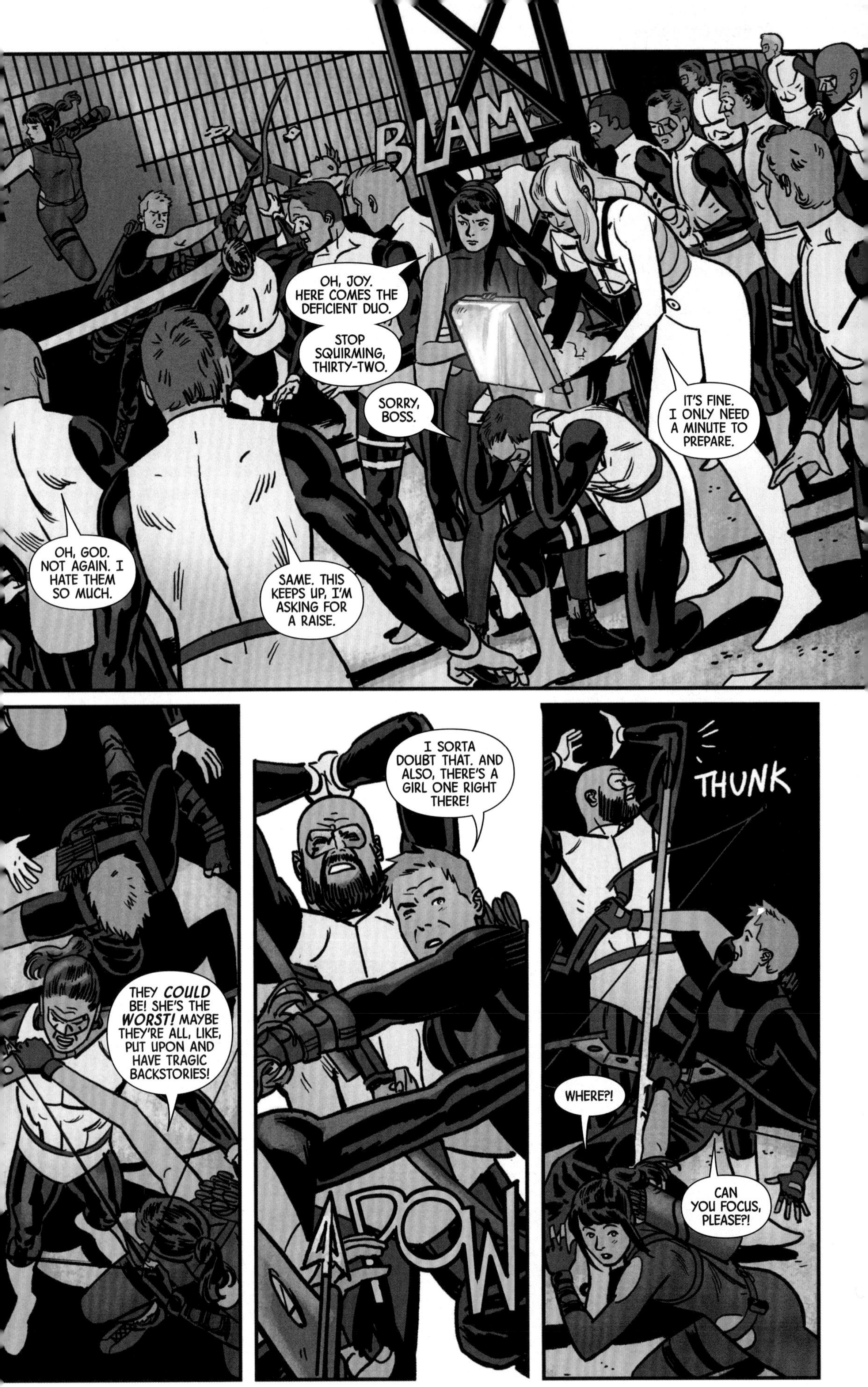
BLAM
OH, JOY. HERE COMES THE DEFICIENT DUO.
STOP SQUIRMING, THIRTY-TWO.
SORRY, BOSS.
IT'S FINE. I ONLY NEED A MINUTE TO PREPARE.
OH, GOD. NOT AGAIN. I HATE THEM SO MUCH.
SAME. THIS KEEPS UP, I'M ASKING FOR A RAISE.
THEY COULD BE! SHE'S THE WORST! MAYBE THEY'RE ALL, LIKE, PUT UPON AND HAVE TRAGIC BACKSTORIES!
I SORTA DOUBT THAT. AND ALSO, THERE'S A GIRL ONE RIGHT THERE!
POW
THUNK
WHERE?!
CAN YOU FOCUS, PLEASE?!

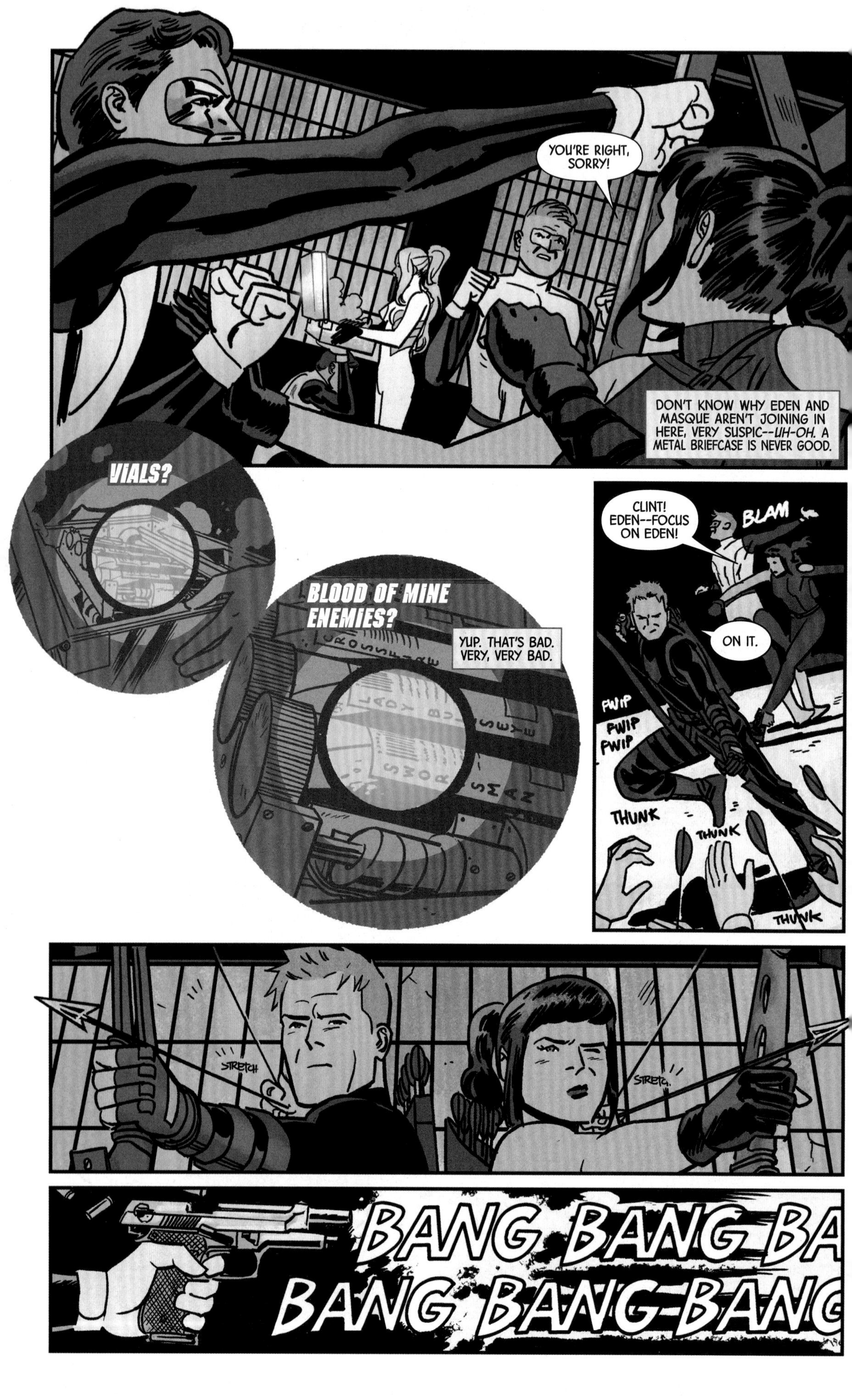

YOU'RE RIGHT, SORRY!
DON'T KNOW WHY EDEN AND MASQUE AREN'T JOINING IN HERE, VERY SUSPIC--UH-OH. A METAL BRIEFCASE IS NEVER GOOD.
VIALS?
BLOOD OF MINE ENEMIES?
YUP. THAT'S BAD. VERY, VERY BAD.
CLINT! EDEN--FOCUS ON EDEN!
BLAM
ON IT.
PWIP
PWIP
PWIP
THUNK
THUNK
THUNK
STRETCH
STRETCH
BANG BANG BA
BANG BANG BANG

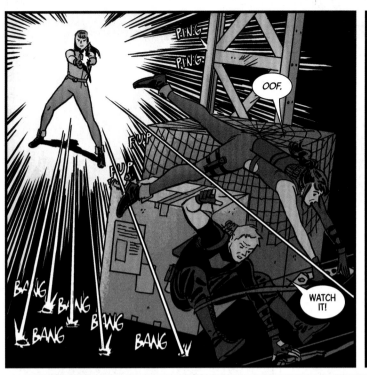

PING
PING

OOF.

FUP
FUP

BANG
BANG
BANG
BANG
BANG

WATCH IT!

SCORE--
GIRL MINION!

ANNNNND...I THINK I JUST GOT AN IDEA?

WAIT. WHAT IS SHE DOING? THIS LOOKS NOT GOOD, KATIE.

IT IS, AS YOU SAY, VERY NOT GOOD.

HNG.

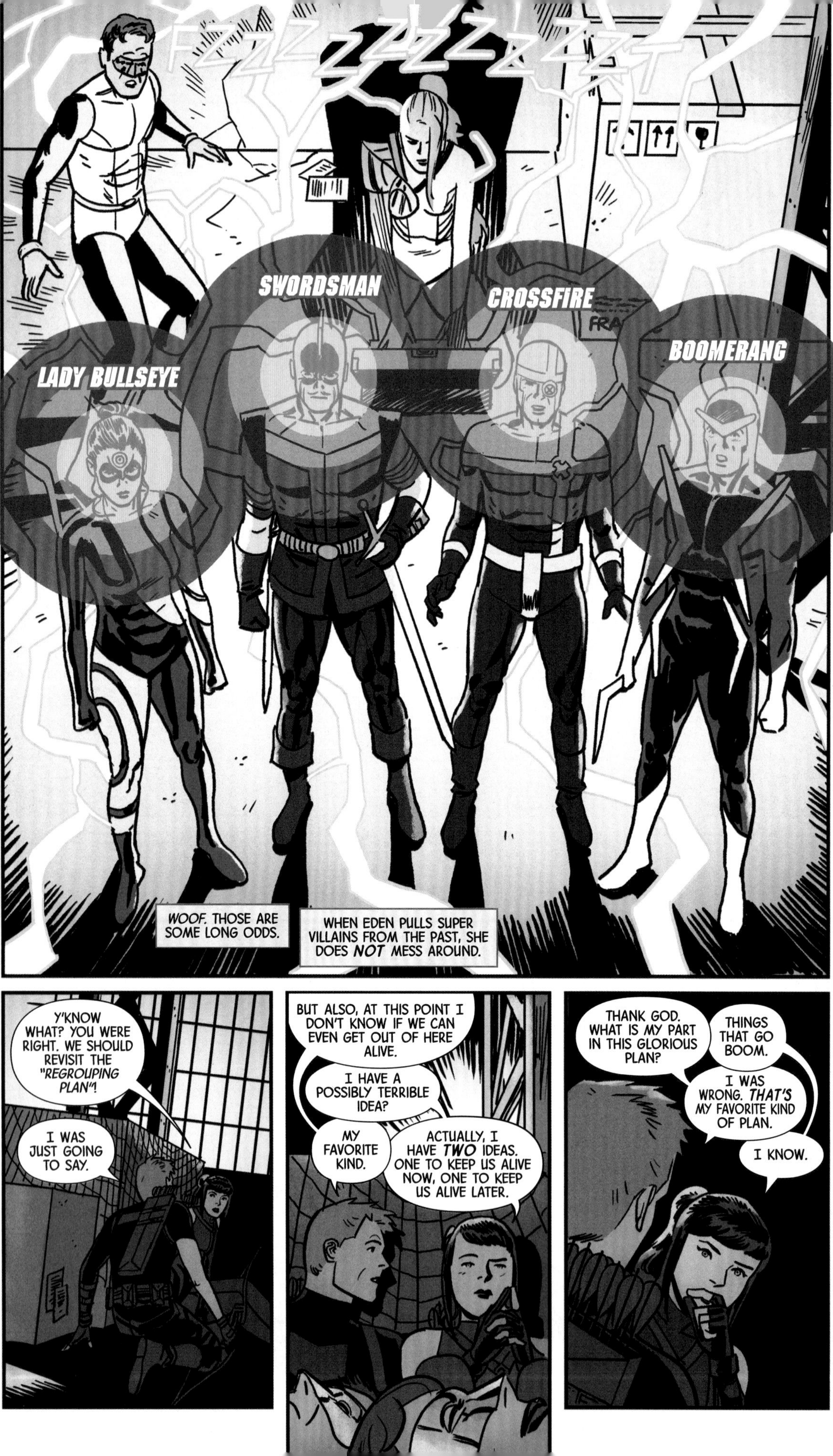
SWORDSMAN
CROSSFIRE
BOOMERANG
LADY BULLSEYE
WOOF. THOSE ARE SOME LONG ODDS.
WHEN EDEN PULLS SUPER VILLAINS FROM THE PAST, SHE DOES ***NOT*** MESS AROUND.
Y'KNOW WHAT? YOU WERE RIGHT. WE SHOULD REVISIT THE *"REGROUPING PLAN"*!
I WAS JUST GOING TO SAY.
BUT ALSO, AT THIS POINT I DON'T KNOW IF WE CAN EVEN GET OUT OF HERE ALIVE.
I HAVE A POSSIBLY TERRIBLE IDEA?
MY FAVORITE KIND.
ACTUALLY, I HAVE ***TWO*** IDEAS. ONE TO KEEP US ALIVE NOW, ONE TO KEEP US ALIVE LATER.
THANK GOD. WHAT IS MY PART IN THIS GLORIOUS PLAN?
THINGS THAT GO BOOM.
I WAS WRONG. ***THAT'S*** MY FAVORITE KIND OF PLAN.
I KNOW.

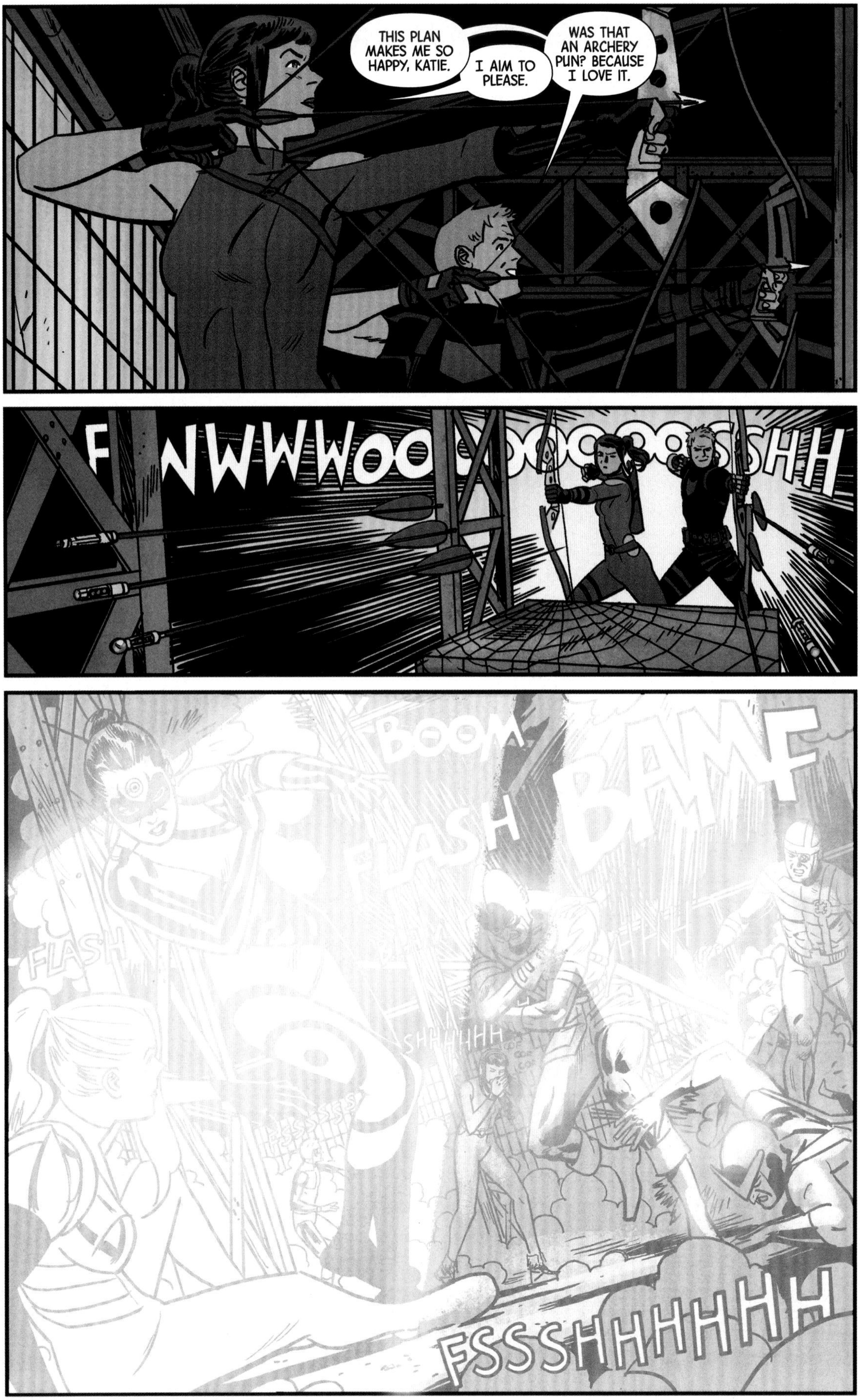

THIS PLAN MAKES ME SO HAPPY, KATIE.
I AIM TO PLEASE.
WAS THAT AN ARCHERY PUN? BECAUSE I LOVE IT.
FNWWWOOOOOOOOSSHH
BOOM
FLASH
BAMF
FLASH
SHHHHHH
FSSSSSS
FSSSHHHHHHH

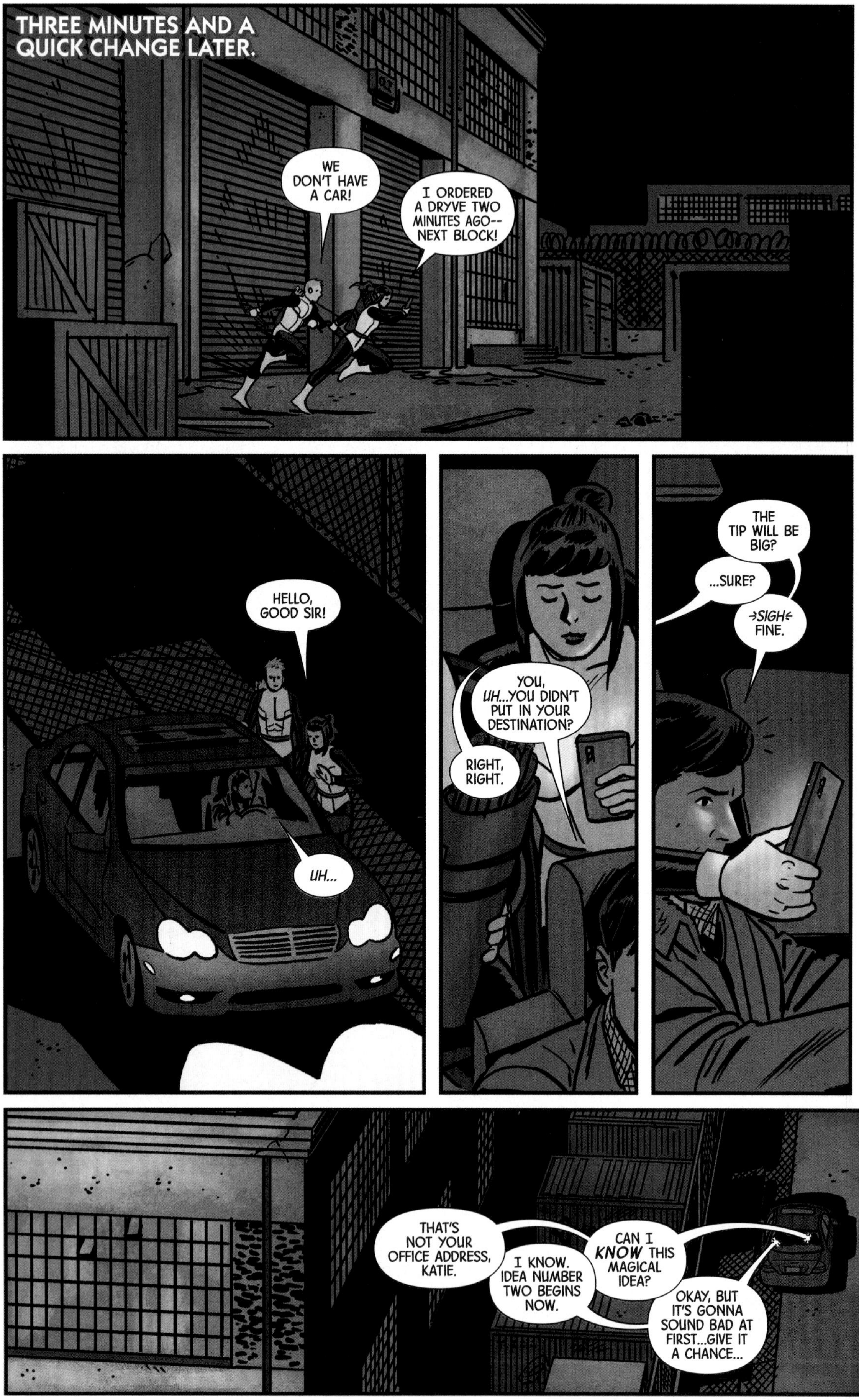
THREE MINUTES AND A QUICK CHANGE LATER.
WE DON'T HAVE A CAR!
I ORDERED A DRYVE TWO MINUTES AGO-- NEXT BLOCK!
HELLO, GOOD SIR!
UH...
YOU, UH...YOU DIDN'T PUT IN YOUR DESTINATION?
RIGHT, RIGHT.
THE TIP WILL BE BIG?
...SURE?
SIGH FINE.
THAT'S NOT YOUR OFFICE ADDRESS, KATIE.
I KNOW. IDEA NUMBER TWO BEGINS NOW.
CAN I KNOW THIS MAGICAL IDEA?
OKAY, BUT IT'S GONNA SOUND BAD AT FIRST...GIVE IT A CHANCE...

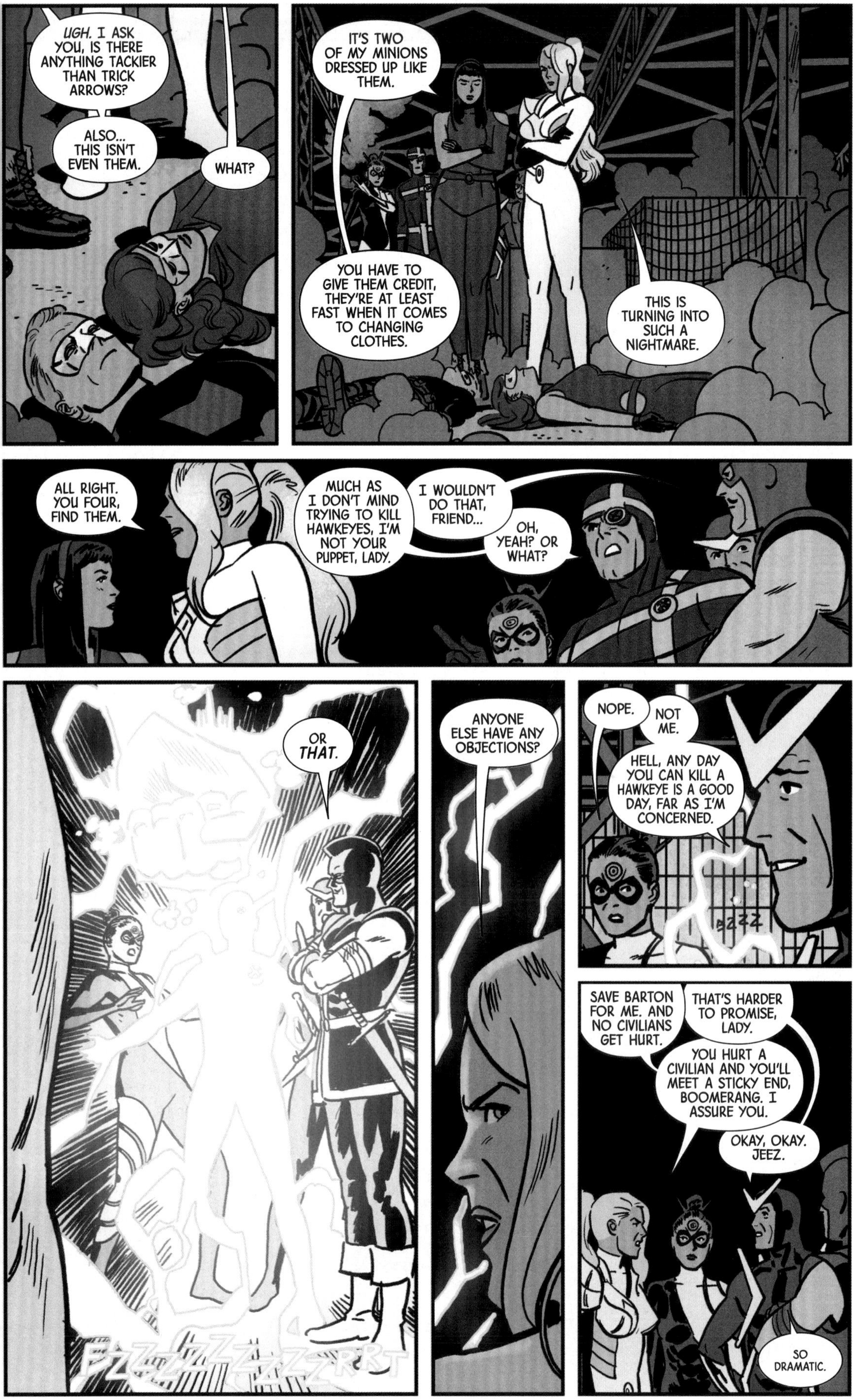
UGH. I ASK YOU, IS THERE ANYTHING TACKIER THAN TRICK ARROWS?
ALSO... THIS ISN'T EVEN THEM.
WHAT?
IT'S TWO OF MY MINIONS DRESSED UP LIKE THEM.
YOU HAVE TO GIVE THEM CREDIT, THEY'RE AT LEAST FAST WHEN IT COMES TO CHANGING CLOTHES.
THIS IS TURNING INTO SUCH A NIGHTMARE.
ALL RIGHT. YOU FOUR, FIND THEM.
MUCH AS I DON'T MIND TRYING TO KILL HAWKEYES, I'M NOT YOUR PUPPET, LADY.
I WOULDN'T DO THAT, FRIEND...
OH, YEAH? OR WHAT?
OR THAT.
FZZZZZZZZZRRT
ANYONE ELSE HAVE ANY OBJECTIONS?
NOPE.
NOT ME.
HELL, ANY DAY YOU CAN KILL A HAWKEYE IS A GOOD DAY, FAR AS I'M CONCERNED.
BZZZ
SAVE BARTON FOR ME. AND NO CIVILIANS GET HURT.
THAT'S HARDER TO PROMISE, LADY.
YOU HURT A CIVILIAN AND YOU'LL MEET A STICKY END, BOOMERANG. I ASSURE YOU.
OKAY, OKAY. JEEZ.
SO DRAMATIC.

MADAME MASQUE'S HIDEOUT-MANSION-THING, ALMOST NOW.

OH. OH, NO.

NO!

I CANNOT BE KICKED IN THE FACE AGAIN TODAY BY A HAWKEYE!

HI, GUYS.

HOW ARE THERE STILL SO MANY OF THEM HERE?! I THOUGHT THEY WERE ALL AT THE WAREHOUSE! ARE THEY SECRETLY RABBITS?!

POF

BLAM

WELL, MASQUE DOES DEAL IN CLONES AND LMDS... MY GUESS IS DUMB WARM BODIES AREN'T A BIG PROBLEM FOR HER!

BLAM

PUNCH

WATCH YOUR BACK.

FWIP FWIP FWIP

THUMP BZZZ

WHAT'S THAT?

BZZZZ

I SAID BEHIND YOU!

BLAM

THOMP

TOC

POW

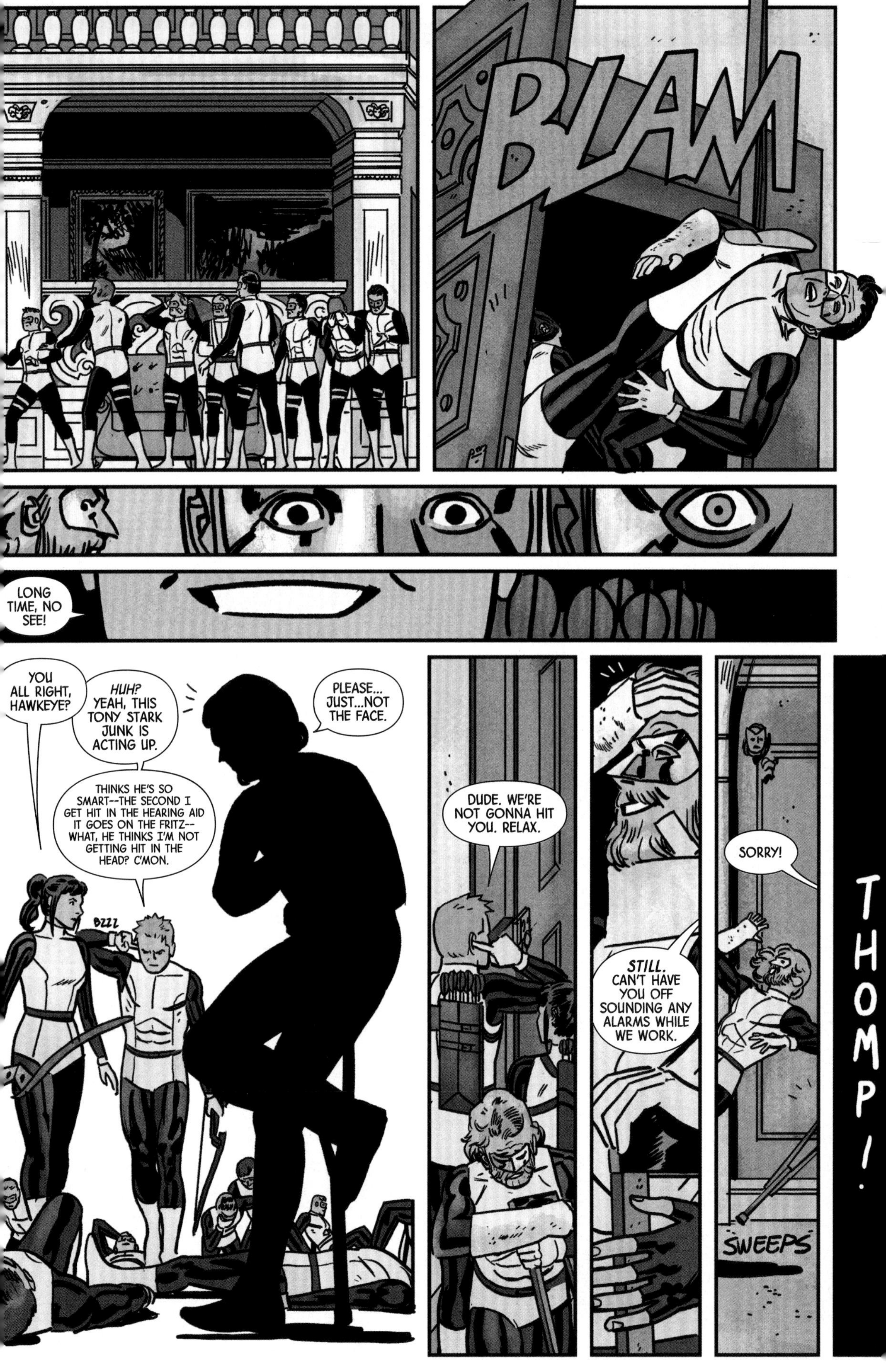
BLAM
LONG TIME, NO SEE!
YOU ALL RIGHT, HAWKEYE?
HUH? YEAH, THIS TONY STARK JUNK IS ACTING UP.
THINKS HE'S SO SMART--THE SECOND I GET HIT IN THE HEARING AID IT GOES ON THE FRITZ-- WHAT, HE THINKS I'M NOT GETTING HIT IN THE HEAD? C'MON.
BZZZ
PLEASE... JUST...NOT THE FACE.
DUDE. WE'RE NOT GONNA HIT YOU. RELAX.
STILL. CAN'T HAVE YOU OFF SOUNDING ANY ALARMS WHILE WE WORK.
SORRY!
SWEEPS
THOMP!

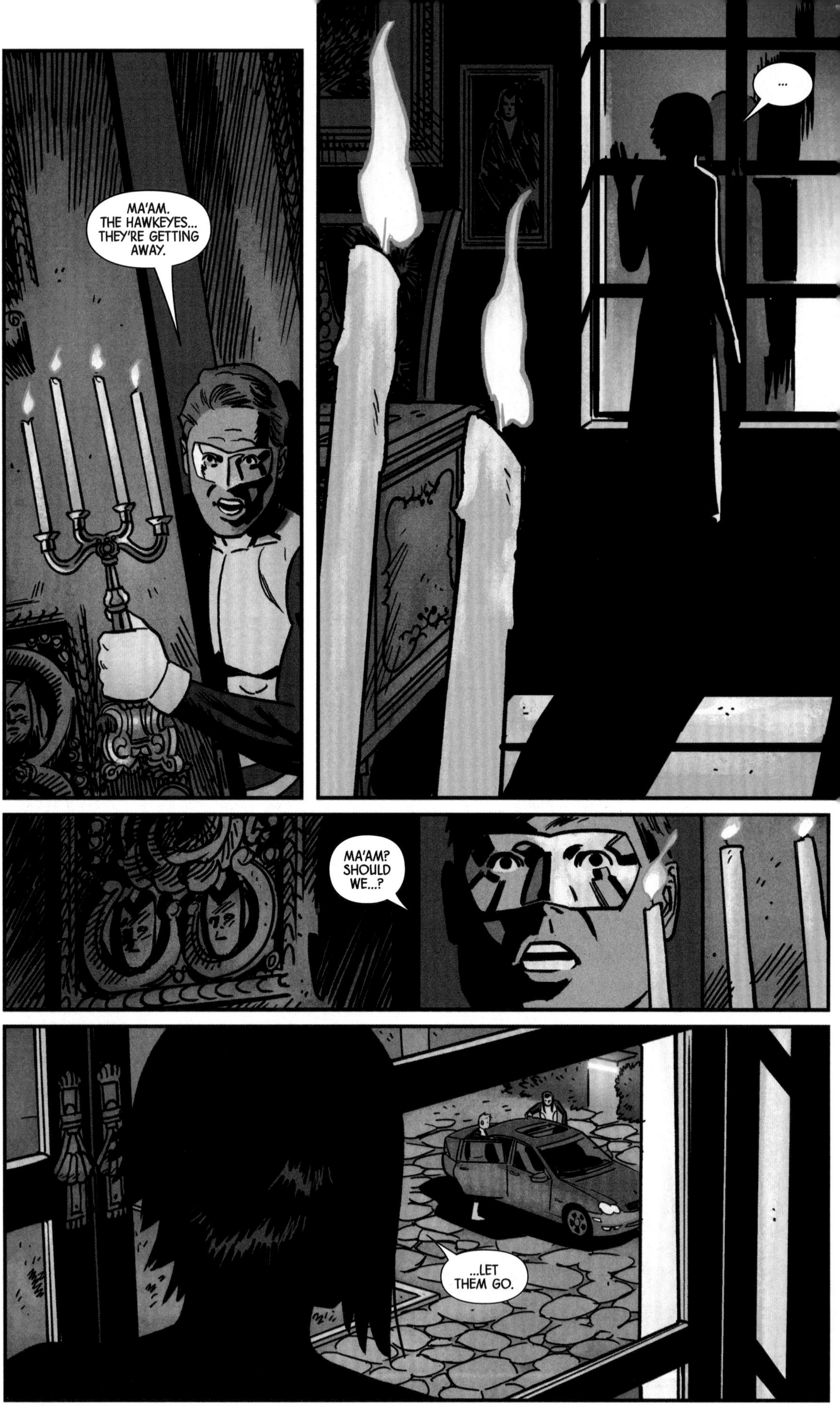
MA'AM. THE HAWKEYES... THEY'RE GETTING AWAY.
...
MA'AM? SHOULD WE...?
...LET THEM GO.

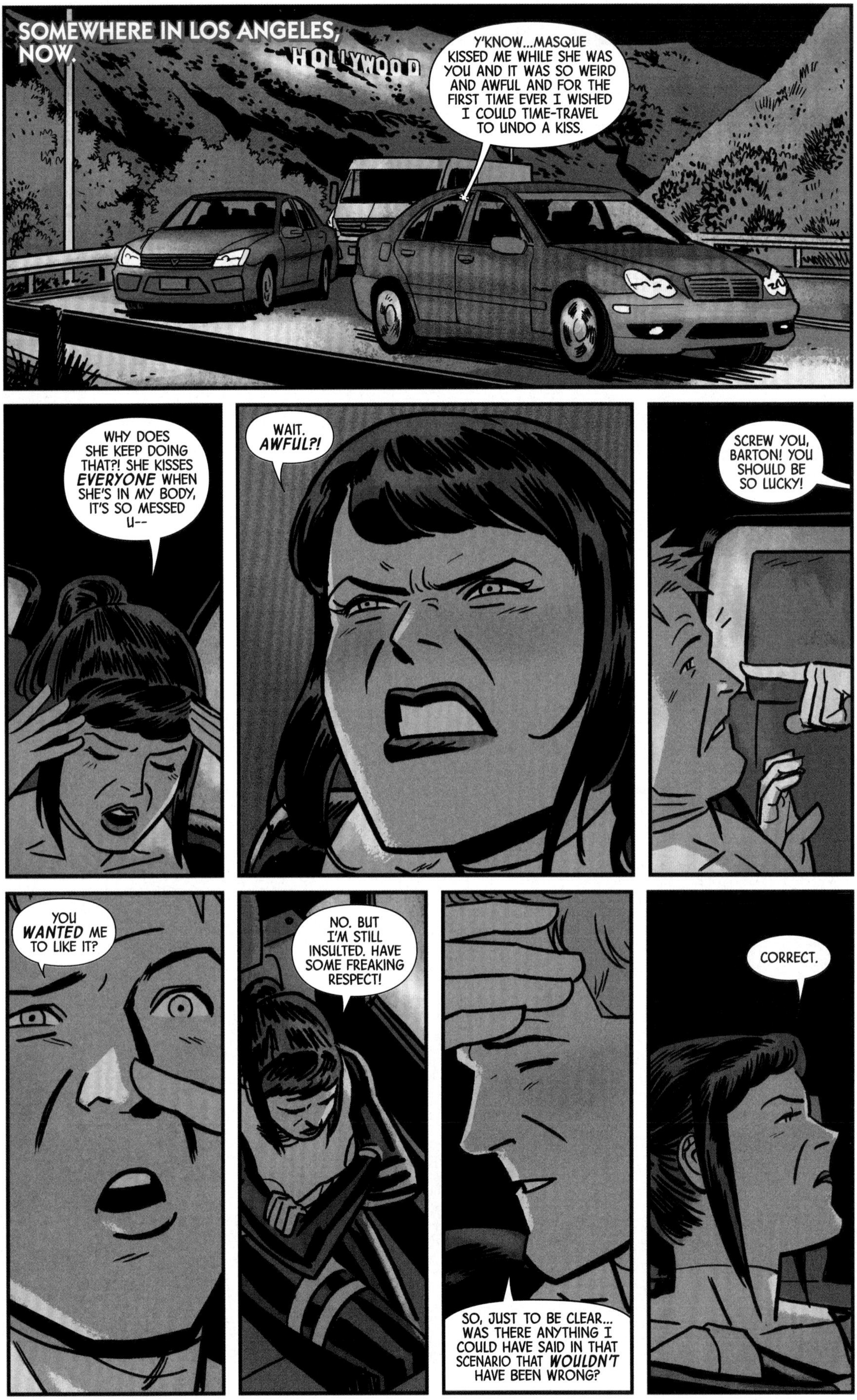
SOMEWHERE IN LOS ANGELES, NOW.
HOLLYWOOD
Y'KNOW...MASQUE KISSED ME WHILE SHE WAS YOU AND IT WAS SO WEIRD AND AWFUL AND FOR THE FIRST TIME EVER I WISHED I COULD TIME-TRAVEL TO UNDO A KISS.
WHY DOES SHE KEEP DOING THAT?! SHE KISSES EVERYONE WHEN SHE'S IN MY BODY, IT'S SO MESSED U--
WAIT. AWFUL?!
SCREW YOU, BARTON! YOU SHOULD BE SO LUCKY!
YOU WANTED ME TO LIKE IT?
NO. BUT I'M STILL INSULTED. HAVE SOME FREAKING RESPECT!
SO, JUST TO BE CLEAR... WAS THERE ANYTHING I COULD HAVE SAID IN THAT SCENARIO THAT WOULDN'T HAVE BEEN WRONG?
CORRECT.

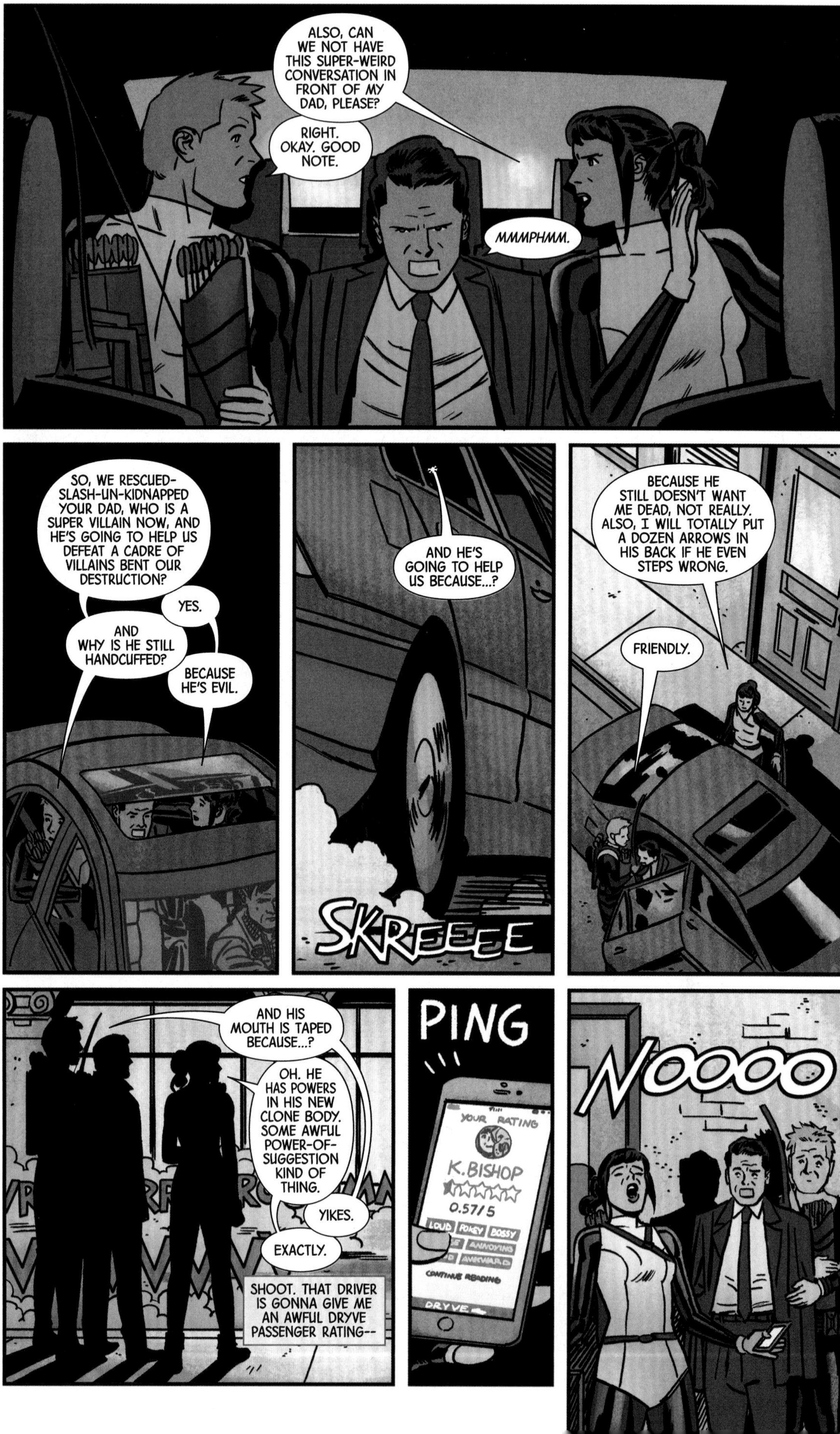
ALSO, CAN WE NOT HAVE THIS SUPER-WEIRD CONVERSATION IN FRONT OF MY DAD, PLEASE?
RIGHT. OKAY. GOOD NOTE.
MMMPHMM.
SO, WE RESCUED-SLASH-UN-KIDNAPPED YOUR DAD, WHO IS A SUPER VILLAIN NOW, AND HE'S GOING TO HELP US DEFEAT A CADRE OF VILLAINS BENT OUR DESTRUCTION?
YES.
AND WHY IS HE STILL HANDCUFFED?
BECAUSE HE'S EVIL.
AND HE'S GOING TO HELP US BECAUSE...?
SKREEEEE
BECAUSE HE STILL DOESN'T WANT ME DEAD, NOT REALLY. ALSO, I WILL TOTALLY PUT A DOZEN ARROWS IN HIS BACK IF HE EVEN STEPS WRONG.
FRIENDLY.
AND HIS MOUTH IS TAPED BECAUSE...?
OH. HE HAS POWERS IN HIS NEW CLONE BODY. SOME AWFUL POWER-OF-SUGGESTION KIND OF THING.
YIKES.
EXACTLY.
SHOOT. THAT DRIVER IS GONNA GIVE ME AN AWFUL DRYVE PASSENGER RATING--
PING
YOUR RATING
K.BISHOP
0.57/5
LOUD
POKEY
BOSSY
ANNOYING
AWKWARD
CONTINUE READING
DRYVE
NOOOO

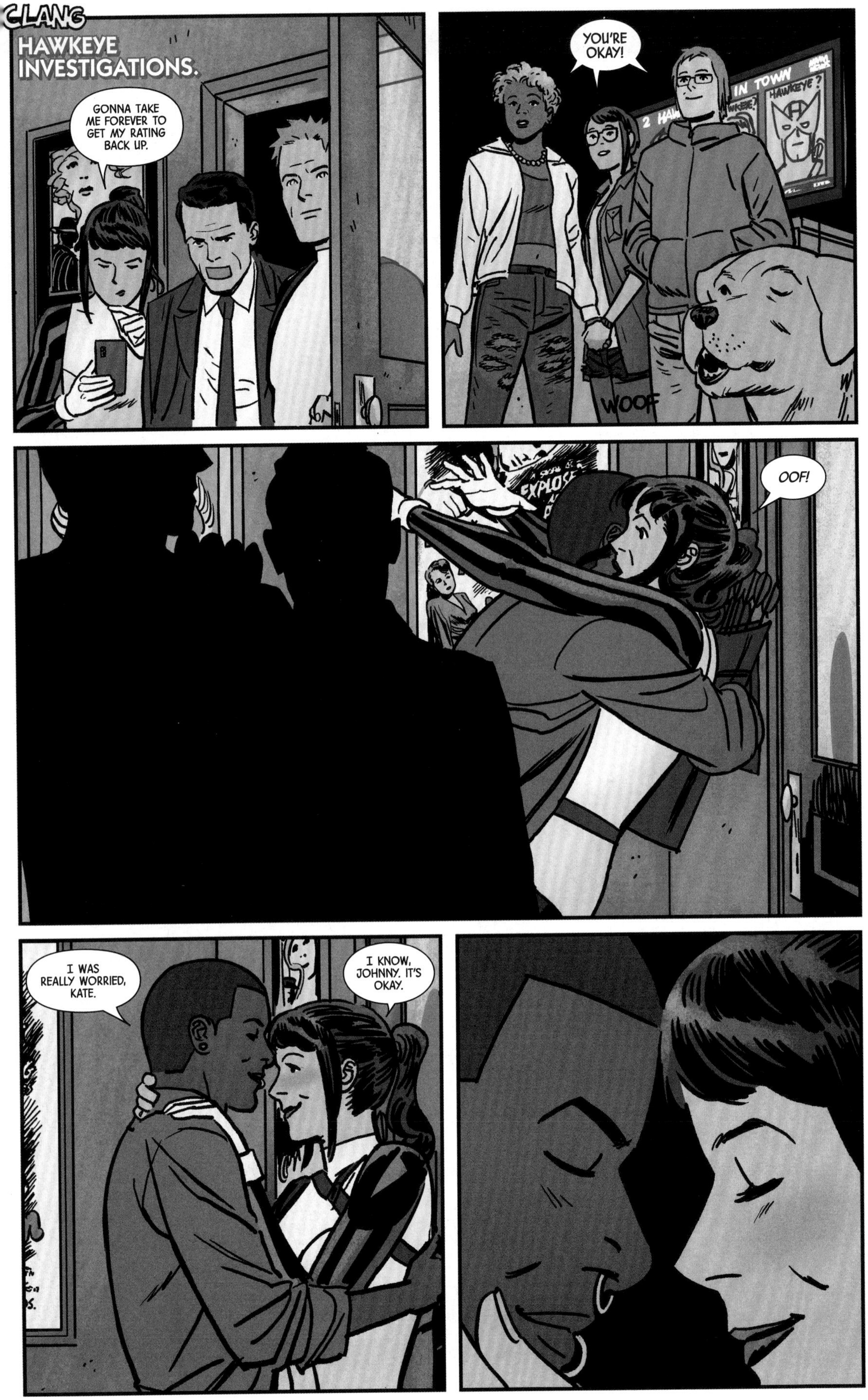
CLANG
HAWKEYE INVESTIGATIONS.
GONNA TAKE ME FOREVER TO GET MY RATING BACK UP.
YOU'RE OKAY!
IN TOWN
HAWKEYE?
WOOF
OOF!
I WAS REALLY WORRIED, KATE.
I KNOW, JOHNNY. IT'S OKAY.

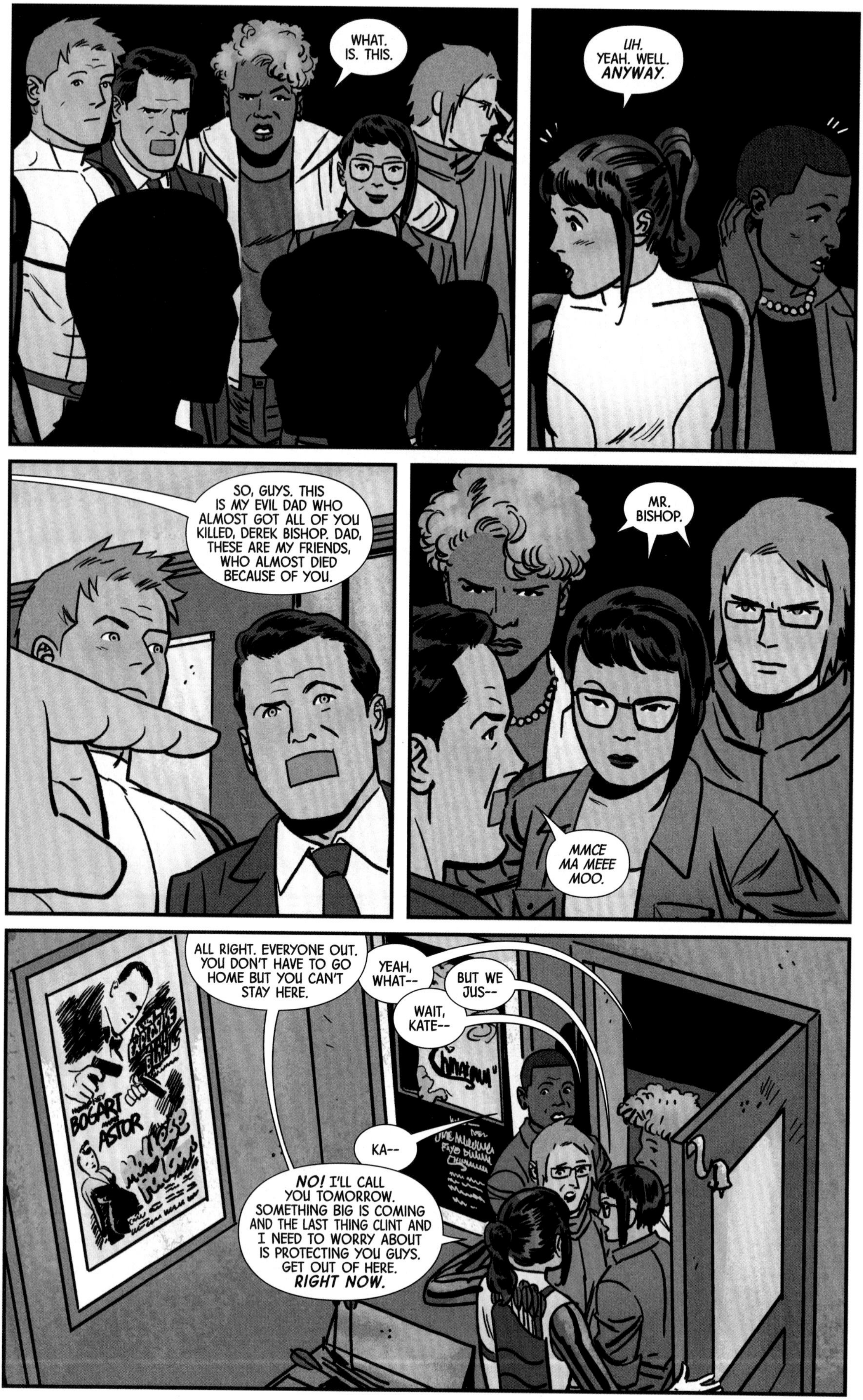

WHAT. IS. THIS.
UH. YEAH. WELL. *ANYWAY.*
SO, GUYS. THIS IS MY EVIL DAD WHO ALMOST GOT ALL OF YOU KILLED, DEREK BISHOP. DAD, THESE ARE MY FRIENDS, WHO ALMOST DIED BECAUSE OF YOU.
MR. BISHOP.
MMCE MA MEEE MOO.
ALL RIGHT. EVERYONE OUT. YOU DON'T HAVE TO GO HOME BUT YOU CAN'T STAY HERE.
YEAH, WHAT--
BUT WE JUS--
WAIT, KATE--
KA--
NO! I'LL CALL YOU TOMORROW. SOMETHING BIG IS COMING AND THE LAST THING CLINT AND I NEED TO WORRY ABOUT IS PROTECTING YOU GUYS. GET OUT OF HERE. *RIGHT NOW.*
BOGART
ASTOR

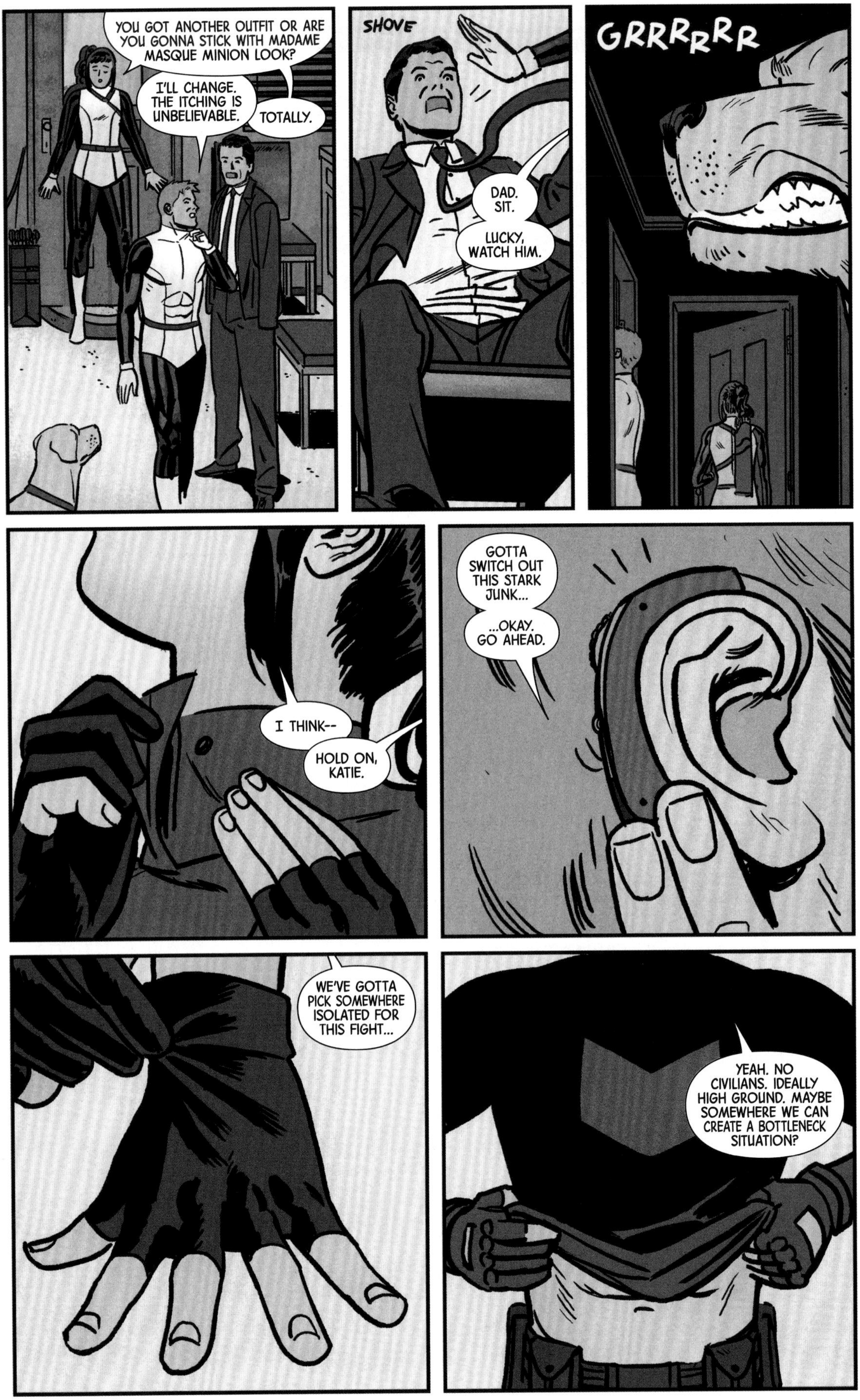

YOU GOT ANOTHER OUTFIT OR ARE YOU GONNA STICK WITH MADAME MASQUE MINION LOOK?
I'LL CHANGE. THE ITCHING IS UNBELIEVABLE.
TOTALLY.
SHOVE
DAD. SIT.
LUCKY, WATCH HIM.
GRRRRRR
I THINK--
HOLD ON, KATIE.
GOTTA SWITCH OUT THIS STARK JUNK...
...OKAY. GO AHEAD.
WE'VE GOTTA PICK SOMEWHERE ISOLATED FOR THIS FIGHT...
YEAH. NO CIVILIANS. IDEALLY HIGH GROUND. MAYBE SOMEWHERE WE CAN CREATE A BOTTLENECK SITUATION?

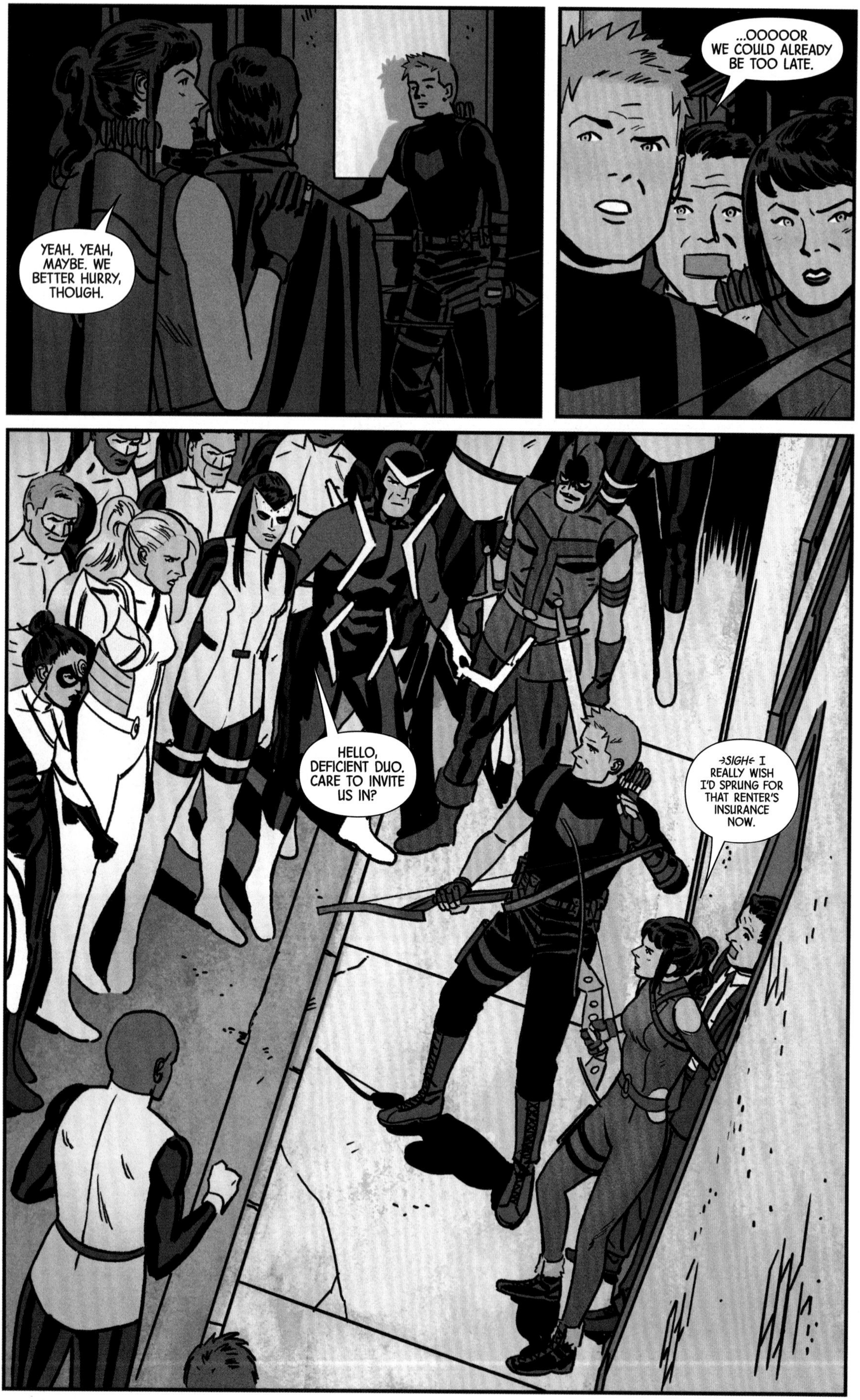
YEAH. YEAH, MAYBE. WE BETTER HURRY, THOUGH.
...OOOOOR WE COULD ALREADY BE TOO LATE.
HELLO, DEFICIENT DUO. CARE TO INVITE US IN?
→SIGH← I REALLY WISH I'D SPRUNG FOR THAT RENTER'S INSURANCE NOW.

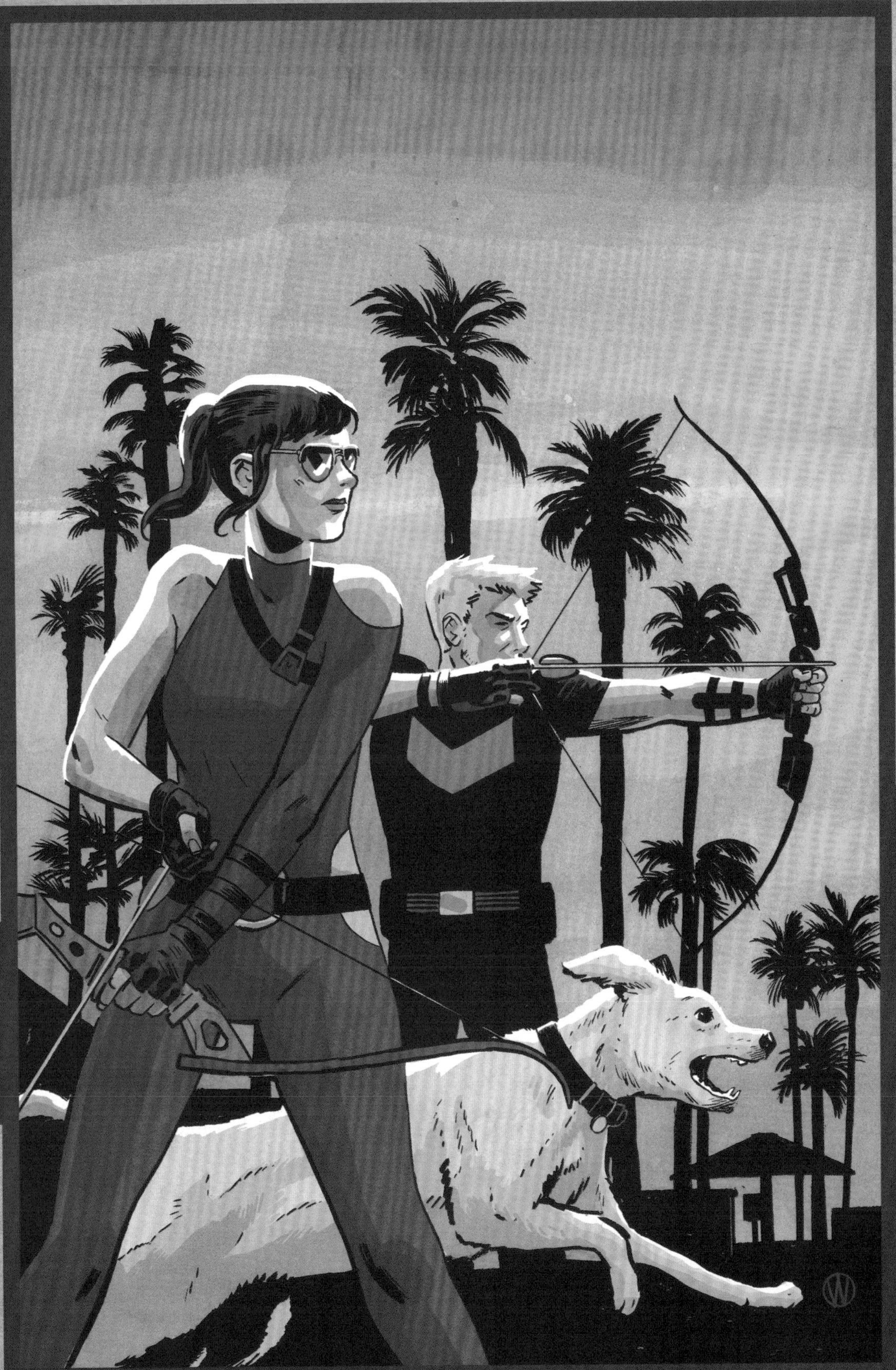

#13 variant by **Michael Walsh**

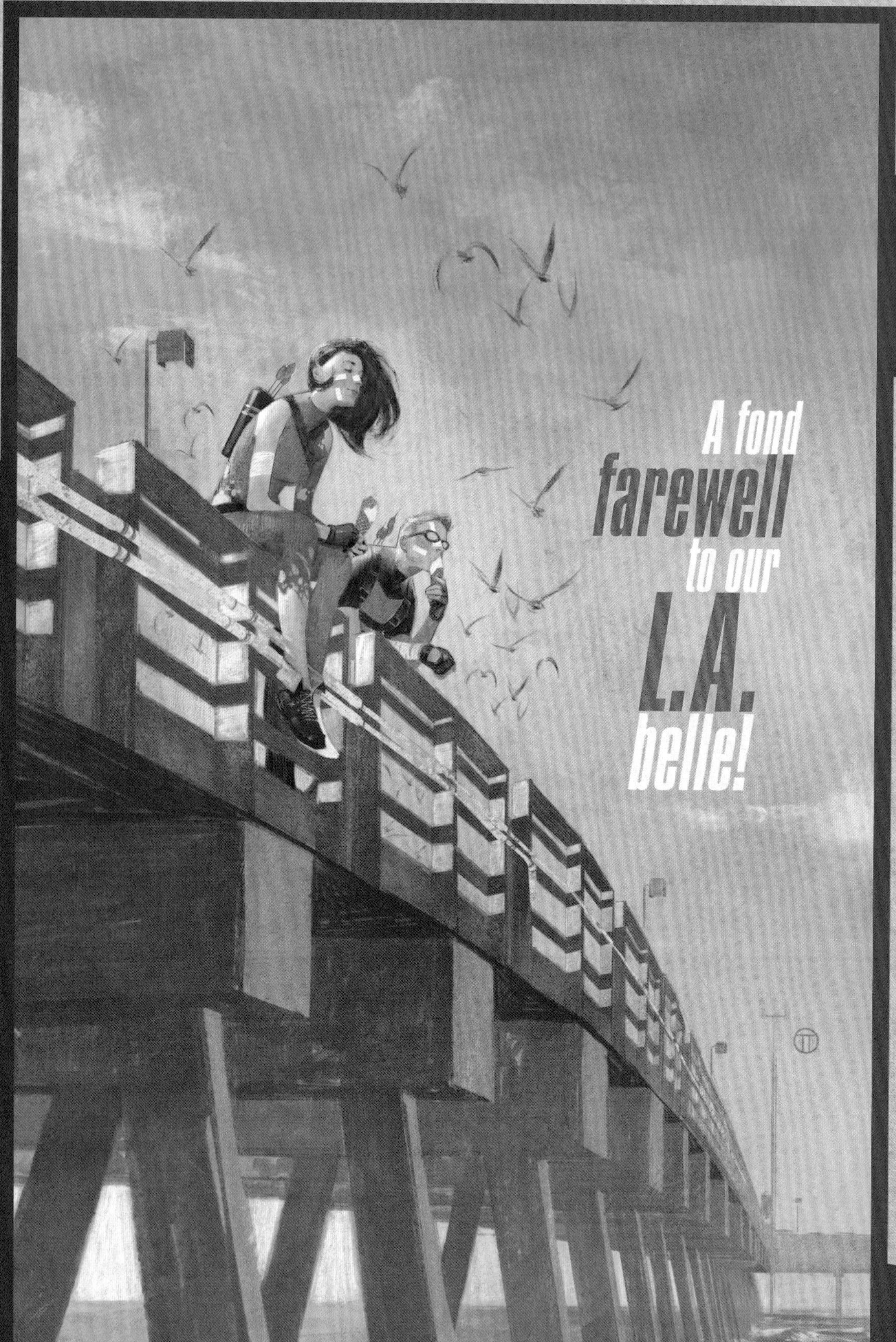

A fond
farewell
to our
L.A.
belle!

16

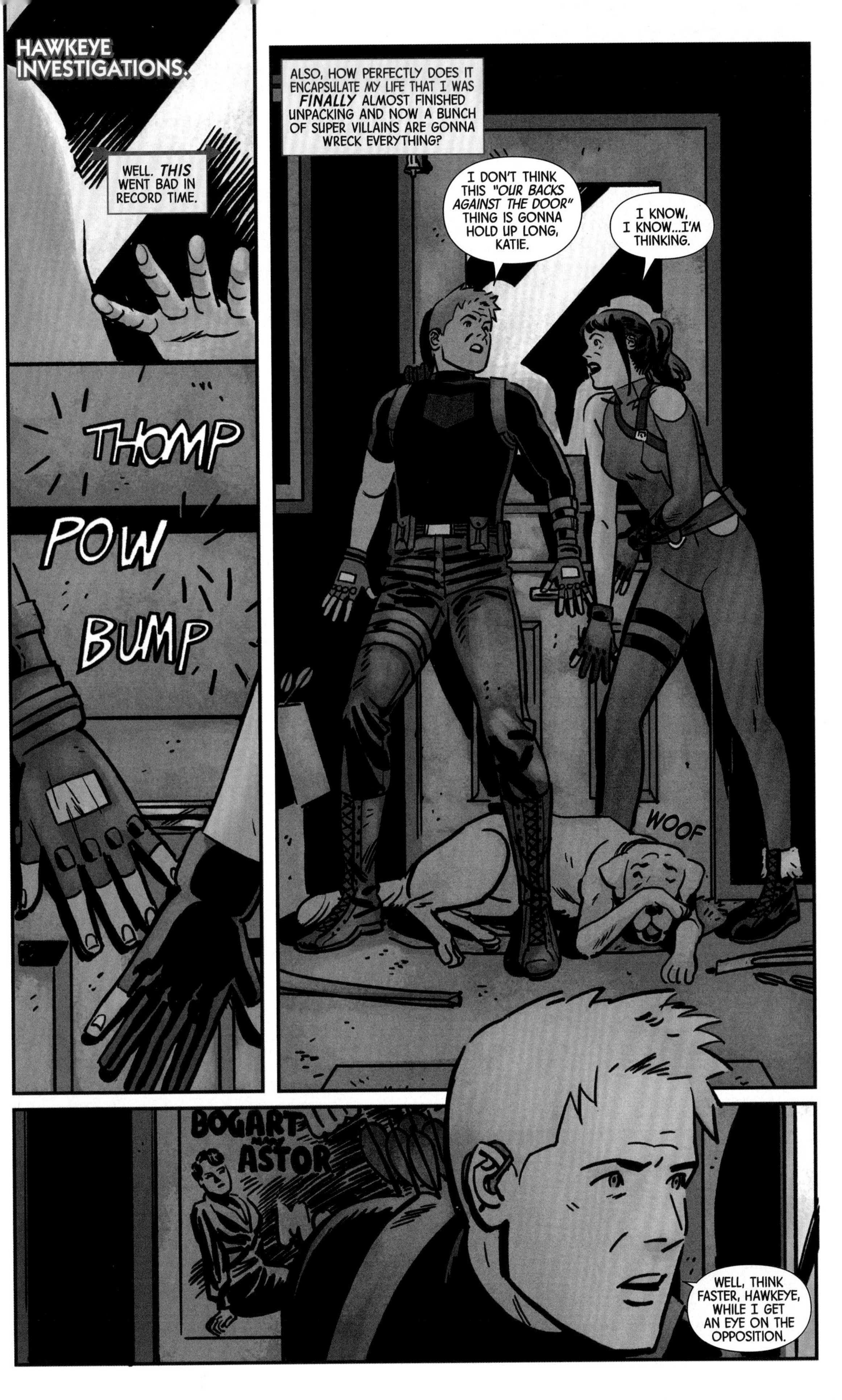
HAWKEYE INVESTIGATIONS.
WELL. THIS WENT BAD IN RECORD TIME.
THOMP
POW
BUMP
ALSO, HOW PERFECTLY DOES IT ENCAPSULATE MY LIFE THAT I WAS FINALLY ALMOST FINISHED UNPACKING AND NOW A BUNCH OF SUPER VILLAINS ARE GONNA WRECK EVERYTHING?
I DON'T THINK THIS "OUR BACKS AGAINST THE DOOR" THING IS GONNA HOLD UP LONG, KATIE.
I KNOW, I KNOW...I'M THINKING.
WOOF
BOGART
ASTOR
WELL, THINK FASTER, HAWKEYE, WHILE I GET AN EYE ON THE OPPOSITION.

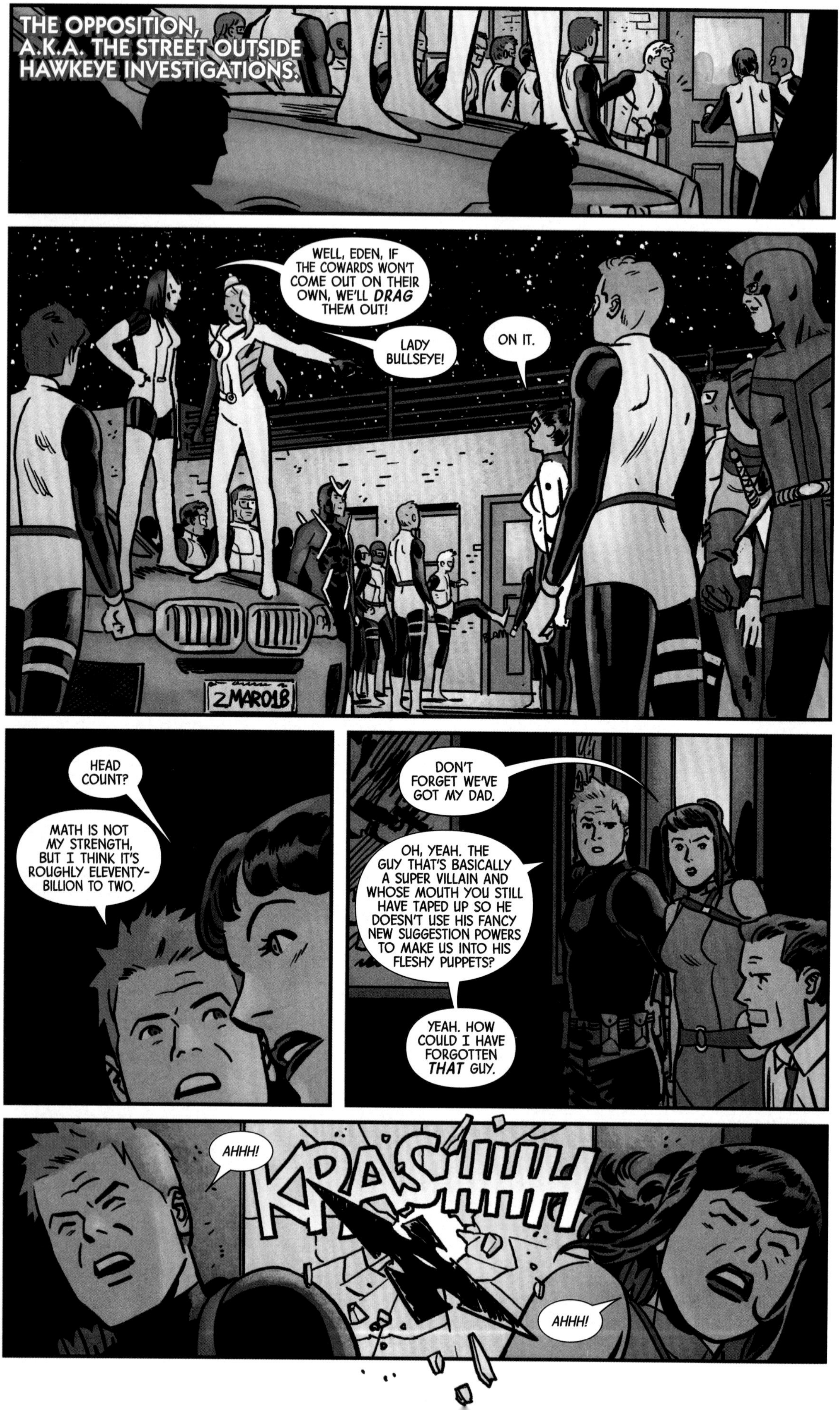
THE OPPOSITION, A.K.A. THE STREET OUTSIDE HAWKEYE INVESTIGATIONS.
WELL, EDEN, IF THE COWARDS WON'T COME OUT ON THEIR OWN, WE'LL DRAG THEM OUT!
LADY BULLSEYE!
ON IT.
BLAM
ZMAR018
HEAD COUNT?
MATH IS NOT MY STRENGTH, BUT I THINK IT'S ROUGHLY ELEVENTY-BILLION TO TWO.
DON'T FORGET WE'VE GOT MY DAD.
OH, YEAH. THE GUY THAT'S BASICALLY A SUPER VILLAIN AND WHOSE MOUTH YOU STILL HAVE TAPED UP SO HE DOESN'T USE HIS FANCY NEW SUGGESTION POWERS TO MAKE US INTO HIS FLESHY PUPPETS?
YEAH. HOW COULD I HAVE FORGOTTEN THAT GUY.
AHHH!
KRASHHH
AHHH!

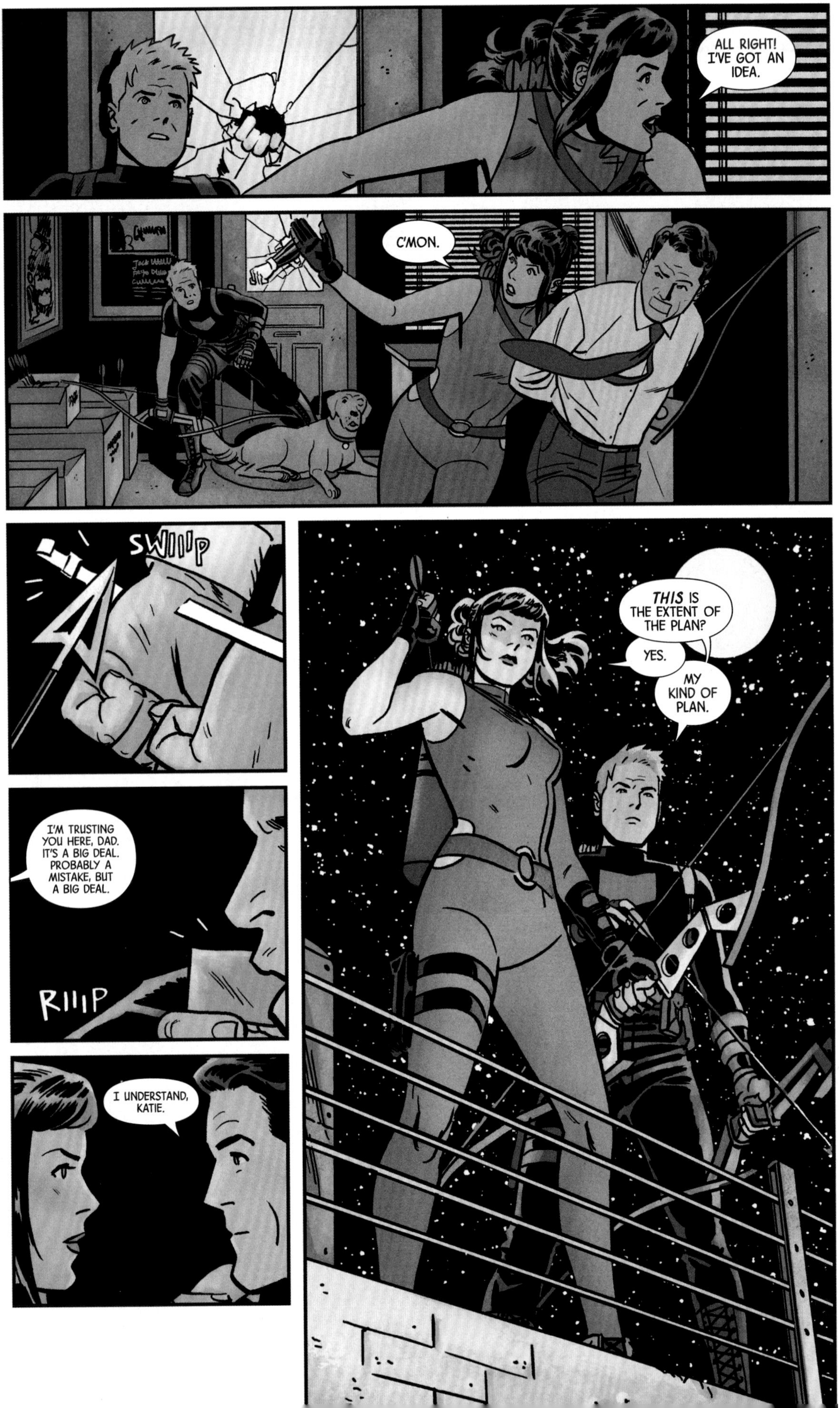
ALL RIGHT! I'VE GOT AN IDEA.
C'MON.
SWIIIP
I'M TRUSTING YOU HERE, DAD. IT'S A BIG DEAL. PROBABLY A MISTAKE, BUT A BIG DEAL.
RIIIP
I UNDERSTAND, KATIE.
THIS IS THE EXTENT OF THE PLAN?
YES.
MY KIND OF PLAN.

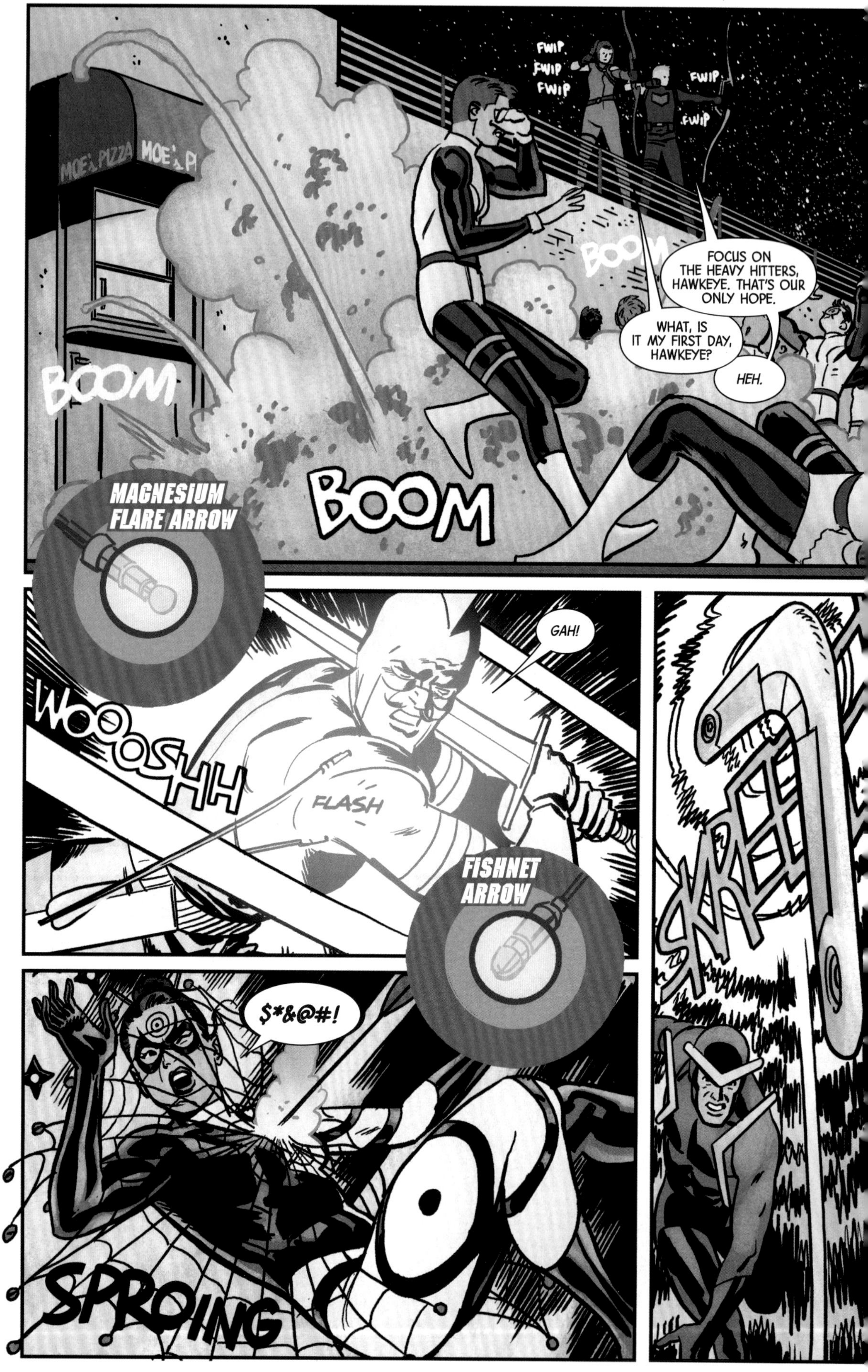

FWIP
FWIP
FWIP
FWIP
FWIP
MOE'S PIZZA MOE'S PI
BOOM
FOCUS ON THE HEAVY HITTERS, HAWKEYE. THAT'S OUR ONLY HOPE.
WHAT, IS IT MY FIRST DAY, HAWKEYE?
HEH.
BOOM
BOOM
MAGNESIUM FLARE ARROW
GAH!
WOOOSHH
FLASH
FISHNET ARROW
$*&@#!
SPROING
SKREE

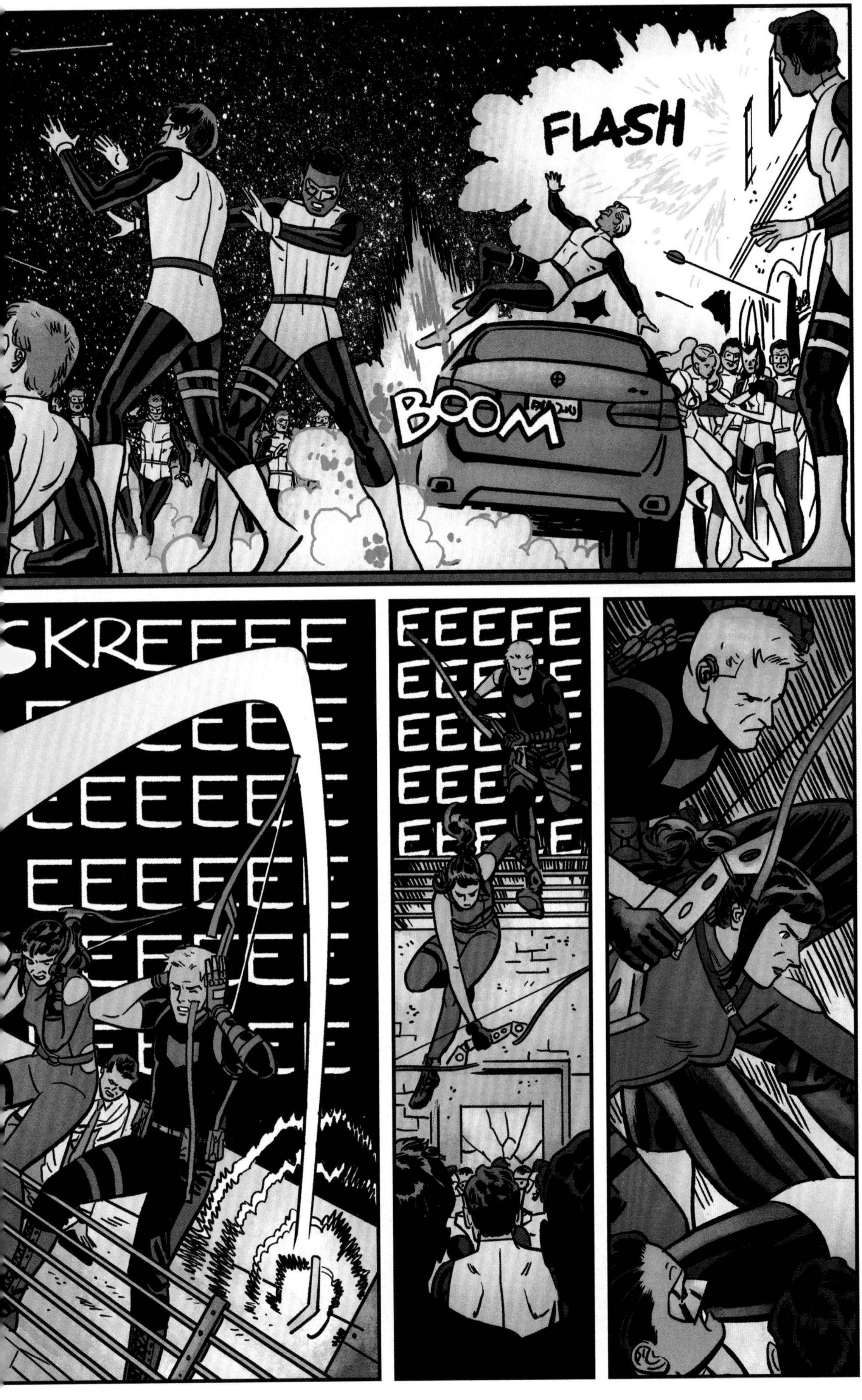
FLASH
BOOM
SKREEEEE
EEEEEE
EEEEEE
EEEEEE
EEEEEE
EEEEE
EEEEE
EEEEE
EEEEE
EEEEE
EEEEE

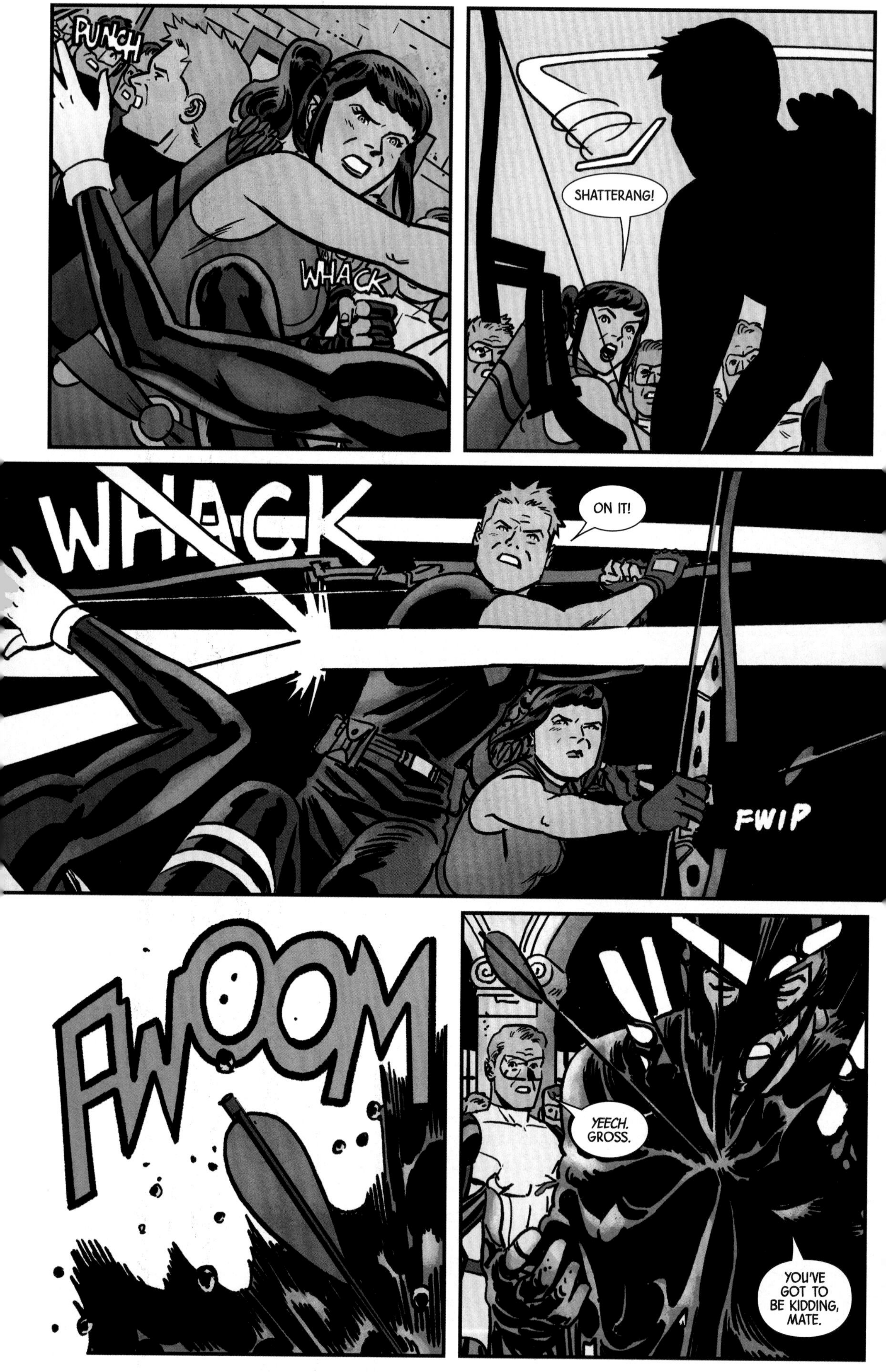
PUNCH
WHACK
SHATTERANG!
WHACK
ON IT!
FWIP
FWOOM
YEECH. GROSS.
YOU'VE GOT TO BE KIDDING, MATE.

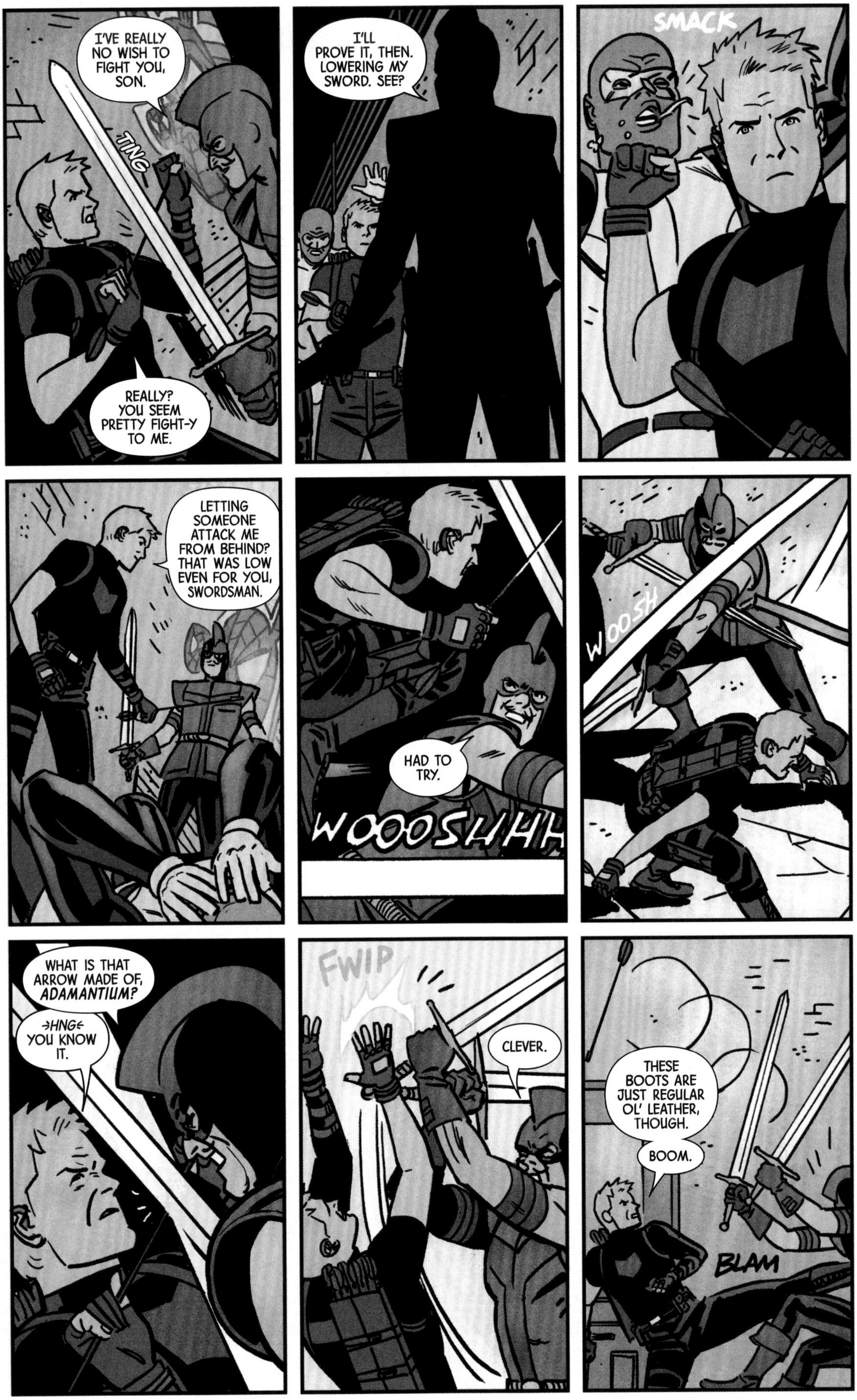
I'VE REALLY NO WISH TO FIGHT YOU, SON.
TING
REALLY? YOU SEEM PRETTY FIGHT-Y TO ME.
I'LL PROVE IT, THEN. LOWERING MY SWORD. SEE?
SMACK
LETTING SOMEONE ATTACK ME FROM BEHIND? THAT WAS LOW EVEN FOR YOU, SWORDSMAN.
HAD TO TRY.
WOOOSHHH
WOOSH
WHAT IS THAT ARROW MADE OF, ADAMANTIUM?
→HNG← YOU KNOW IT.
FWIP
CLEVER.
THESE BOOTS ARE JUST REGULAR OL' LEATHER, THOUGH.
BOOM.
BLAM

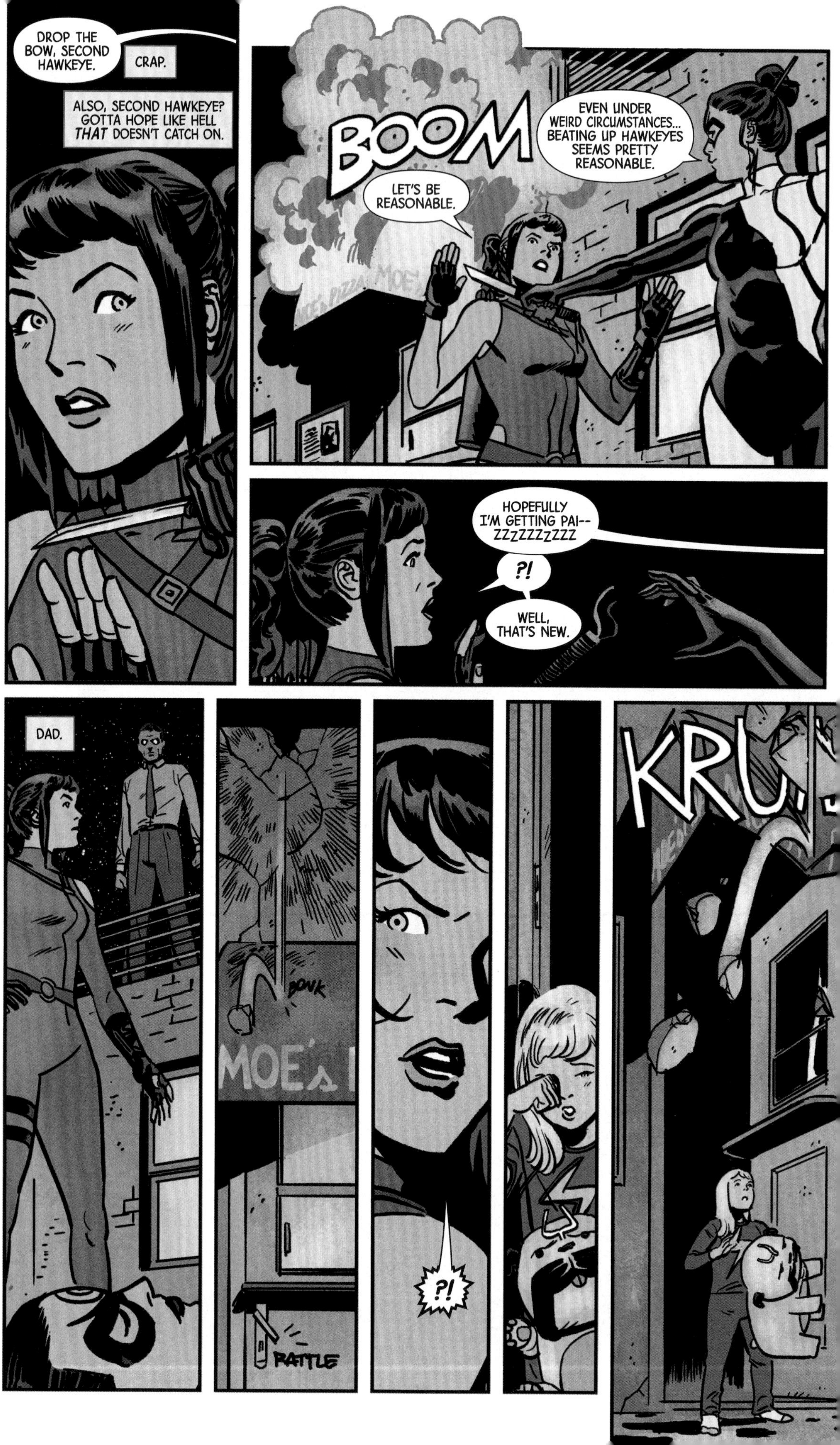
DROP THE BOW, SECOND HAWKEYE.
CRAP.
ALSO, SECOND HAWKEYE? GOTTA HOPE LIKE HELL *THAT* DOESN'T CATCH ON.
BOOM
LET'S BE REASONABLE.
EVEN UNDER WEIRD CIRCUMSTANCES... BEATING UP HAWKEYES SEEMS PRETTY REASONABLE.
MOE'S PIZZA MOE'S
HOPEFULLY I'M GETTING PAI-- ZZZZZZZZZZ
?!
WELL, THAT'S NEW.
DAD.
BONK
MOE'S
RATTLE
?!
KRU..

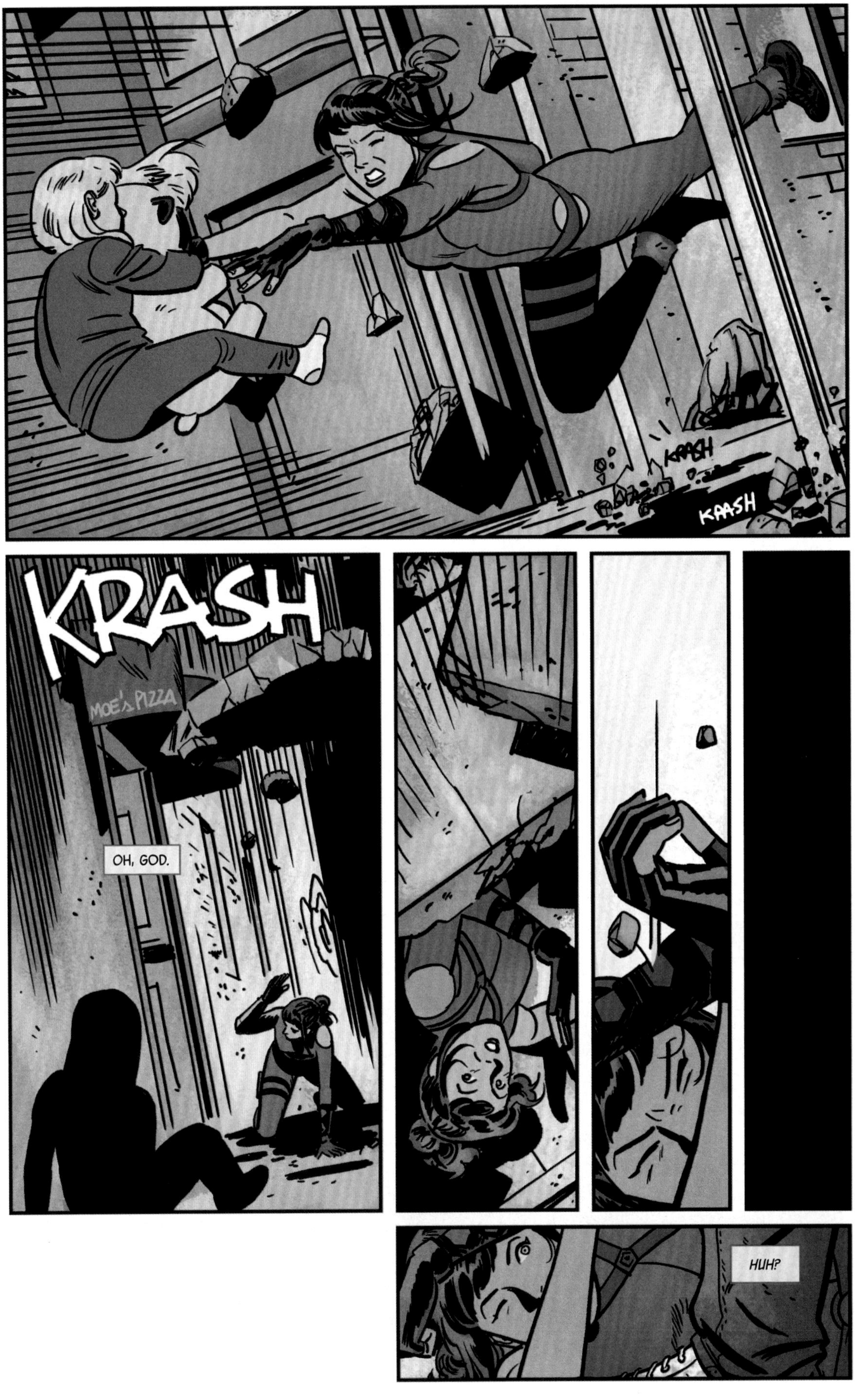
KRASH
KRASH
KRASH
MOE's PIZZA
OH, GOD.
HUH?

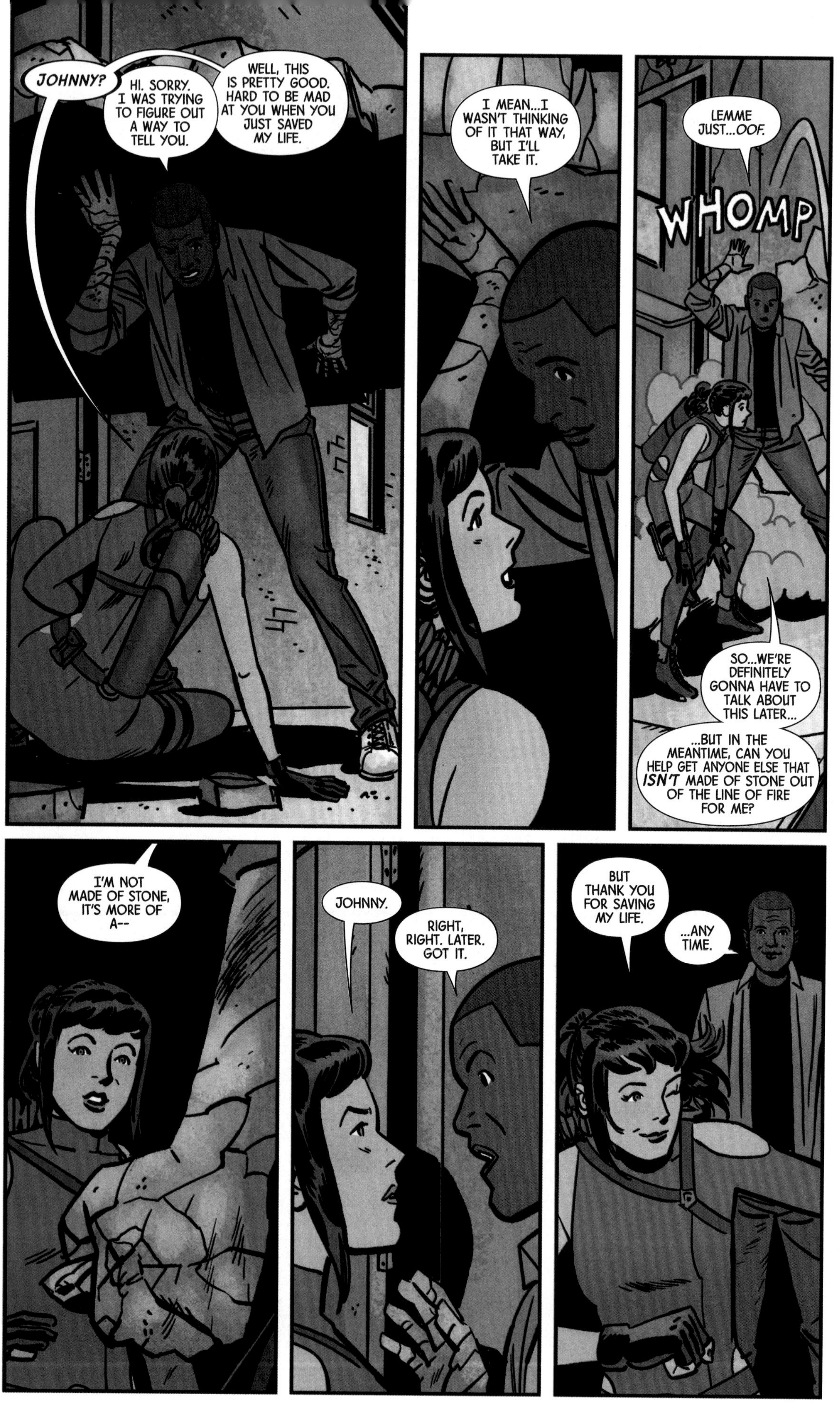
JOHNNY?
HI. SORRY. I WAS TRYING TO FIGURE OUT A WAY TO TELL YOU.
WELL, THIS IS PRETTY GOOD. HARD TO BE MAD AT YOU WHEN YOU JUST SAVED MY LIFE.
I MEAN...I WASN'T THINKING OF IT THAT WAY, BUT I'LL TAKE IT.
LEMME JUST...*OOF.*
WHOMP
SO...WE'RE DEFINITELY GONNA HAVE TO TALK ABOUT THIS LATER...
...BUT IN THE MEANTIME, CAN YOU HELP GET ANYONE ELSE THAT ***ISN'T*** MADE OF STONE OUT OF THE LINE OF FIRE FOR ME?
I'M NOT MADE OF STONE, IT'S MORE OF A--
JOHNNY.
RIGHT, RIGHT. LATER. GOT IT.
BUT THANK YOU FOR SAVING MY LIFE.
...ANY TIME.

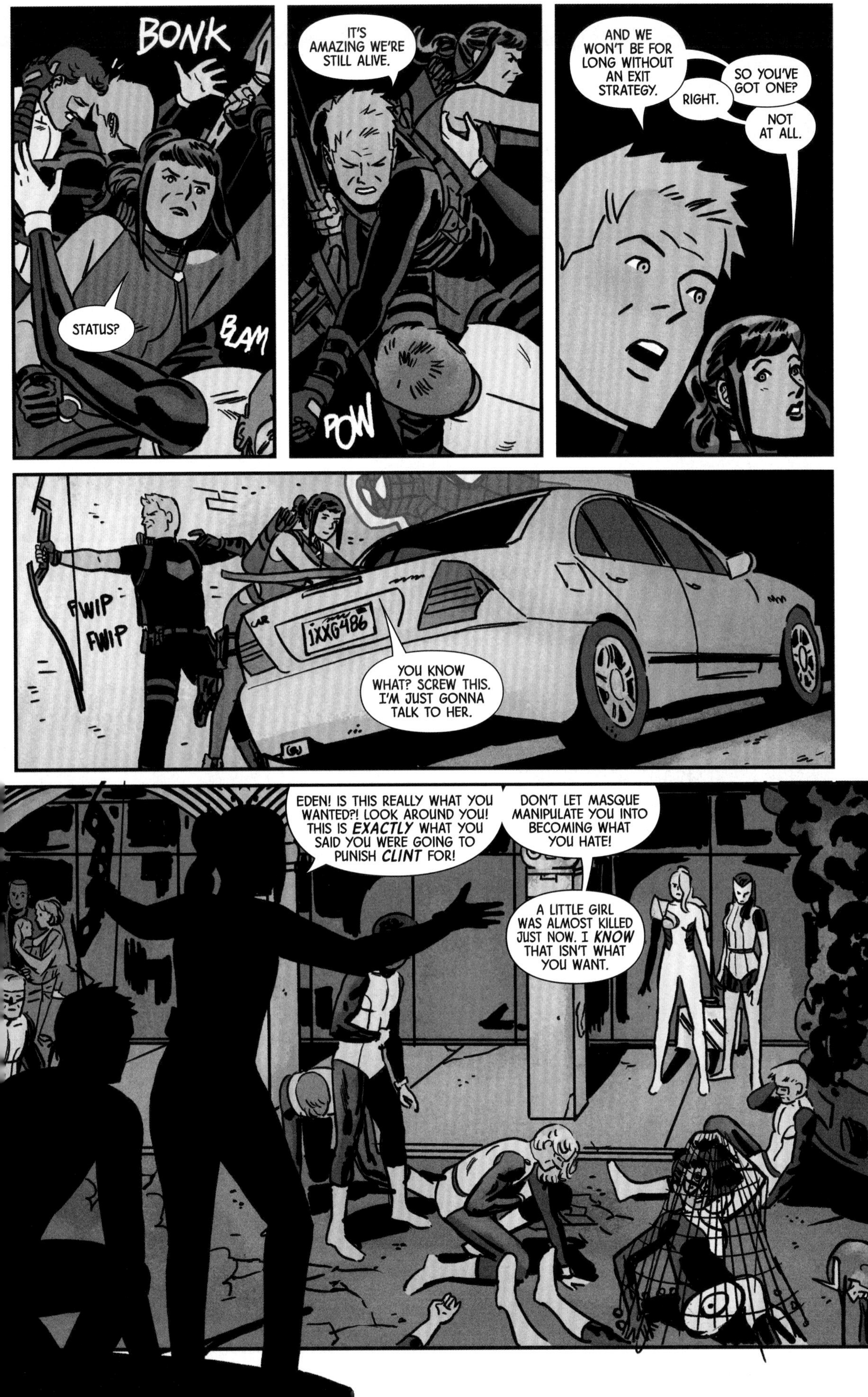
BONK
STATUS?
BLAM
IT'S AMAZING WE'RE STILL ALIVE.
POW
AND WE WON'T BE FOR LONG WITHOUT AN EXIT STRATEGY.
SO YOU'VE GOT ONE?
RIGHT.
NOT AT ALL.
FWIP
FWIP
1XXG486
YOU KNOW WHAT? SCREW THIS. I'M JUST GONNA TALK TO HER.
EDEN! IS THIS REALLY WHAT YOU WANTED?! LOOK AROUND YOU! THIS IS EXACTLY WHAT YOU SAID YOU WERE GOING TO PUNISH CLINT FOR!
DON'T LET MASQUE MANIPULATE YOU INTO BECOMING WHAT YOU HATE!
A LITTLE GIRL WAS ALMOST KILLED JUST NOW. I KNOW THAT ISN'T WHAT YOU WANT.

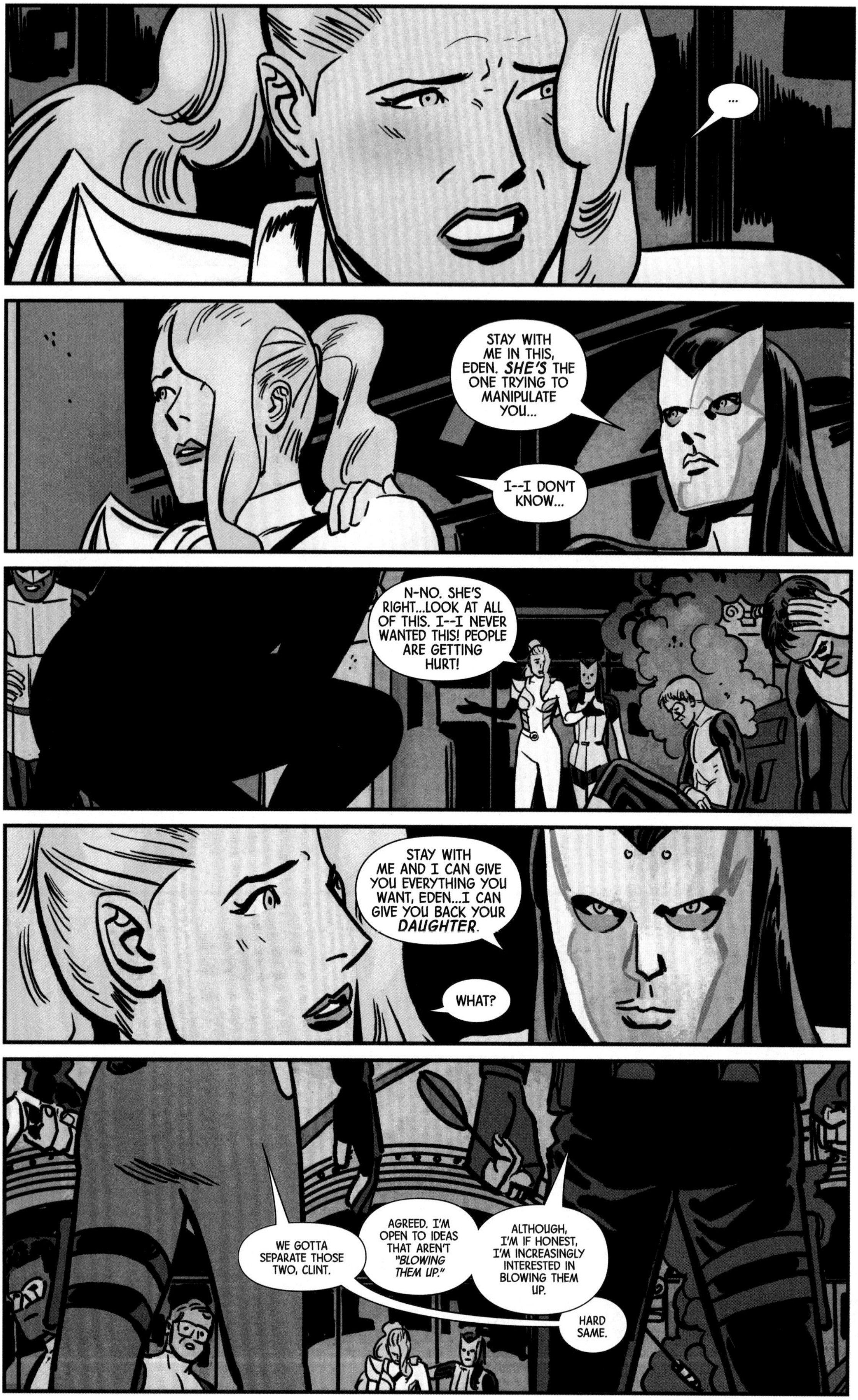
...
STAY WITH ME IN THIS, EDEN. SHE'S THE ONE TRYING TO MANIPULATE YOU...
I--I DON'T KNOW...
N-NO. SHE'S RIGHT...LOOK AT ALL OF THIS. I--I NEVER WANTED THIS! PEOPLE ARE GETTING HURT!
STAY WITH ME AND I CAN GIVE YOU EVERYTHING YOU WANT, EDEN...I CAN GIVE YOU BACK YOUR DAUGHTER.
WHAT?
WE GOTTA SEPARATE THOSE TWO, CLINT.
AGREED. I'M OPEN TO IDEAS THAT AREN'T "BLOWING THEM UP."
ALTHOUGH, I'M IF HONEST, I'M INCREASINGLY INTERESTED IN BLOWING THEM UP.
HARD SAME.

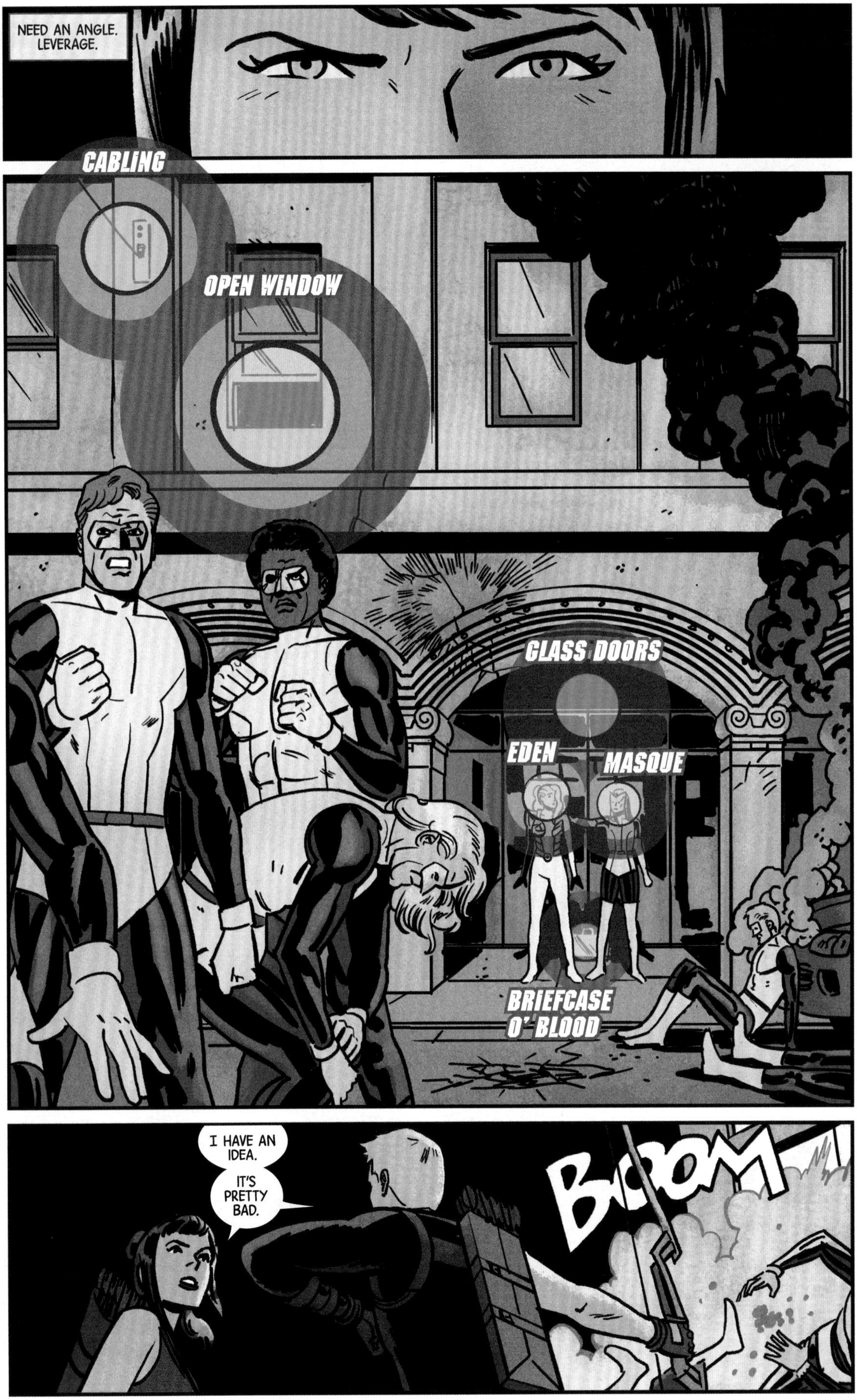
NEED AN ANGLE. LEVERAGE.
CABLING
OPEN WINDOW
GLASS DOORS
EDEN
MASQUE
BRIEFCASE O' BLOOD
I HAVE AN IDEA.
IT'S PRETTY BAD.
BOOM

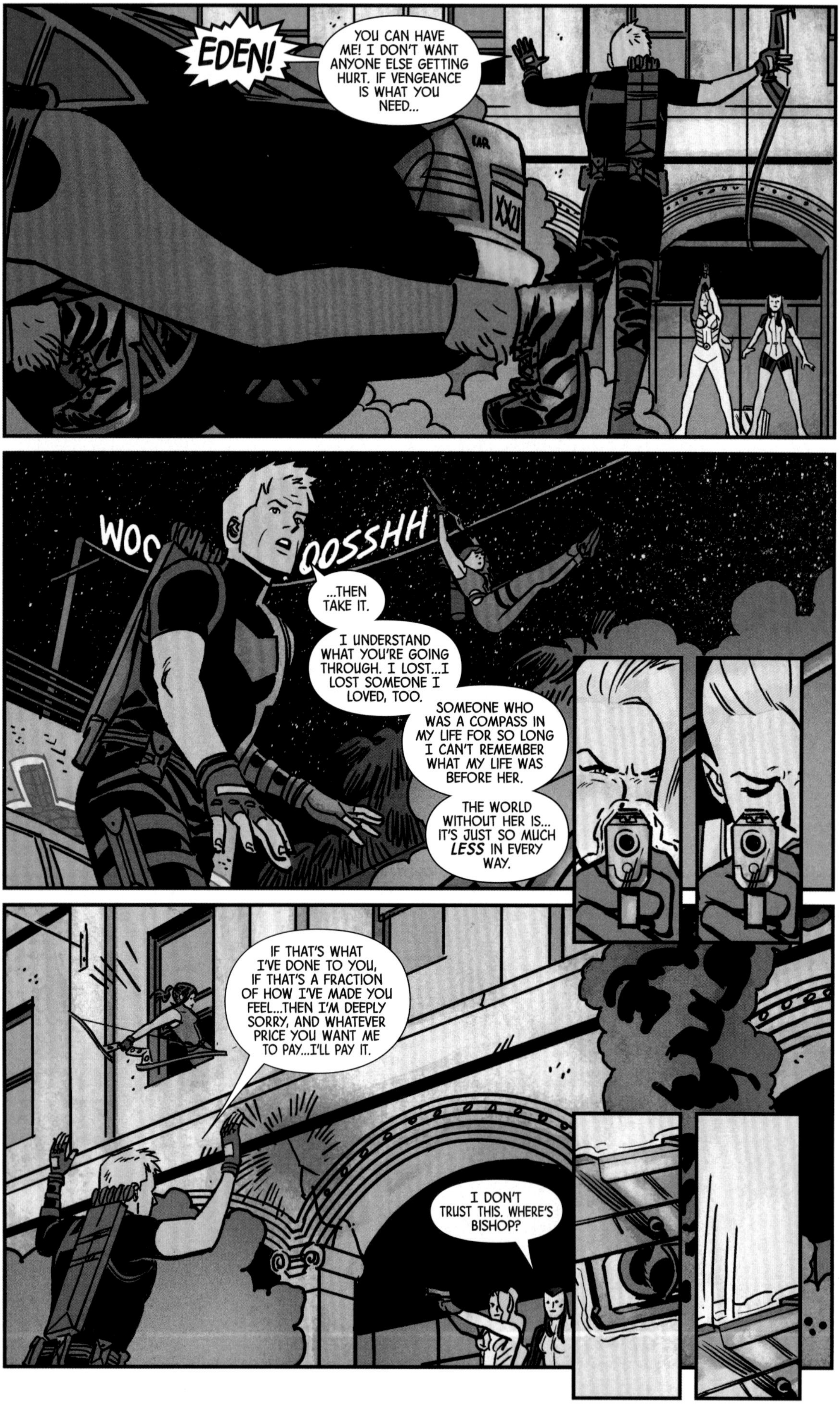
EDEN!
YOU CAN HAVE ME! I DON'T WANT ANYONE ELSE GETTING HURT. IF VENGEANCE IS WHAT YOU NEED...
WOOOSSHH
...THEN TAKE IT.
I UNDERSTAND WHAT YOU'RE GOING THROUGH. I LOST...I LOST SOMEONE I LOVED, TOO.
SOMEONE WHO WAS A COMPASS IN MY LIFE FOR SO LONG I CAN'T REMEMBER WHAT MY LIFE WAS BEFORE HER.
THE WORLD WITHOUT HER IS... IT'S JUST SO MUCH LESS IN EVERY WAY.
IF THAT'S WHAT I'VE DONE TO YOU, IF THAT'S A FRACTION OF HOW I'VE MADE YOU FEEL...THEN I'M DEEPLY SORRY, AND WHATEVER PRICE YOU WANT ME TO PAY...I'LL PAY IT.
I DON'T TRUST THIS. WHERE'S BISHOP?

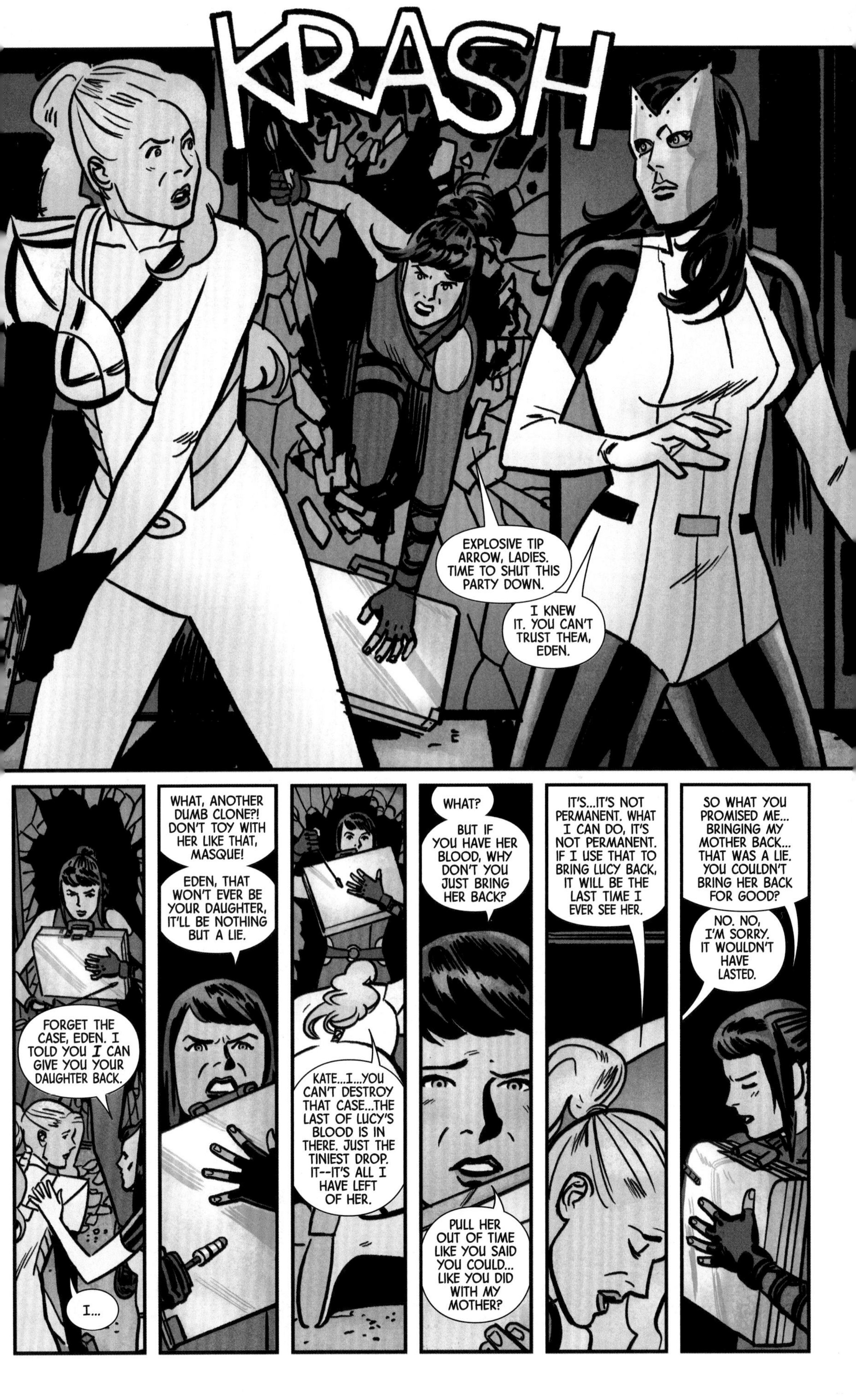
KRASH
EXPLOSIVE TIP ARROW, LADIES. TIME TO SHUT THIS PARTY DOWN.
I KNEW IT. YOU CAN'T TRUST THEM, EDEN.
FORGET THE CASE, EDEN. I TOLD YOU *I* CAN GIVE YOU YOUR DAUGHTER BACK.
I...
WHAT, ANOTHER DUMB CLONE?! DON'T TOY WITH HER LIKE THAT, MASQUE!
EDEN, THAT WON'T EVER BE YOUR DAUGHTER, IT'LL BE NOTHING BUT A LIE.
KATE...I...YOU CAN'T DESTROY THAT CASE...THE LAST OF LUCY'S BLOOD IS IN THERE. JUST THE TINIEST DROP. IT--IT'S ALL I HAVE LEFT OF HER.
WHAT?
BUT IF YOU HAVE HER BLOOD, WHY DON'T YOU JUST BRING HER BACK?
PULL HER OUT OF TIME LIKE YOU SAID YOU COULD... LIKE YOU DID WITH MY MOTHER?
IT'S...IT'S NOT PERMANENT. WHAT I CAN DO, IT'S NOT PERMANENT. IF I USE THAT TO BRING LUCY BACK, IT WILL BE THE LAST TIME I EVER SEE HER.
SO WHAT YOU PROMISED ME... BRINGING MY MOTHER BACK... THAT WAS A LIE. YOU COULDN'T BRING HER BACK FOR GOOD?
NO. NO, I'M SORRY. IT WOULDN'T HAVE LASTED.

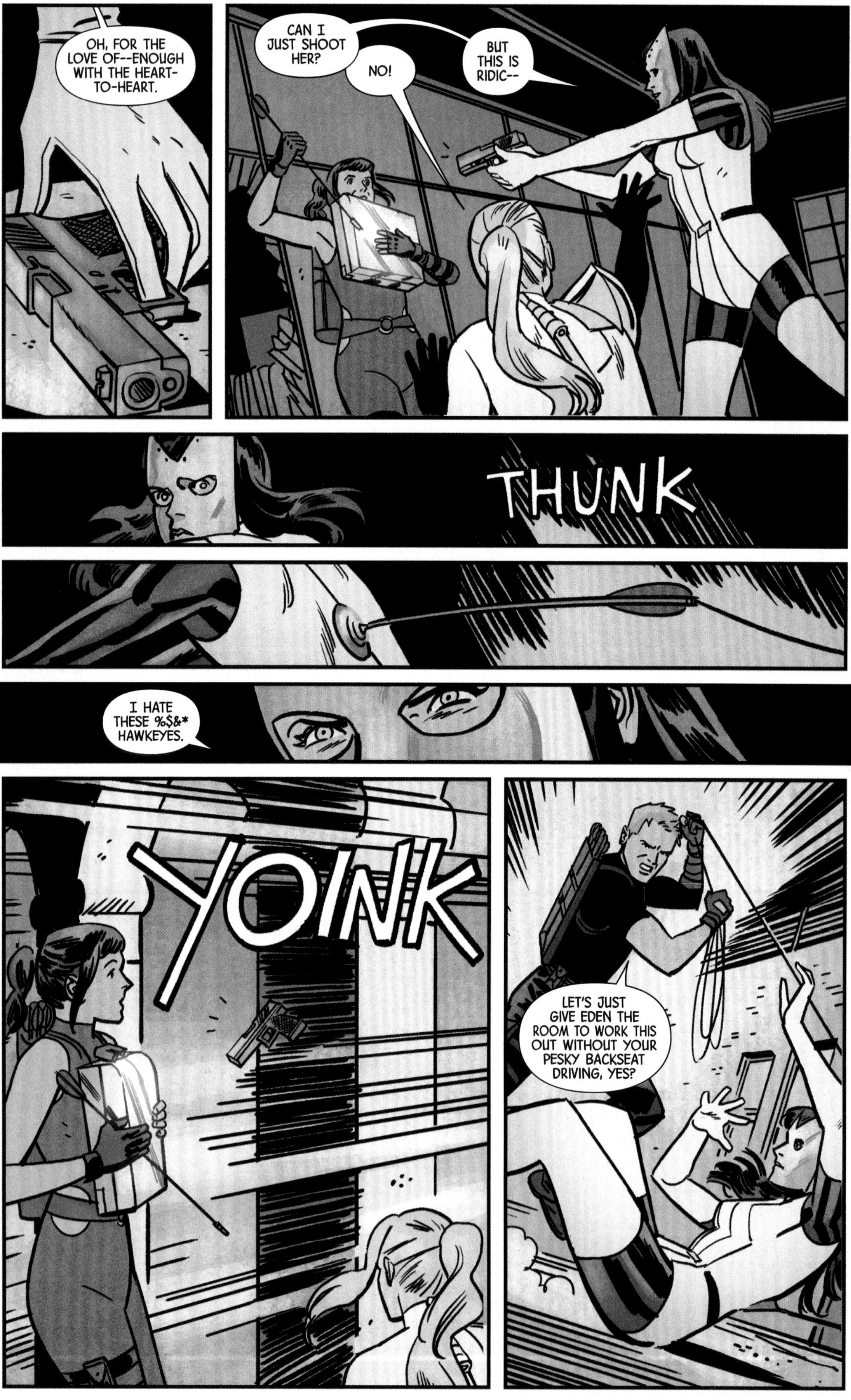

OH, FOR THE LOVE OF--ENOUGH WITH THE HEART-TO-HEART.
CAN I JUST SHOOT HER?
NO!
BUT THIS IS RIDIC--
THUNK
I HATE THESE %$&* HAWKEYES.
YOINK
LET'S JUST GIVE EDEN THE ROOM TO WORK THIS OUT WITHOUT YOUR PESKY BACKSEAT DRIVING, YES?

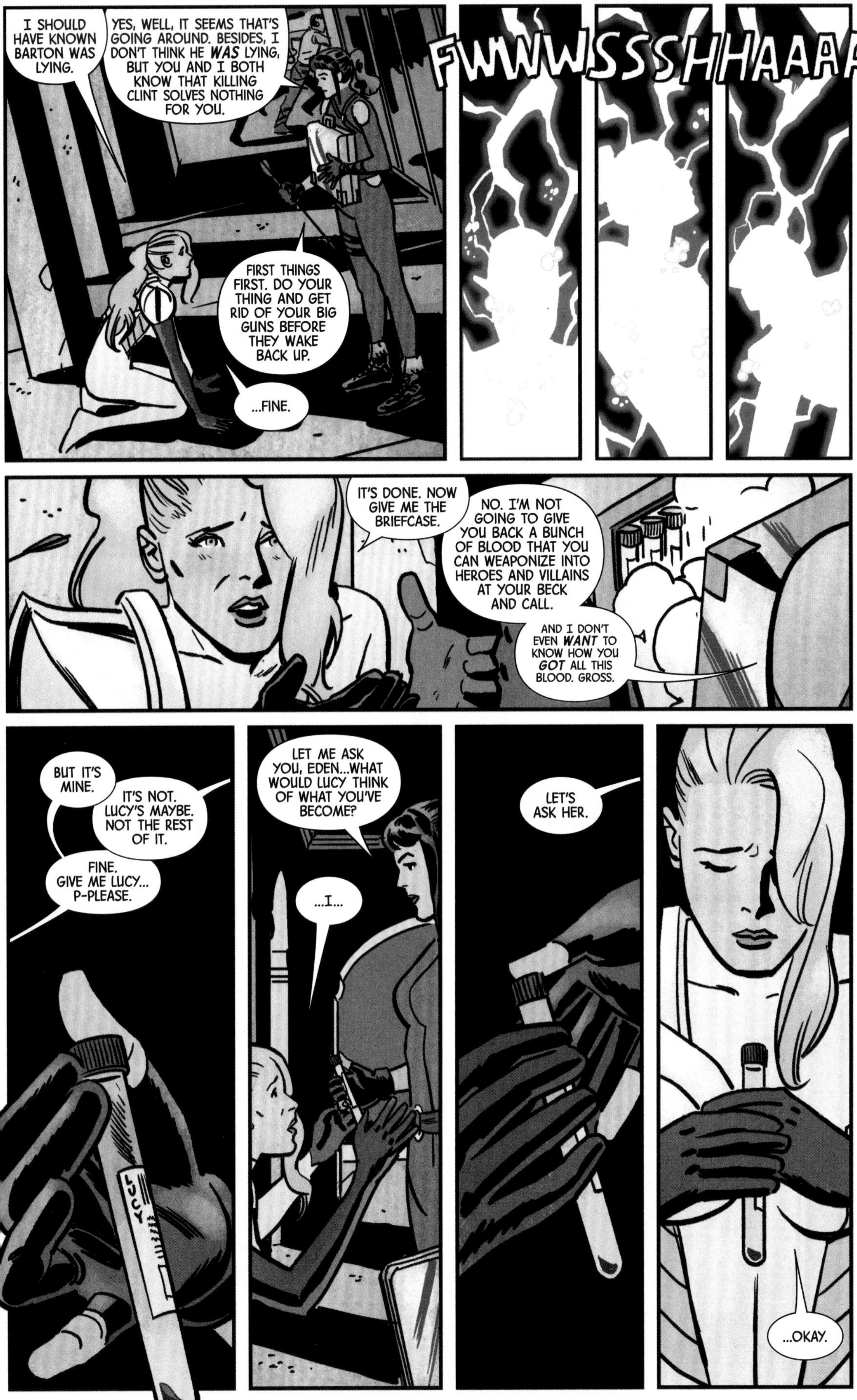
I SHOULD HAVE KNOWN BARTON WAS LYING.
YES, WELL, IT SEEMS THAT'S GOING AROUND. BESIDES, I DON'T THINK HE WAS LYING, BUT YOU AND I BOTH KNOW THAT KILLING CLINT SOLVES NOTHING FOR YOU.
FIRST THINGS FIRST. DO YOUR THING AND GET RID OF YOUR BIG GUNS BEFORE THEY WAKE BACK UP.
...FINE.
FWWWSSSHHAAAA
IT'S DONE. NOW GIVE ME THE BRIEFCASE.
NO. I'M NOT GOING TO GIVE YOU BACK A BUNCH OF BLOOD THAT YOU CAN WEAPONIZE INTO HEROES AND VILLAINS AT YOUR BECK AND CALL.
AND I DON'T EVEN WANT TO KNOW HOW YOU GOT ALL THIS BLOOD. GROSS.
BUT IT'S MINE.
IT'S NOT. LUCY'S MAYBE. NOT THE REST OF IT.
FINE. GIVE ME LUCY... P-PLEASE.
LUCY
LET ME ASK YOU, EDEN...WHAT WOULD LUCY THINK OF WHAT YOU'VE BECOME?
...I...
LET'S ASK HER.
...OKAY.

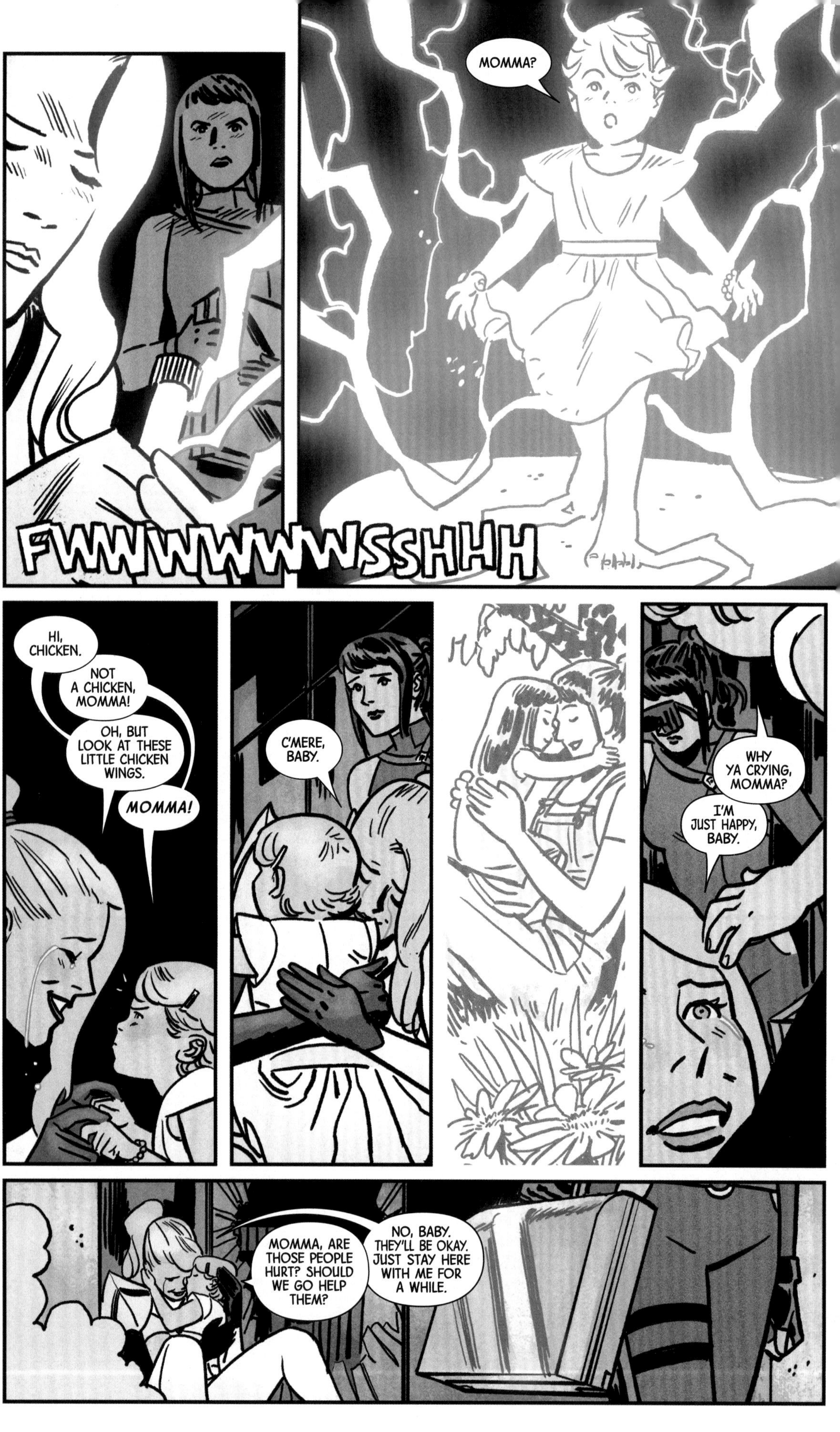
MOMMA?
FWWWWWWWSSHHH
HI, CHICKEN.
NOT A CHICKEN, MOMMA!
OH, BUT LOOK AT THESE LITTLE CHICKEN WINGS.
MOMMA!
C'MERE, BABY.
WHY YA CRYING, MOMMA?
I'M JUST HAPPY, BABY.
MOMMA, ARE THOSE PEOPLE HURT? SHOULD WE GO HELP THEM?
NO, BABY. THEY'LL BE OKAY. JUST STAY HERE WITH ME FOR A WHILE.

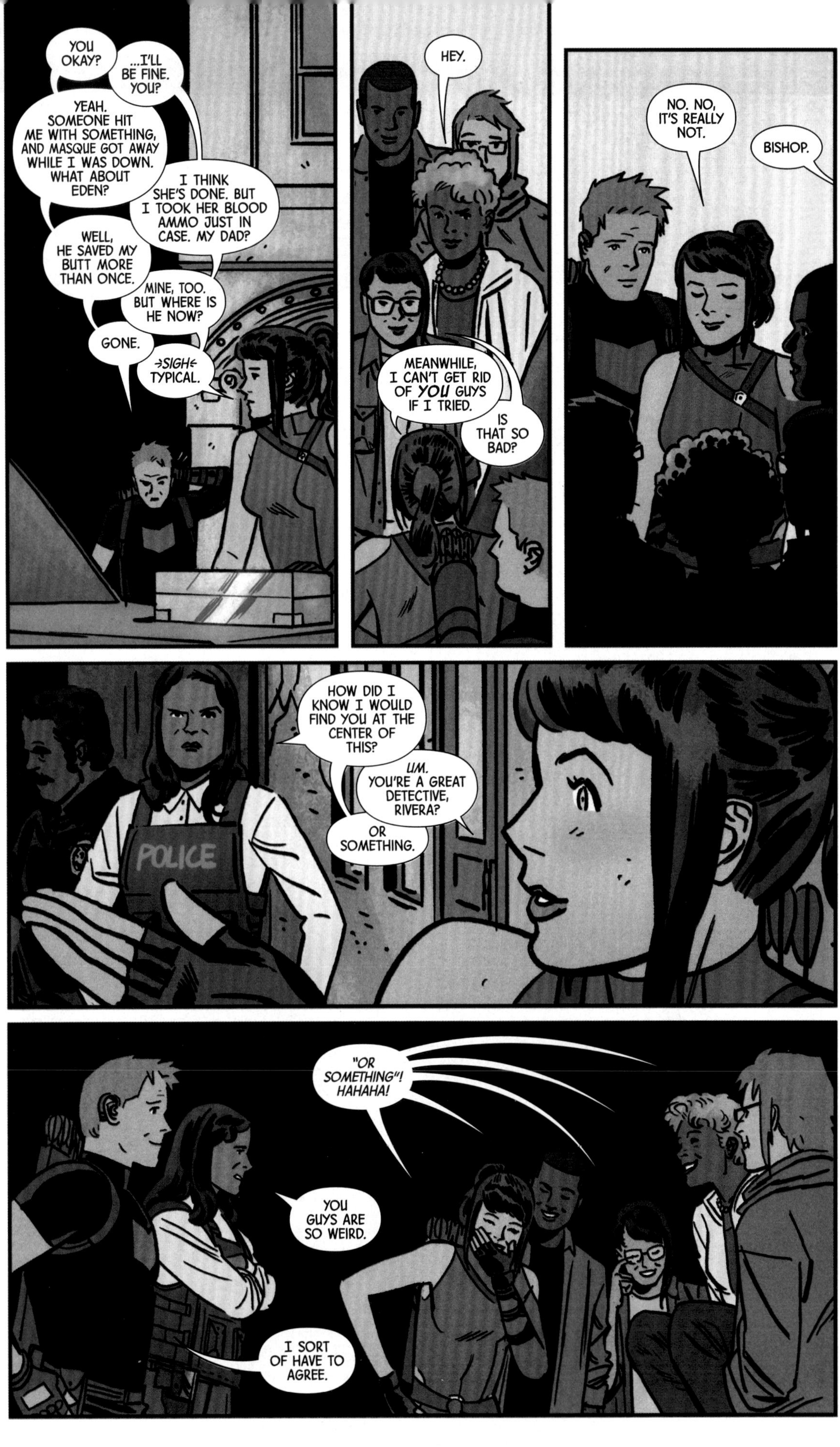
YOU OKAY?
...I'LL BE FINE. YOU?
YEAH. SOMEONE HIT ME WITH SOMETHING, AND MASQUE GOT AWAY WHILE I WAS DOWN. WHAT ABOUT EDEN?
I THINK SHE'S DONE. BUT I TOOK HER BLOOD AMMO JUST IN CASE. MY DAD?
WELL, HE SAVED MY BUTT MORE THAN ONCE.
MINE, TOO. BUT WHERE IS HE NOW?
GONE.
→SIGH← TYPICAL.
HEY.
MEANWHILE, I CAN'T GET RID OF *YOU* GUYS IF I TRIED.
IS THAT SO BAD?
NO. NO, IT'S REALLY NOT.
BISHOP.
POLICE
HOW DID I KNOW I WOULD FIND YOU AT THE CENTER OF THIS?
UM. YOU'RE A GREAT DETECTIVE, RIVERA?
OR SOMETHING.
"OR SOMETHING"! HAHAHA!
YOU GUYS ARE SO WEIRD.
I SORT OF HAVE TO AGREE.

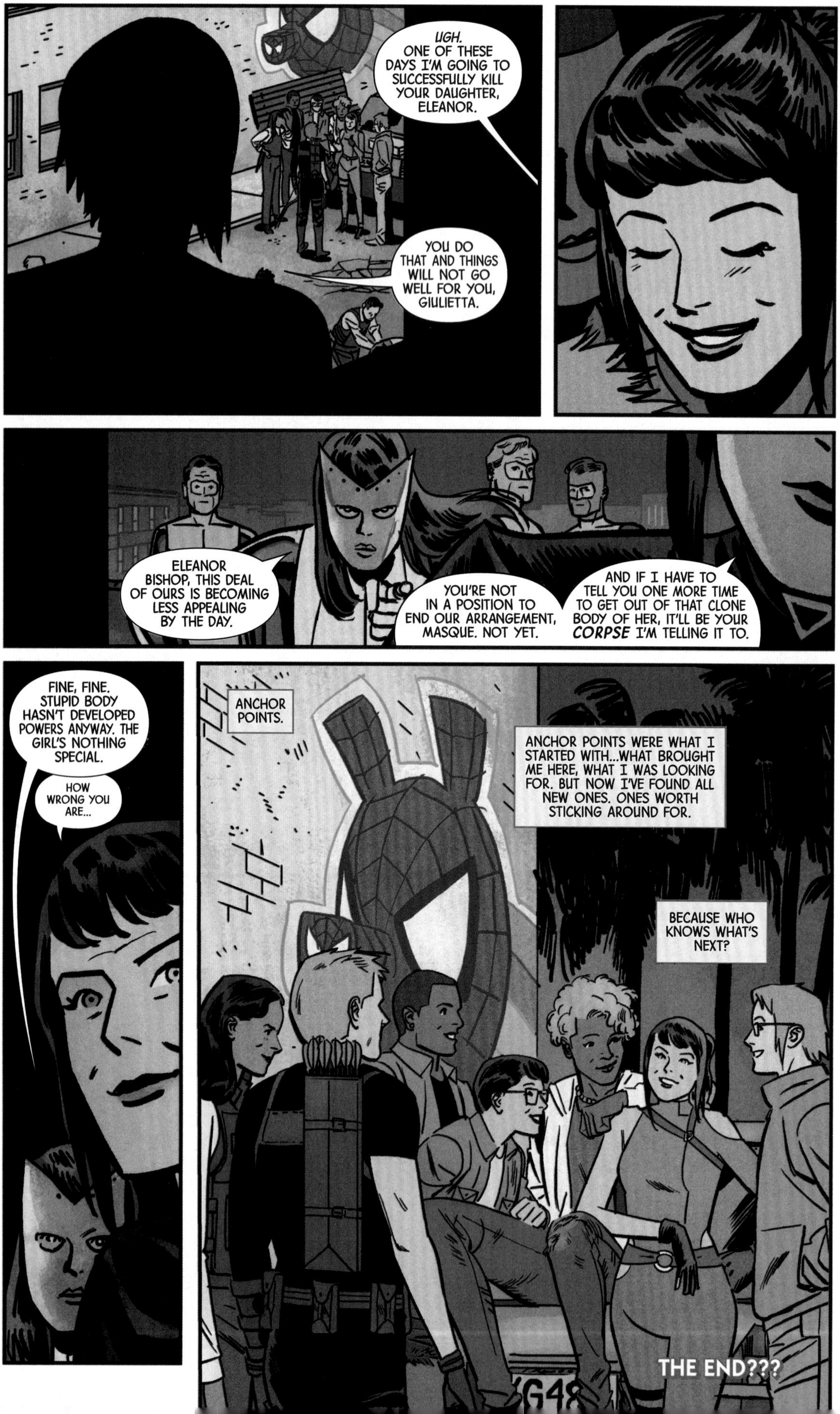
UGH. ONE OF THESE DAYS I'M GOING TO SUCCESSFULLY KILL YOUR DAUGHTER, ELEANOR.
YOU DO THAT AND THINGS WILL NOT GO WELL FOR YOU, GIULIETTA.
ELEANOR BISHOP, THIS DEAL OF OURS IS BECOMING LESS APPEALING BY THE DAY.
YOU'RE NOT IN A POSITION TO END OUR ARRANGEMENT, MASQUE. NOT YET.
AND IF I HAVE TO TELL YOU ONE MORE TIME TO GET OUT OF THAT CLONE BODY OF HER, IT'LL BE YOUR CORPSE I'M TELLING IT TO.
FINE, FINE. STUPID BODY HASN'T DEVELOPED POWERS ANYWAY. THE GIRL'S NOTHING SPECIAL.
HOW WRONG YOU ARE...
ANCHOR POINTS.
ANCHOR POINTS WERE WHAT I STARTED WITH...WHAT BROUGHT ME HERE, WHAT I WAS LOOKING FOR. BUT NOW I'VE FOUND ALL NEW ONES. ONES WORTH STICKING AROUND FOR.
BECAUSE WHO KNOWS WHAT'S NEXT?
THE END???

Back in 2015, when I first began trying to pitch a book called HAWKEYE INVESTIGATIONS to Marvel, I was so naive I basically ignored the fact that I was asking to follow up one of the best and most critically acclaimed runs in all of super hero comics.

Seriously, what kind of fool is like--"oh yeah, that book is brilliant! Let me--a newbie at best--try to follow up that genius thing"?

Well, THIS kind of fool, it turns out. But the truth is, of course, I'm that foolish. As a creator you never look at stuff that's NOT brilliant and try to follow that up, you look at the things that inspire you...you aim for the stars.

Luckily for me, Sana Amanat is an exceptional editor who saw my passion for Kate Bishop and knew that she could shape it into something wonderful. And so she did. Understanding that it takes a very talented village to make a great comic book, she and wondrous editor Charles Beacham put me together with the insanely gifted artist Leonardo Romero, Eisner-winning colorist (of what seems like roughly a thousand monthly books) Jordie Bellaire, savvy Joe Sabino on letters and the miraculous Julian Totino Tedesco on covers--and honestly...magic began to happen. We added the magnificent Michael Walsh for art on our alternate arcs, the marvelous Manny Mederos for some cool design work and sensational editor Alanna Smith...and together we stormed the beach of comics and made something beautiful. We're not the perfect book for everyone, but the people we're perfect for get us SO MUCH.

Though it may be considered gauche to write, I could not be more proud of what we accomplished together, and I'll be chasing this experience--both in what we created and in what a joy it was to actually create together--probably for the rest of my professional life. I couldn't have asked for a better team. KATE couldn't have asked for a better team. We love her madly, and I know many of you do, too.

Which brings us to the fans. Thank you. Thank you for loving Kate and for loving us. It was a spectacular journey, and my most fervent hope is that the adventure is not quite over. Alanna and I have been cooking something up for our beloved Kate-eye... and I truly think you guys are going to love it. So stay tuned...and keep yours Marvel!

Finger guns forever, you guys!

Kelly "Kate-eye" Thompson

(That's not actually a thing but I'm trying to make it catch on. Shhhh!)

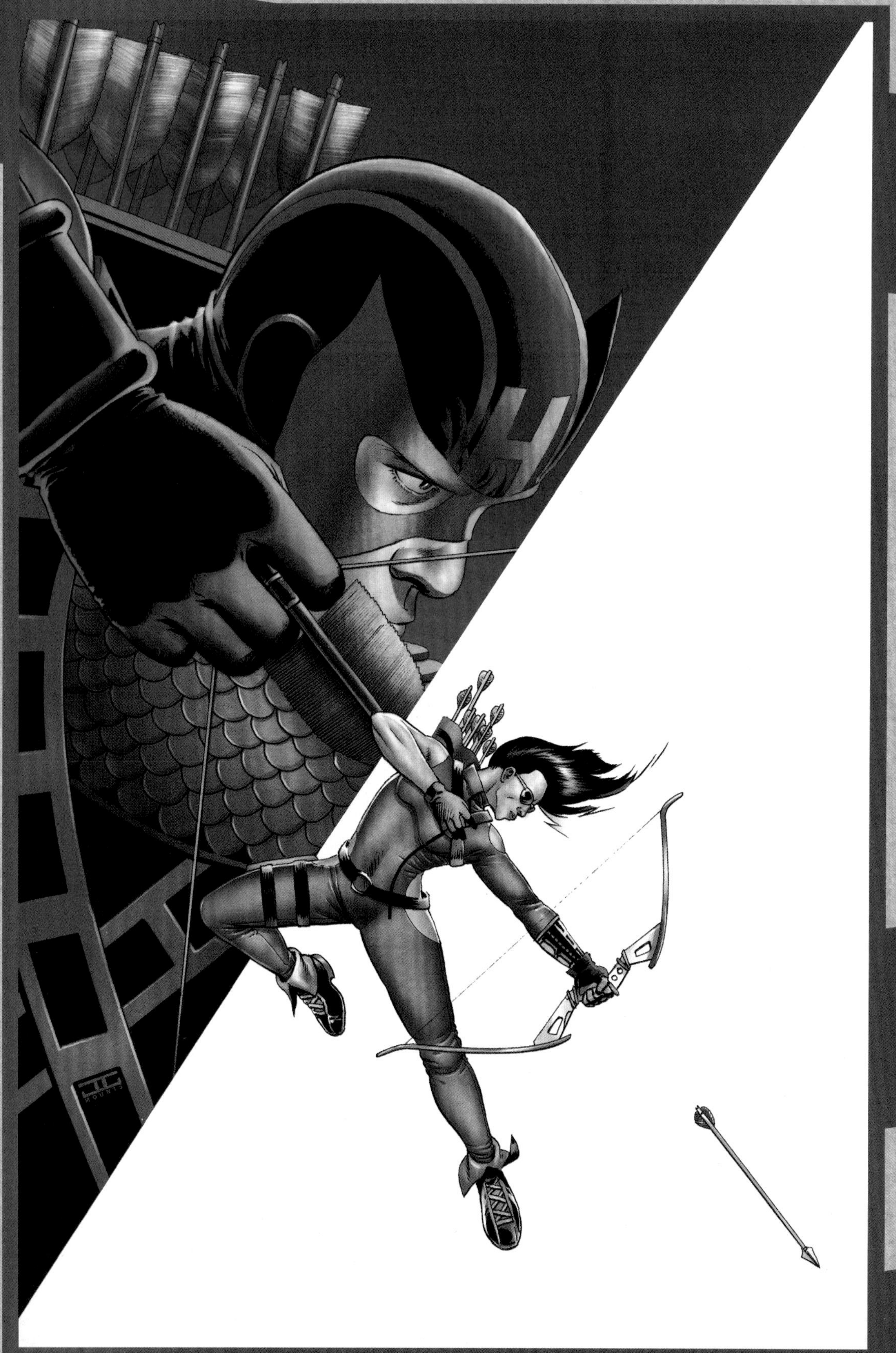

Generations: Hawkeye & Hawkeye #1 variant
by John Cassaday & Paul Mounts

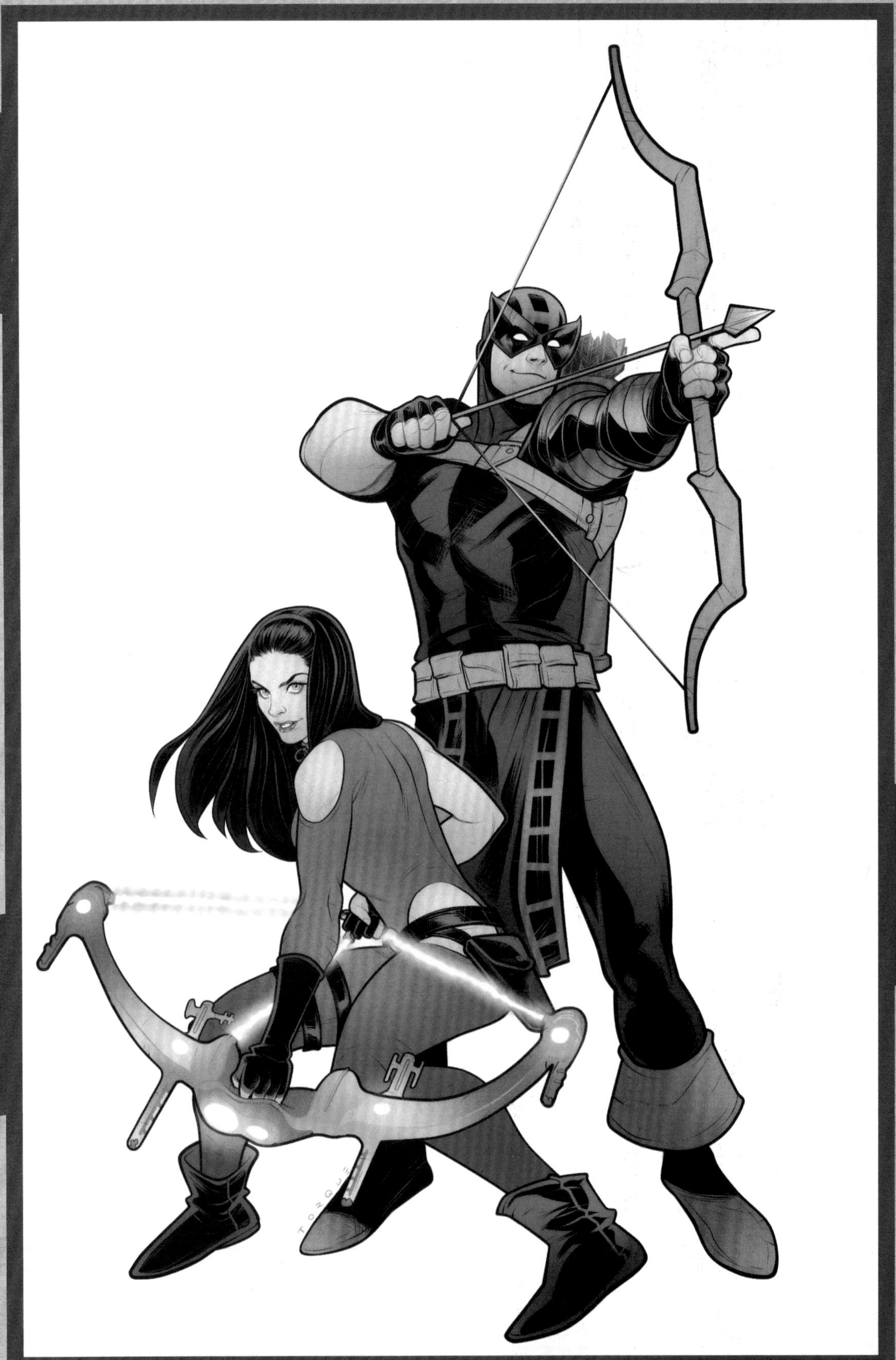

Generations: Hawkeye & Hawkeye #1 variant
by Elizabeth Torque

HAWK

INVESTIGATIONS

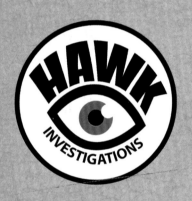